SECRETS, SPIES & SPOTTED DOGS

JANE EALES

MH
PRESS

SECRETS, SPIES AND SPOTTED DOGS
Discovering mysterious family connections hidden in a secret adoption

Published by Middle Harbour Press Pty Ltd Australia
Email: middleharbourpress@bigpond.com
http://www.middleharbourpress.com

National Library of Australia Cataloguing-in-Publication Entry
Author: Eales, Jane, 1947– author.
                   Secrets, Spies and Spotted Dogs: discovering mysterious family
                   connections hidden in a secret adoption
                   Includes bibliographical references.
ISBN: 978 0 9925276 4 8 (paperback)
                   978 0 9925276 5 5 (eBook)
Subjects   Eales, Jane.
                   Adopted children – Biography.
                   Adoption.
                   Families.
                   Spies.
                   World War, 1939–1945 – History
                   Arnhem, Battle of, Arnhem, Netherlands, 1944.
Dewey Number   306.874

For Rob and our children

With love

CONTENTS

List of Illustrations *vii*

Family Trees *viii*

Preface *x*

PART ONE: WHO AM I? *1*

1   The letter *3*

2   Salisbury *6*

3   Jonathan and me *9*

4   Forbidden territory *14*

5   Questions *22*

6   Mum's early life in London *24*

7   Mum and Dad in London – 1933–40 *27*

8   From London to Southern Rhodesia – 1947–1954 *29*

9   Holidays, birthdays and boarding school – 1949–54 *37*

10   Dad and Granddad in Germany, 1876–1933 *41*

11   Our family secret – 1954 *48*

12   Middle childhood – 1955–61 *52*

13   Growing up – 1961–65 *59*

14   Living in Johannesburg and the summons home *68*

15   Adjusting, meeting Rob and wedding plans *69*

16   'Please elope' *74*

17   Rewarding times, challenging times – 1971–87 *78*

PART TWO: INTRODUCING PHYLLIS *87*

18 The search begins *88*

19 London – 2002 *92*

20 Finding Paul, Phyllis' son *97*

21 Contact with Paul – Easter 2005 *100*

22 Face to face with Paul – 30 March 2005 *104*

23 Resolving the question 'Who am I?' *110*

24 The Hogg family, London – From July 1906 *118*

25 What is it like to be a bastard? *127*

26 Phyllis' childhood – 1906–18 *131*

27 Was Phyllis a product of her time? *137*

28 Growing up in England during WWI – 1914–18 *142*

29 Phyllis and her introduction to Dalmatians – 1918–27 *145*

30 Phyllis' marriage to Jim – 1927 *153*

31 Paul's story *158*

32 Phyllis and John Leonard Kleyn in Europe – 1937–39 *167*

33 Phyllis and John Kleyn - back in England – 1939 *179*

PART THREE: PHYLLIS'S WORLD WAR II CAREER *183*

34 Phyllis and John Kleyn – 1940–432 *184*

35 Phyllis' army record goes blank –
     11–13 November 1943 *203*

36 Phyllis is sent to Arnhem *212*

37 Checking Phyllis' spying story *215*

38 Solving the logistical issues *226*

39 The dissemination of military intelligence *230*

PART FOUR: PHYLLIS'S LIFE AFTER WORLD WAR II *237*

40   General Pieters and *Dick Barton Special Agent 1946* *238*

41   My twelve months with Phyllis *244*

42   East Anglia – 1949–63 *255*

43   My mother and me *273*

Epilogue *280*

Acknowledgments *283*

APPENDICES *286*

Endnotes *286*

Chronology of the life of Phyllis Margaret Hogg/Whicker/Kleyn/
   MacRobert *289*

References *292*

List of Illustrations

Page

93   Jonathan and the author enjoying some time together, 2003

106   Phyllis Margaret and Paul, 1938

111   The author and her half-brother, Paul

123   Hogg family, 1932 – the author's extended family

150   Advertisement in the Kennel Club Catalogue, 1956

167   John Leonard Kleyn, Phyllis Margaret's second husband

187   Ethel Hogg (Big Granny), Boy and Phyllis Margaret, 1941

219   The author and her husband outside Phyllis's wartime home: 5 Little Chester Street, Belgravia. SW1, 2005

219   Map showing proximity of 5 Little Chester Street, Belgravia to Eaton Square and Chester Square, London

225   Phyllis Margaret Kleyn's War Medals "221999 JNR CMDR PM KLEYN ATS, War Medal and Defence Medal, 1939–1945"

249   12 Lancaster Drive, Hampstead, where the author was born

253   Dr Davidson's surgery in Park Square East, N.W.1, Regents Park, 2007

258   Cheney's Lane, Tacolneston, Norfolk, 2005 where we assumed Mother's thatched house had been

260   Paparazzi around a prize-winning Dalmatian and its owner, 1960's

261   Phyllis Margaret MacRobert (Mother) and her prize-winning Dalmatian winning a prize at The Kennel Club, 1955

269   The Old School House

Adoptive Family Tree

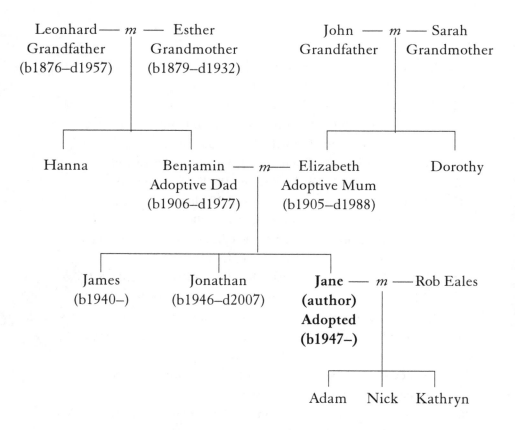

BERGMAN

Leonhard— *m* — Esther
Grandfather | Grandmother
(b1876–d1957) | (b1879–d1932)

Hanna

Benjamin — *m*— Elizabeth
Adoptive Dad | Adoptive Mum
(b1906–d1977) | (b1905–d1988)

WATSON

John — *m* — Sarah
Grandfather | Grandmother

Dorothy

James
(b1940–)

Jonathan
(b1946–d2007)

Jane — *m* —Rob Eales
(author)
Adopted
(b1947–)

Adam   Nick   Kathryn

Biological Family Tree

HOGG

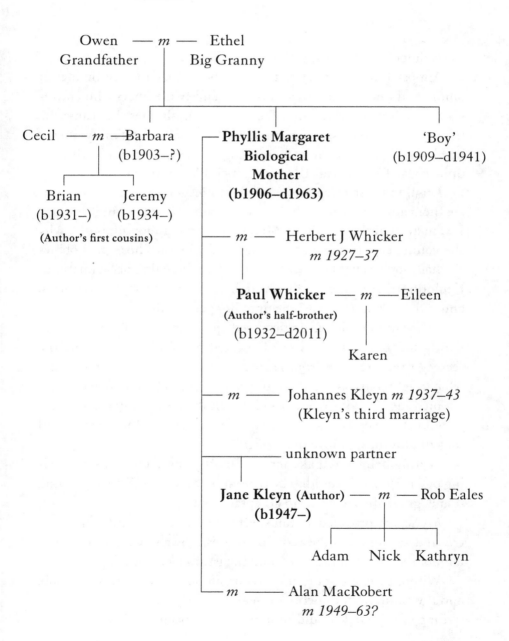

Owen — *m* — Ethel
Grandfather   Big Granny

Cecil — *m* — Barbara
            (b1903–?)

Brian   Jeremy
(b1931–)   (b1934–)

(Author's first cousins)

Phyllis Margaret
Biological
Mother
(b1906–d1963)

'Boy'
(b1909–d1941)

— *m* — Herbert J Whicker
            m 1927–37

Paul Whicker — *m* — Eileen
(Author's half-brother)
(b1932–d2011)

Karen

m — Johannes Kleyn *m 1937–43*
            (Kleyn's third marriage)

unknown partner

Jane Kleyn (Author) — *m* — Rob Eales
(b1947–)

Adam   Nick   Kathryn

m — Alan MacRobert
            m 1949–63?

Preface

I was nineteen when I was told I was adopted.

Almost forty years later, I began the search for my biological family and uncovered a wealth of new family members who enthusiastically welcomed me into their hearts and homes. I became the happy recipient of some remarkable and poignant family stories involving abandonment and espionage, often intertwined with the upheavals of World War II, about which I knew very little.

I couldn't just accept these family stories – I wanted to substantiate them and understand their social, historical and cultural context. I wanted to understand why Mother gave me up for adoption, why she volunteered to spy for the Allies, and why she chose the hobbies she had, such as her bridge playing and her breeding of Dalmatians. Exploring these avenues of research led to wonderful adventures, and provided valuable insights into her personality.

As events unfolded, unanswered questions about my adoptive family too began to emerge; I wanted answers to questions the secrecy prevented me from asking. I wanted to better understand what might have been their perspective in relation to why they adopted me. Good, sincere people, with the best of intentions, they generously accepted me into their home and lives. I appreciated all they did for me and love them dearly.

Writing helped to make sense of most things. The constant feeling of wonder, 'this couldn't be true' and 'this couldn't be happening to me' gradually gave way to acceptance and peace.

My search provided an unexpected bonus: an expanded perspective and awareness of the adoption process, the changing face of contemporary adoption practices, and the issues faced by adoptees.

Without the constant and loving support of my husband, Rob, and my children, the successful search for my birth identity and the writing of this book would simply not have been possible.

Preface

The names of a few people, including some family members, have been changed out of respect for their wishes and to protect their privacy.

PART ONE

Who Am I?

CHAPTER ONE

The letter

The letter arrived in a drab brown envelope stamped 'official'. At that moment I had no idea how big a change in my life this innocent-looking letter would make. It was October 1966. I was nineteen, and had been living in Johannesburg for a year. I was staying in the YWCA, a centrally-located, purpose-built modern hostel for women. My room was on the fifth floor with a pleasant outlook over the city. Mum and Dad (Elizabeth and Benjamin) lived in Salisbury (now known as Harare) in Rhodesia (now called Zimbabwe) and a year earlier they had encouraged me to move to Johannesburg, and had also supported the choice of the YWCA as a place where I could live. Some years before this, James, my brother, who was seven years my elder, had moved to Australia.

It was standard practice for the South African Department of Immigration to contact newcomers at the end of their first year to ask if they were planning to stay permanently in South Africa and if so, to invite them to complete an application for permanent residency.

It seemed fairly straightforward; however I needed my birth certificate. I looked for it in the document file in my cupboard, but it wasn't there. Where could it be?

Then I remembered, Mum and Dad had done all the paperwork for my passport application a few years earlier, so maybe they still had it. In my next weekly letter home, I asked Mum and Dad to post my birth certificate to me. They probably kept it with my other personal documents in their safe at home in Rhodesia. With that done, I put it out of my mind.

After supper on the very next Sunday night, I was sitting on the edge of my bed in my hostel room choosing clothes to wear for the week ahead. The curtains were half open and the city lights twinkled in the dark of the night. It had been a sociable weekend – with a great party the previous evening filled with new friends, guitar playing, and folk singing.

'Jane, room fifty-two, please take a phone call in the lobby!'

The intercom announcement boomed into the bedrooms of all seventy residents. I had never had a phone call during my stay at the hostel, so generally took no notice of these broadcasts. There was a brief pause and the proclamation rang out again, and this time the voice was more insistent. I suddenly realised the announcement was for me! How embarrassing. I jumped up, pressed the intercom button, acknowledged the message, and dashed downstairs.

Who was it? Who would be phoning me?

This was long before the days of mobile phones, and at that time in Johannesburg, there was a long wait to get a phone connected at home. We were fortunate as the hostel had two public telephones in the lobby. No privacy though! The motherly concierge, as well as any residents with their guests, could hear every conversation. This did not bother me, as I was not planning to have any personal conversations. But who could be phoning?

'Hello. Good evening,' I said in my most confident voice.

'Hello, Jane. It is Dad. How are you?' Of course as soon as I heard his heavy German accented voice, I knew it was Dad. But why was he phoning me? What was the urgency?

'Fine – thank you, Dad. How are you? How is Mum?'

Dad, characteristically, came straight to the point.

'We are all right, Jane. Thank you for asking. We received your letter.'

Oh, yes. I remembered now.

Dad continued in the tone I knew so well that meant, 'Do not question me; let me finish what I want to say, then please follow my instructions!' Perhaps he was aware of where I was and that there was no privacy.

'Jane, I won't beat about the bush. I will say immediately why I am phoning you. Mum and I want you to fly home for the weekend next Saturday. It will be nice for you to visit and we can give you the documents you ask for.

Fly home, for just a weekend! I liked the idea of going home. It was quite a few months since they had visited me in Johannesburg. But, why did they want me home suddenly, at such short notice? Why fly all that way for only a twenty-four hour visit? This would be my first trip home since Christmas the year before.

Feeling apprehensive, I knew Dad did not want me to question anything over the phone.

'Okay, Dad. That's fine,' I said.

He continued. 'I'll book the flight and organise for the ticket to reach you before you leave. Take a taxi to the airport on Saturday morning and I will pay. I will meet you at the airport.'

'Thanks, Dad,' I said. After asking Dad to give Mum my love, we rang off.

Wow! How exciting! The pleasure of looking forward to flying to Salisbury diminished any doubts or uncertainties about why I had been called home so suddenly. Life at nineteen was exhilarating and I felt as if nothing could go wrong.

There was little that could have prepared me for what was to follow.

CHAPTER TWO

Salisbury

Six days later, I flew home to Salisbury in a Viscount aeroplane. The loud drone in the cabin of the aircraft surprised me, but it couldn't dampen my excitement. I felt very special having a window seat and enjoyed looking at the scenery below. It was like a living geography lesson. The farmland soon gave way to bush veldt as we flew over the Northern Transvaal. I was fascinated by the silvery glint of the meandering rivers as the sun reflected off the water. Gradually, the countryside was obscured by the gathering of soft woolly clouds. They were starting to pile loftily upon each other in preparation for the afternoon rains, changing into various tones of lighter and darker grey, capped in white. In the gaps between the gathering clouds, it was possible to see the mud brown of the Limpopo River and the faded yellow grass plains of Rhodesia.

After more than two hours in the air we landed at Salisbury. It was already after lunch.

Dad was waiting for me at the airport and very soon we were driving home. We chatted and I asked how Mum was, but his response was evasive. That was curious.

Salisbury was mostly flat and spread out, with the exception of the Kopje, a solitary hill with a pretty outlook. From there, in August and September, one could look out over the city and see the masses of jacaranda trees with their blue/purple flowers that lined the streets and filled the parks. In October the flowers began to slowly fade and fall, with apple-green leaf shoots taking their place. The fallen flowers then became a mauve carpet along the grassy pavements. In 1966, Salisbury was a young, clean 'modern' city with wide, tree-lined avenues and a botanical garden near the city centre. It was an attractive African town full of hope and a positive atmosphere.

I took everything at face value and felt totally safe there.

As soon as we arrived home, I went looking for Mum and found her sitting in the study. I said hello and bent to give her a hug. To my horror and fright, she stiffened at my touch. What was wrong? First Dad wouldn't speak about Mum and now she recoiled from me — what was all this about?

Mum clearly didn't want me with her, and with Geoffrey, our cook, in the kitchen next door, within earshot, I understood she would be reluctant to talk to me about anything upsetting or personal. So, I quietly left her and went to the kitchen to say hello to Geoffrey.

'Helloo, Missy Jen.' He smiled broadly as I entered the kitchen and we shook hands. He looked happy and as smart as usual in his white uniform and white chef's hat. He had been our chef for many years. It was good to see him and we had a short chat. Then he went to his quarters across the lawn for his afternoon time off.

Mum, Dad and I now had the house to ourselves.

I took my bag upstairs to my bedroom; it was just as I'd left it a little over a year earlier. Glancing out the window at the familiar landscape, I noted with a twinge of regret that my tree house had been taken down. I left my bedroom and as I came down the stairs, Dad called me into the study, where Mum was already waiting.

Upon entering the small oak-panelled room, I caught a whiff of Dad's favourite cigars. I had grown to love the complex aromas of his cigars. I was home again. I took in the large, familiar oil paintings of Granddad Leonhard and Grandmother Esther looking down at me. To my left was a heavy, elaborately-carved, wooden chair upholstered in dull brown, well-worn leather on the seat, high back, and armrests. Behind the chair was a large framed photograph of Aunt Hanna and Dad as children. Opposite the door was a window, and to the right of that, a large oak desk with a glass top. Dad sat at this desk when he worked at home. Behind the desk and running across the width of the room were bench-height oak cupboards, also with glass tops. Immediately to the right of the door and against the wall, in front of the desk, was a comfortable, soft green velvet, winged-back chair – one of my favourites.

As I had often done in past years, I sat in front of the window on a well-worn and comfortable Moroccan leather pouffe. This lower seating option completed an equilateral triangle in front of Mum and Dad's chairs. I would be looking up at them, and hoped this would make them feel at ease.

I did not particularly like the study. It was dimly lit, partly because of the wood panelling, but also because the only window looked out onto the open carport, which had a roof that cut out much of the light. The room was south-facing as well. All in all making it seem dark and cold.

Mum sat stiffly on the edge of the green velvet chair. She was always conscious of her posture. Dad moved the heavy wooden chair out of the way, took down the large, ebony-framed photograph of him and his sister, and opened the heavy safe door hidden behind. He took out a buff-coloured file, retrieved some papers from it and put the file back into the safe.

I presumed these would include my birth certificate.

Mum fixed me with her blue eyes and started the conversation, but I was distracted by her demeanour. She had always seemed age-less to me - she would have been sixty-one at the time - but looked younger than that. She was still attractive and slender and, as usual, dressed impeccably in a pretty, blue and white floral dress with a dainty round white collar. She wore clear nylon stockings with pat-terned white and tan, low-heeled Italian shoes. Her hands were nervously folding and unfolding a hand-embroidered white hand-kerchief.

CHAPTER THREE

Jonathan and me

Mum came straight to the point and I was struck again by her use of language and the beautiful way she spoke. She was proud of being able to speak the 'Queen's English.' However, today she was certainly not herself. She looked at me and in a stilted voice said, 'Jane, this is a long story. You know Dad and I married in London, that James was born there in 1940, and that after WWII, we had Jonathan. We've told you about him.'

I nodded. Jonathan was my secret brother.

Mum changed position in her chair, and now looked down, avoiding eye contact with me. My apprehension grew. Dad, still standing and holding the papers in his left hand, moved closer to Mum. He looked most unhappy.

'I do not think you know, but during the WWII, while still living in England and before I was pregnant with Jonathan, I had two mis-carriages. This was extremely traumatic and disappointing. Then, to our delight, I became pregnant with Jonathan and the pregnancy went well. We were so hopeful.' Her eyes welled with tears and she paused, struggling to regain her composure.

I felt helpless, only able to sit and quietly listen.

She swallowed, looked down, and spoke again in a low soft voice.

'When Jonathan was born, we discovered he was born with Down's syndrome. We were devastated. We asked Dr Davidson for advice and he told us Jonathan would probably not grow up normally and might not be able to learn basic skills like talking or dressing himself. He would probably be retarded and most likely would need special care and help all his life. He also had health issues, including heart problems.'

Tears rolled down her face.

'Why did you ask Dr Davidson for advice?' I asked.

'He was our family's doctor in London. Dad chose him because he was German and Jewish and from Berlin, like Dad.' Mum glanced at Dad, and then vehemently said, 'I didn't much like him, but Dad felt he would understand our family's situation.'

'Oh, come on, Elizabeth – is this relevant?' He looked cross and uncomfortable.

Mum continued, saying, 'We knew that having a child with Down's syndrome quite often happened to older mothers. Dr Davidson told us about that. He also advised us to put Jonathan into a home where he would receive proper care. This was considered best for someone like him in those days.'

She wiped her eyes with her handkerchief.

A question crept into my mind with all the talk about Jonathan. What has this to do with me? I wished I could relieve her distress, but I knew so little and especially did not know anyone who had Down's syndrome.

Her voice quivered and she looked at me earnestly.

'We had to think of our whole family. It was a terrible time. We were both extremely distressed.'

Dad spoke up at this point, his agitation showing in his voice.

'Elizabeth, do not upset yourself. Do you have to go into this now?'

Mum struggled again to regain composure. After two miscarriages, having Jonathan, with his disability, must have been devastating. She looked up at Dad and gave him a determined nod, as if to say: be patient, I'm getting there.

Taking a breath to steady herself, she went on. 'Jonathan stayed with us for a few months. We had a nurse to help, but we struggled. We thought carefully about Dr Davidson's advice. We had already decided to migrate to Southern Rhodesia. We wanted a new life. But, how could we care for Jonathan in Rhodesia? He would have had special needs and we would not have been able to provide him with the support – his schooling and the health care he needed.' She paused and took a breath.

'And so, when a position became available in a special home for babies like Jonathan, we took him there. We met the nurses, who were nuns and very kind to us, and who knew how to take good care of babies like Jonathan.' She sobbed and sobbed then. It was almost as if she was reliving how they made that heart-wrenching decision.

'We did not feel we had a choice, Jane. We believed this was the best decision not only for him, but also for our family.' Mum continued to sob, her shoulders heaving and her face buried in her handkerchief.

I felt overwhelmed by the waves of her pain coming at me. I was struck by her sadness, despite saying she believed they had done the best thing for Jonathan.

But – why was I part of this? Why were they telling me about Jonathan? I struggled up off the cushion and went to her, putting my arms around her.

Dad was silent, and then sternly said, 'Oh, come now, Elizabeth! Let us get on with it. Let us get to the point. It doesn't help to talk like this.'

I knew he could not bear to watch Mum cry.

Mum stiffened in my encircling arms. I backed away and sat down again.

She drew in a ragged breath and continued. 'Soon after Jonathan was born, after we decided that Jonathan would go into care, Dr Davidson told us that there was a newborn baby girl whose mother could not care for her – and that she needed a home. Dr Davidson said they were looking for a good home and a loving family for the baby girl. We thought about it, Jane, and decided to go ahead.' The next sentence came out in a soft rush. 'That baby girl was you.'

She stopped talking and there was silence.

I was stunned, struggling to understand. So, I'm not their daughter. I'm someone else's daughter! They had known all along and didn't tell me! Why? What did this mean? I frantically began to scan back through my childhood, sensing this revelation might explain many things. But I was numb and there was too little time. This was more than I could process.

Mum and Dad sat in front of me looking worried and anxiously waiting for me to respond. Mum began to cry softly and Dad put his arm around her. Their wait may have been only a few moments, but it seemed an eternity.

'Mum and Dad' I said, and then stopped. I was confused, but also afraid. Would they still want to be my mum and dad? I had such mixed feelings, gratitude – waves of gratitude – followed by a flood of questions, doubts, worry. I did not know what to say.

Time stood still.

Who was I, after all? Who were my real mother and father? Where were they? Would I ever find out about them, meet them, or get to know them? Why did they give me up for adoption?

I looked at Mum and Dad. Would my relationship with them change? Would they still love me? Would I still have a home to come back to? And where was Jonathan now? What had happened to him? I felt helpless, pushed along by thoughts and questions swirling around my head, each one far too much to absorb. I could do nothing. The blood drained from my face, and I felt cold and clammy. For a dark moment that seemed to last forever, I panicked. But no – this was not the time to do that! I vividly remember the effort it took to maintain my composure and control my reactions. I had to preserve my family relationships. An enormous gulf seemed to open between us – amid a stunning realisation that it might have been there all along. They had known about this all the years I lived with them.

Enough! I could not face that. Stop. Stay grounded. I had to stay in control despite the erupting feelings – feelings I could not name yet. But there was no time to think. The seconds were passing and Mum and Dad were still waiting. I sensed the immensity of the tragedy Jonathan's disability had been for them; the loss of the child they had so desperately wanted. I wanted them to explain and talk more about what had happened, but most of all, I needed reassurance that they would still want to be my parents.

'Mum and Dad – I love you. You are still the only mum and dad I have known. You are all I have.' I struggled to get up off the pouffe and hugged them.

'Oh, Jane,' they said in unison, with immense relief. 'We were so worried! We did not know how you would take this.'

But was there more to come?

CHAPTER FOUR

Forbidden territory

Even with my attempt at reassuring Mum and Dad, the tension in the study stayed high. Why? I found this hard to understand. At the same time, unanswered questions whirled around my head. I helped myself and Mum to a couple of tissues from a box on the desk and we all took a few deep breaths. I sat back down on the pouffe.

Now, it was *my* turn to speak.

'I have questions, of course, but what I want to say first is: thank you Mum and Dad! Thank you for all that you have done for me!' I tried to control the quivering in my voice and I could see they understood and appreciated that I was trying to keep calm. The impact of Jonathan's life on Mum and Dad, and his long-lasting influence on all our family flooded into consciousness, not as words, but as a series of feelings. There was so much I wanted to convey but words were strangely elusive.

'It must have been extraordinarily difficult for you when Jonathan was born,' I said.

Mum nodded, looking at me soulfully, as tears rolled down her cheek.

I felt tears coming, too, as their generosity and the enormity of what they had done for me sank in.

Moreover, I had known about Jonathan since childhood, but not the special connection between us. I couldn't imagine what it must have been like to take me home as a baby, so soon after taking Jonathan, also still a baby, to the children's home. How could they possibly have come to terms with having to leave Jonathan in that time? I was shocked. After losing their much anticipated baby, what did this mean as far as how they related to me?

Dad fetched Mum another tissue. I felt alone and cold and started to shiver uncontrollably, as the chill of their message began to sink in. I struggled once again to maintain control. I knew this discussion would not easily happen again and certainly could not have occurred over the telephone. I did not know when we would be together again – possibly only for Christmas – and that was months away. I felt increasingly anxious and also concerned about Mum and Dad. I knew that if I was restrained, it would go a long way toward relieving and containing their hurt, and might help them to continue talking about it. I desperately needed to safeguard our relationship, and I thought that was their aim, too. Feelings could be explored later, but my need to know pushed me on to ask more questions.

We talked further and gradually both Mum and Dad relaxed. Dad sat down on his large leather chair and Mum slowly eased back into her into the padded green velvet of her chair.

We talked about the circumstances of my adoption. Where, when, and how they received me? Did they meet my biological mother or father and what they were like? Mum did most of the talking.

'On the day we arranged to adopt you, we visited Dr Davidson. His practice was located in a terrace in Regents Park. In fact, he had beautiful rooms in one of the Nash terraces. It was a very exclusive address. We found you there in a pram in the surgery. Then, we realised that we had seen your mother, from the back, as she left the surgery. She was tall and smartly dressed in high heels. It was raining and she wore a long black raincoat with a belt and she had an umbrella.'

I remember Mum's description of my mother was so good that I could picture her silhouette.

'What did Dr Davidson tell you about my parents?' I asked, anxious to know.

'He said that your Mother was English, and of an age similar to mine. He also said you were the result of mixed parentage, from a good class of person.'

'Oh,' I said, trying to absorb what she was saying. 'What did that mean?'

15

I kept asking more questions, but Mum explained that adoptive parents were often not told much about the parents of their adopted baby.

'Dr Davidson led us to believe that your parents were similar to us. Dad and I are mixed both in nationality and religion, for example. Dad is from Germany and I am English. Your parents might have had a different nationality and religion, though I'm not sure about this.'

She went on. 'You know, Jane, Dr Davidson was a private doctor and it cost a lot to consult him. It's quite possible that your mother couldn't afford Dr Davidson's fees, so perhaps your father arranged for your mother to see Dr Davidson and paid for it.'

This raised all sorts of questions. I assumed Mother was English, like Mum, but what nationality was Father? If he was the person who arranged for Mother to go to Dr Davidson, could he have been, like Dad: German, Jewish and from Berlin?

'Why did my biological mother not keep me?' I asked. I felt very vulnerable. How could she give me away? I felt raw with pain.

'Dr Davidson said that she was not in a position to keep you. She probably could not cope financially and was not able to marry her partner.'

I could not help but feel disappointed and rejected.

Mum continued. 'This happened a lot then, especially just after the war. Years ago, there was no way of a woman being able to survive if she wasn't married and could not work. There were no pensions in those days.'

'Why could she not marry her partner?'

'I do not know. It could be that your father was not in a position to marry her. Maybe he was already married. Perhaps his wife was in an asylum.' Mum mentioned this again several times later on that afternoon. What did this mean for me?

'Do you actually know that?' I asked.

Mum was evasive. 'We were told very little Jane, but I do remember that she, too, was an older mother. Dr Davidson told me that. During the war, it was difficult for everybody. A single mother would not have been able to provide for you.'

We talked a while longer, and then the atmosphere strangely changed and Mum's voice took on a completely different tone when, with her voice raised for emphasis, she said, 'There is one thing you must promise us, Jane!'

She fixed me with her blue eyes and Dad stared at me as she continued.

'Nobody in Rhodesia knows you are adopted. We wanted to give you the best life possible – just as if you were our real daughter,' Mum said, and then added, 'We think you should keep it that way.'

I asked them if James, my brother, knew about me – he was seven when I was adopted. I was upset and was struggling to keep my feelings contained and hidden.

'Yes. He knew,' Dad said. Much later, nearly forty years later, James told me that, as a seven year old little boy, he was with Mum and Dad when they went to collect me from Dr Davidson's surgery.

'How come James did not tell me while I was growing up? Did you tell him not to tell me?'

'Yes,' they both said.

So, my adoption had been a secret between the three of them. For all my nineteen years, while I grew up believing them to be my biological parents, they kept this secret from me. I felt betrayed and so alone. I felt degraded and devalued. How connected could they feel towards me? Was I ever considered a full member of their family? I had always been on the outside. I began to shiver again. I could not absorb much more. I needed time out. I tried to make light of it.

'I have often wondered why we do not look like each other Mum. Now I know why!' My voice sounded artificially bright and cheery. I was not yet in control of myself. Mum nodded, looking at me and perhaps understood my attempt at levity was a signal that I was reaching the end of my endurance.

But they had still more to say. Mum's demeanour became very serious and Dad leaned forward with an intense look on his face.

'Jane, there is one more important thing,' she said. The tone of her voice was again very stern. 'You must promise us–' She paused a moment. 'You must promise us *never* to look for your mother and father.'

I gave an involuntary gasp. How *could* they ask this?

She leaned toward me and spoke slowly, pronouncing each word clearly and unequivocally. 'Jane, please promise us never to search for your mother and father.'

'But – why?' I asked, feeling crushed and defeated. It was a familiar feeling by now. I had no idea what to think or do.

'Because you do not know what you will find. You must *promise* us, Jane!'

'Promise us!' Dad insisted.

'What do you mean, I won't know what I will find?' I asked.

'Well, your mother may not be living in good circumstances. She may well be poor and you may find that she wants help. Sometimes people have contacted their families only to find out all sorts of things they did not want to know, and their families have come begging.'

Why were Mum and Dad so insistent? Did they know something more? Were they hiding something?

'If you love us Jane, do not look for your mother! Promise us that you will not search for your mother and father!'

I looked at them both. Surely my need to find out about my real parents was natural. I was confused. I had a tight feeling in my chest and my throat thickened. I felt as if I were suffocating. I looked into their faces. There was concern there, but I was not sure what it meant or what they knew.

'All right, I promise,' I replied, looking down. Yet again, I felt overwhelmed and so alone. I could not make sense of their motivation for asking me to do this. Could I be a daughter of a relative? I did not think Mum's sister, Aunt Dorothy, had any children. Were there some further family secrets involved? Were they under an obligation to ask this of me? If so, then why?

'And Jane, you must let this be our family secret. We do not want anybody here in Rhodesia knowing you are adopted. That would start too many questions.'

'What do you mean?' I asked mischievously.

'Oh, you know what we mean!' Dad replied in a stern voice.

I did know what they meant. They meant that no one in Rhodesia at this time knew about Jonathan's existence or the fact that I was adopted, and they wanted to keep it that way. But was this all?–

As was often the case with my parents, it was what was left unsaid that was important. They seemed anxious to reassure me about how lucky I was and began to remind me how privileged I had been, growing up in a nice home and having them for parents. I had heard this kind of talk before – many times in the past. 'You are very fortunate, Jane,' they often said when I was growing up. But this time they went further, reminding me about the plight I might have found myself in if they hadn't adopted me. They spoke of how babies often did not find families to adopt them, let alone families who could afford to bring them up in the manner I had enjoyed.

I sincerely felt grateful for all they had done for me, but it didn't feel good to be reminded of it – especially under the heavy veil of their long-kept secret. But it was an expectation of theirs. I found myself all through my childhood saying thank you and how much I appreciated what they did for me – to the extent that once my brother James asked me why I kept 'sucking up' to them.

I had been puzzled for years about their oft-repeated reminders to be grateful. It is something my husband and I would never feel the need to say to our children. Now, two generations later, I understand more. Expressing my gratitude was my way of asking for confirmation of their love and of establishing that I was indeed secure in my relationship with them.

Much, much later, I discovered this is a common experience of adoptees.

They paused for a moment, and then debated asking Geoffrey to come back from his afternoon rest and make us some tea, but decided against it; we could make our own tea and keep our privacy.

After tea, Mum spoke more freely about what being adopted meant. I had never met anyone who was adopted. At my age, one hated to be different to one's peers, so it was not something I would want to talk about with friends. In addition, how acceptable was it to be adopted? Mum reminded me about one of my Jewish boy friends who had been keen to marry me, but with whom I had long since broken up. She said that if this boyfriend had known that I was adopted, he might not have even started going out with me. Knowing him, I agreed with her – but it forcibly brought home the social stigma attached to being 'a bastard' and 'illegitimate'. She urged me again to keep our family secret and warned me that if I told my friends about my adoption, they might be sympathetic to my face, but would not necessarily be so when they were not with me. On the positive side, Mum said true friends would accept me for who I was. This was clearly sound advice.

I cannot remember much more about that Saturday, except that we all tried to make it a pleasant one. Mum and Dad, with some other Jewish families, were starting a Reform Jewish congregation. They asked if the next time I came home I would like to sing at one of their celebrations. I happily agreed.

So, they did want me to come home again and to continue to be part of their lives. It was clear that they planned my visit home and their talk with me very carefully. They wanted it to end on a good note, and so did I.

They would always be my mum and dad.

Then, they told me of their plans to sell the family home and build a new home on the other side of town. I felt strong pangs of regret; this was where I had grown up. I was pleased for them, and said it was lovely they had such a creative and constructive project to look forward to.

The next day, I took my last walk around our house and garden. Memories flooded in. I remembered reading my favourite books about Biggles by the light of the moon streaming through my bedroom window. And gazing through that window, I looked longingly at the tree I loved to climb as a child and the thatched garden house I used to play in.

I had always loved Mum's bedroom and the little anteroom next to hers, a glassed-in porch where I used to sew with my Singer sewing machine. I remember Mum watching over me, giving me advice as I went along. I remember the landing at the top of our stairs where our much-loved dachshund, Pluto, gave his last breath.

Downstairs, the kitchen was a place I sometimes shared with Geoffrey, who was ever ready to talk with me and teach me, always with a smile. The room next to the kitchen was where I used to help Mum as she arranged flowers for the dining table and hallway when we had guests.

I said goodbye to Geoffrey and Charles in the garden, wondering when next I would see them.

That afternoon, Mum and Dad drove me to the airport, and I flew back to Johannesburg a totally different person, harbouring serious secrets – the new and shadowy presence of my biological parents – lurking like ghosts in the back of my mind. I had little choice but to doggedly try to resume my 'normal' life, whatever that might be.

CHAPTER FIVE

Questions

Fortunately, lapses in memory can be wonderfully soothing. When thinking became too painful or overwhelming, I stopped thinking. I remember commenting to a boyfriend at the time that being able to shut out painful events in one's life was a huge relief. I did my best to ignore what had happened. If thoughts and memories did pop back into consciousness, as they had a habit of doing, I pushed them back down into a darker corner of my mind.

I had been forbidden to search for my birth family and told it was in my best interest to keep my adoption a secret. So, what could I do? There was no way I could even work through it. I didn't know anyone else who was adopted.

Once again, what was left unsaid was important.

Sometimes I feel as if being adopted is rather like swimming in the sea with goggles on. Most people, when they swim in the sea, can look up and have a clear view of the sky and the scenery around them and it is tangible and real. When an adopted person chooses to search for their biological family, it is rather like choosing to wear goggles. A whole new world emerges below the water line; sometimes clearly, sometimes not, that is just as real.

After returning to South Africa from Rhodesia the hurt and questions grew. Why couldn't I know the truth about who I am? Why was it so necessary for my adoptive parents and family, those who arranged my adoption, and my biological mother and father and their families to have these secrets? Whose interests were they serving? Why must I be excluded from information that everyone else takes for granted? Why can't I know who my mother and father are?

What I believed to be true, what I thought real and could depend on, seemed to slip away. I grew up believing I was one person, and now I was somebody else. My sense of reality became tenuous and keeping the sense of rejection at bay was a constant effort. Who was I after all? And how do I find out?

It took decades to integrate this new identity into a 'new' me. Many childhood experiences, with the meanings and interpretations I had attributed to them, now needed to be revisited through the new prism of adoption. I needed to re-establish and confirm who I was to myself. Perhaps there were clues I had missed that could provide explanations to the myriad other questions I seemed to have.

What I really hated most was not being able to be completely open and frank with my close friends, acquaintances, and others that I knew. From my perspective, this really interfered with those I most wanted to connect with and was both awful and very painful.

Decades passed, and it slowly dawned on me that if I re-examined my childhood, my relationship with Mum and Dad, and our lives together, it might help to clarify some things. I had taken them at face value and now I needed to look more closely at their lives and history. If they weren't my biological parents – who were they? Were there clues and nuances I had missed that would shed light on my origins and my relationship with them? And did I understand all there was to know about why they made the decisions they did?

And why insist on the secrecy? Why were they so vehement and insistent that I never search for my biological parents? I wanted to be loyal to them and to feel secure in my relationship with them. I couldn't imagine any circumstances or reason not to keep my promise. Nevertheless, the strength of their insistence that I keep this promise was curious and out of character. And made me wonder: what more was there to discover?

They were people of their times and it is possible that a better understanding of their social and historical perspective could shed more light on this need for secrecy. This search for understanding would become a rewarding, healing, and vital part of the process for me. And what's more, I could start to re-examine my childhood and explore their history without breaking my promise.

CHAPTER SIX

Mum's early life in London

The process of examining my childhood started in a strange way. I was mining – mining my memories.

Some of my very first memories date back to when I was three or four when James, my brother, was away at boarding school. I would listen to Elizabeth, my adoptive mother, reminiscing about our life in England. These story times took place in her bedroom upstairs in our home in Salisbury.

On Sunday mornings, Dad would take Mum's breakfast tray into her room, and after a quick chat, he would leave for work. About an hour after Dad left, I would knock softly on Mum's door; wait for her invitation to enter, and then say 'Good morning, Mum. How are you?' If she was well or in a good mood, she would chat with me. I would usually find her sitting in bed in her dressing gown, reading the newspaper or a book, or sitting at her dressing table.

Mum was particularly fond of her bedroom because she had designed it. It was added on a year or two after the house was built. A large north-facing room, painted a soft powder blue, with heavy royal-blue damask curtains hanging either side of a large window, it overlooked our sunburnt rose garden. Shafts of sunlight would bathe the room in light and warmth. Next to her bed was a royal blue velvet armchair and matching velvet footstool. The footstool was my favourite seat when she chatted to me. I remember looking up at her as she put on make-up at her dressing table. It was at times like those that I felt closest to her. When her familiar scent wafted over me, I felt at home.

I loved sitting on the velvet footstool during those mornings, listening to her stories about her childhood and our family in England. They became embedded into my own sense of self. Like most young children, I accepted everything without question. If, at the end of our time together, she was happy she would give me a hug. Remembering those mornings still gives me a warm glow.

Mum's stories painted her history for me. She was born Elizabeth Watson in March, 1905 in London. She had an older sister, my Aunt Dorothy, and two younger brothers. Her family was poor, but they made the best of their circumstances and were a happy family.

Her father was injured in World War I (WWI) and her mother, cared for him. She was a fiercely independent woman who paid the bills from the laundry she took in.

Mum adored her older sister, they really enjoyed growing up together and sharing the responsibility of caring for their two younger brothers. Interestingly, I remember the envy in her voice when she spoke of how her brothers were adored by her parents.

Her family belonged to the Church of England and they attended church regularly. They lived in a small, two-storey, semi-detached brick terrace house with a tiny backyard in the working-class part of Chelsea. She was proud of living in Chelsea, which even in 1905 was quite Bohemian, well-known for its artists, painters, and Pre-Raphaelites.

One of her stories was about the family cat. During winter in the bitter cold, their cat would often climb into the coal-fired kitchen range oven (sometimes called a kitchener) to get warm. One day, the oven door closed and the poor cat was discovered a few hours later, roasting! Her three-year-old brother said, 'Look Mother, (Mum's mother, Sarah), there is the cat with some gwavy!'

Mum and her sister walked to school even when it was sleeting or snowing. Mum enjoyed singing in the school and church choirs and did well at school. She was given parts in school plays and in her last year at school she played the lead in an end-of-year Gilbert and Sullivan musical performance.

Soon after her fourteenth birthday, a year after WWI had ended and when she could legally leave school, her school principal visited her parents and asked if she could stay at school. This was not to be though, as Mum's parents needed her income. Her father could no longer work and her sister, now a milliner, was already contributing her earnings to the family purse. They needed Mum's help too. Mum accepted her fate with grace.

Soon after that, she was offered a junior position at Harrods, the beautiful department store in Knightsbridge. She was thrilled. Mum joined Harrods in 1919 when she was fourteen and soon progressed up the hierarchy. She became a buyer of young women's fashions. In 1920, Harrods was a British icon of fashion, elegance, and class. Besides attending fashion shows and going on buying trips to Paris or Berlin in the 1930s, she also travelled seven times to New York on the ocean liner, *The RMS Queen Mary*. She had a wonderful career and wasn't affected by the depression of the 1930s.

When her father died and once her brothers had left home, Mum and her sister moved to an apartment with their mother, staying there until she married Dad.

Mum had a close relationship with her mother, Sarah, and sister, Dorothy. Dorothy's skills as a milliner came in handy when together, they made their own suits, coats, and beautiful hats. Mum always had a clear understanding of style, design, and dressmaking, as well as how clothes should fit.

Sadly, Mum's mother, Sarah, passed away before I was born, so I never knew her.

Mum grew to be a very attractive woman. She had large, pale blue eyes, high wide cheekbones, even features, and lovely wavy brown hair. Her slender figure meant that she always looked like a model in her clothes. People often said she was a 'real lady'.

A year or two before she died, Mum gave me a lovely photograph taken of her while she worked at Harrods. She was beautifully dressed in the fashion of the time as a flapper. I used the photograph as a subject soon after I started painting. It has a special place in our home and is a fond memory of our story times together.

In the mid-1930s she met Dad.

CHAPTER SEVEN

Mum and Dad in London – 1933–40

Mum told me that soon after Dad and Grandfather Leonhard arrived in London in 1933, they rented an apartment and Dad started work at Dickins and Jones. He was in ladies fashion in the Regent Street store owned by Harrods, the same company where Mum was working. Dad met Mum through work and he courted her for years. Mum's career in the world of fashion made her very attractive to Dad given his background. While they courted, Mum helped Dad improve his English and Dad would sometimes take her to Paris for the day in a small aeroplane.

I thought this was so romantic, and rather extravagant.

It was clear that Dad was a person of some means and that Leonhard approved of his choice. Perhaps he thought that Mum's expertise would be a great asset to Dad as he endeavoured to learn about the fashion trade in London.

Mum found Dad's courting very hard to resist. He was very charming and he had a twinkle in his eye. Although Mum was a member of the Church of England when Dad proposed to her, she agreed to convert to Judaism. Dad and his father attended the West London Synagogue, Britain's oldest Jewish Reform Synagogue. Mum really liked the Rabbi – he was inclusive and welcomed her warmly into the congregation. They married in late 1938. Their marriage certificate is a beautiful document written in both Hebrew and English. Mum told me she took her conversion seriously; she studied Hebrew, attended prayers, and learned how to run a Jewish household.

Soon after Mum and Dad married WWII started – in September 1939 – and interrupted everything. Dad's status changed from being an alien to being an 'enemy alien'. Also, in the spring of 1940, WWII was not going well and there was an increased fear of spies. All Germans over the age of sixteen were called before special tribunals and many were sent to camps. The fact that Dad was a Jewish refugee, hardly likely to be sympathetic to the Nazis, seemed not to influence the outcome.

Dad was interned, but I don't know where he was sent. Initially, married women were not allowed into the camps to see their husbands. However, by August 1940, visits were permitted, and in late 1941, a family camp was established.

My brother, James, was born in 1940. I cannot imagine a more stressful time for Mum, a new mother with an infant baby boy to care for, just as WWII was progressing badly. She was shocked and distressed to discover after she married Dad, that although she was born British, she had to relinquish her British citizenship and register as a German national. After extensive administrative lobbying, she was re-admitted to British nationality in 1941. Dad was re-admitted to British nationality in 1947, with the recorded address as East Sheen, Richmond, and his occupation as 'gown manufacturer.'

East Sheen near Richmond Park must have been a frightening place to live during the war. Just outside Sheen Gate, the British Army had set up an anti-aircraft gun that was used to shoot down German aircraft flying over London.

During one of our morning talks, while sitting on the royal blue velvet footstool, I remember asking Mum, 'What about Dad's childhood, Mum? Can you tell me about his life before he met you?' I remember Mum smiling at my enthusiasm and saying, 'Not yet, Jane. Let's talk about you first. Dad's story will make more sense then.'

CHAPTER EIGHT

From London to Southern Rhodesia – 1947–1954

I was born in April 1947 in London, England. Mum told me I was a very small baby and that I cried often because I had colic. Soon after I was born, Mum and Dad invited Marty, a young girl from Switzerland, to stay with us and help care for me. She spoke German, like Dad, and brought a happy atmosphere into our home.

When I was about two months old, Leonhard came with our family on a holiday to Malta and he and I were the subject of a newspaper article with a lovely photograph. When Mum told me about it, I thought it was a wonderful story.

Although Britain offered a safe place for our family to live, Britain had been at war with Germany and Germans. Dad was both German and Jewish. Mum explained that he didn't feel at home and wanted to start over somewhere without the hangover of WWII. So, soon after I was born, Mum and Dad started to think about moving to Southern Rhodesia. Eventually, Dad travelled to Salisbury, decided to settle there, and employed an architect to build a house for us.

Moving to Southern Rhodesia must have seemed a very constructive way for them to cope. They could leave the sadness and destruction of World War II behind them. They could start a new life in a country far away from Europe. They could create a business of their own again and build their own home. There was a Jewish community in Salisbury, so they hoped to join a Jewish congregation. It would cost less to live in Rhodesia than in England, so they could travel back to England or Europe at any time. They felt confident the move was a wise decision.

In November 1949, Mum and Dad, my nine year old brother and

I, all said goodbye to Mum's sister, her other family, and Marty (who then returned to Switzerland) and boarded one of the Union Castle trans-Atlantic ocean liners, the Edinburgh Castle in Southampton. Our destination was to be Southern Rhodesia.

I was two and a half years old.

When we arrived in Salisbury in November 1949, our family of four was part of the wave of new immigrants that took the white settler population to about 125,000. White settlers, along with the Coloured and Asian people, comprised only about five per cent of the total population. A large number of the immigrants came from Britain and were welcomed because of the money they brought and the jobs they generated. This influx of people led to a post-war boom in the Southern Rhodesian economy, a welcome change after the world-wide depression and WWII.

Dad chose to live in a pleasant part of Salisbury, Southern Rhodesia's most industrial city, and the business capital. It was an attractive, clean African city, with lovely gardens and parks and beautiful bougainvillea. We lived in an English-looking, two-storey brick house. Our garden took up half of the five acres of land, with grass, bushes, roses, and other plants reminiscent of England. The jacaranda, pine, and pomegranate trees, with the bougainvillea, provided glorious colour in spring and summer. Along our street, which was a dirt road at that time, grew a long row of tall Australian eucalyptus trees.

Soon after arriving, Dad started a business importing a wide range of stationery and other goods to supply to retailers throughout the country. Mum and Dad worked hard. Dad would leave for work early, around 6.30 or 7am, while Mum left home around 9.30am, after organising the meals the cook should prepare for lunch and dinner. She would also talk with my nanny. They would come home for lunch at 1pm, drive back to work at 2pm, and return for dinner around 7pm. When they came home in the evenings, I would be allowed to be with them while they enjoyed a glass of sherry. I was sent to bed before their evening meal.

They would discuss the business at every mealtime - the weekly or monthly sales figures, their customers, who to sell their new stock to, and how to sell the old stock. The business did not always go well – finding suitable people to work for them was always an issue.

Sometimes, Dad would go alone to England and Europe on buying trips. Understandably, Mum hated having to stay behind to mind me and the business alone.

Within a few months of arriving, I was sent to nursery school and my brother, James, was sent to boarding school. From then on, he was only at home during school holidays. Mum had a special relationship with my brother and missed him terribly.

I enjoyed nursery school and being with the other children. I particularly enjoyed trying on the clothes and hats in the dressing up corner. Unfortunately, a few months after starting at the nursery school, I caught ringworm in my head – probably from trying on the hats. I had long, wavy brown hair, which all had to be cut off, and then my head was shaved two or three times a week. The ring-worm was contagious, so this meant that Mum couldn't take me to play with other children. It also prevented Mum from meeting other mothers, too. The local doctors did not know how to treat it, so it wasn't cured until two years later in Johannesburg.

I never returned to nursery school.

Mum went back to work in the family business with Dad, while indigenous African nannies, often recent arrivals to the city, looked after me during the day ensuring I was bathed, fed, and in my pyjamas ready for bed when Mum and Dad came home at 7pm. If I laughed and played with my nanny, Mum used to ask me why I was laughing or what I was playing at with her, and often, for reasons I didn't understand, Mum would ask the nannies to leave.

Those were very long, lonely, boring years.

Mum went into work every day during the week. However, on nanny's half-day off on Thursday afternoons, Mum would stay and read me nursery rhymes or stories. Once or twice, she showed me how to cut chains of people out of newspaper, which was fun. Later, she also encouraged me to read. She loved reading and believed that being self-reliant, independent, and having imagination was more valuable than expensive toys. I valued those principles and respected her views.

The first five years in Southern Rhodesia were tough for all our family. We were all aware that Mum was often depressed. When she was sad, Dad would ask that I leave the room. They would talk, and often he would forbid her to talk about the things that upset her. She missed her friends and her dear sister in England. Often, I was the only person around she could speak to, and she sometimes asked me not to tell anyone else what we had talked about. I felt helpless and there was very little I could do or say that could help her.

Now I know that the things that really upset her, she couldn't tell me about anyway. She would enjoy reminiscing about England and often compared her life in Rhodesia to her life in London. She talked about how she loved pushing the pram around beautiful Richmond Park, and how she loved to visit my Aunt in Upper Richmond Road, Putney or to walk along the Thames. She talked about the jonquils, daffodils, and all the English spring flowers she loved. She missed the lovely green English countryside with bluebells and roses. She was disappointed in her Rhodesian garden, because it did not look anything like her English garden. The grass went yellow in summer and plants seemed to shrivel or grow so slowly by comparison.

Sometimes, Dad would come home irritable or upset, especially when business was difficult, and then she would calm him down. She helped him a lot in this way.

Not long after we had arrived in Rhodesia, Dad came home with a pet dog, a dachshund, we called Pluto. He provided a happy distraction and I often played with him. Dad adored him.

By then, Mum and Dad had separate bedrooms, because Dad snored so loudly Mum could not sleep. I knew what she meant, as Dad's bedroom was next to mine, and even after closing my bedroom door I could hear him snore.

Mum often told me that her childhood was quite unlike mine.

Recently, I began to read about London in the early 1900s. This, together with my memories of the stories she told about her childhood, deepened my appreciation of the world she lived in, her attitudes, values, and her role as a parent at that time.

Mum and Dad were fairly strict parents and most of the time I was the only child at home. We had no extended family. They insisted I always say thank you and be grateful for whatever they did for me. Looking back, I now know that this was largely positive. They came from the era when children were expected to be seen, but not heard.

At times it must have been hard for Mum to understand me. When I was four and a half years old, Mum and I visited Johannesburg to obtain a cure for the ring worm I had contracted two years before; as a treat, she bought tickets to the film, The Wizard of Oz. She so looked forward to going out and spent a lot of time telling me how lovely the film was and about the characters. However, I was petrified. Unbeknown to her, I was terrified of the possibility of seeing sad or violent movies. I cried bitterly until she threw away the tickets. I still avoid violent or very sad movies.

The first few years settling into Rhodesia were also stressful for Mum and Dad.

Living as a child in the suburbs of Salisbury in the 1950s, with the hot summers and warm winters, the sunburnt veldt and tall eucalyptus, the flame trees and the lazy African summer sun, WWII seemed to be a world away, remote, and irrelevant to our day-to-day lives. Only much later did I become aware of the impact of WWII and the genocide of the Jews on a huge scale all over Europe.

But, for my adoptive parents, the opposite was true. Years later, Dad was still actively grieving, but I was too young to understand. Sometimes, he would begin to enthusiastically talk with Mum about an experience in his youth in Germany or Berlin or he would put a record on our gramophone and listen to a song by the famous and much loved German singer, Marlene Dietrich. He would start singing along only to end up choking up, and then silence and sadness would take over. Mum would ask me to leave the room and I would wonder if I had said or done something to make Dad sad. Now I know this wasn't so, but their WWII experiences became a source of heartache between us I could never really share. All through my childhood, on the occasions when this came up, I would find it hard to show that I understood. Sometimes they would be angry with me for not understanding and would try and explain, but after a while they would give up. This was far too far from my life experience. Inadvertently, I felt shut out and in the end I learnt to avoid these discussions.

Mum and Dad never liked speaking about their experiences during WWII. 'What is the point?' Dad would say. 'It does not help to go back over everything.' This was his way trying to cope.

Later, I wondered whether this kind of experience was an unexpected consequence of being adopted. But, more recently, it dawned on me that this could be a common occurrence among many of my generation born after WWII to parents traumatised by their wartime experiences and reluctant to talk about them.

This had a further unfortunate consequence. I associated 20th century history at school with what happened at home. If learning history meant I had to relive my parents' hurt, I wasn't interested. I didn't understand that at the time, nor did they. But it meant that when they were alive I avoided talking with them about WWII, perpetuating my lack of understanding of their early lives. Now, many decades later, history has a wonderful relevance leading to a richer understanding of our past as a family, respect for my parents, and unexpected insights into their values and attitudes.

In England, before and during WWII, they were active members of the North London Jewish Reform Congregation. As soon as they arrived in Salisbury, Mum and Dad wanted our family to resume their membership of a Jewish congregation. Unfortunately, a Reform Jewish congregation did not yet exist in Salisbury and the Jewish synagogue community was traditional and conservative. Mum was not born Jewish and her conversion to Judaism, welcomed by the Reform Congregation in London, was not recognised by the orthodox Jewish congregation in Salisbury. All their attempts over those first years to be accepted into the local Jewish community were rejected. Mum and Dad were devastated!

Eventually, as my brother and I were growing up, Mum and Dad decided that it was important that we be taught the values and ethics of a Judeo/Christian religion; and so, when my brother was twelve and I was five, we were baptised at our local Anglican Church.

The local rector, Father Cranswick, a charming, compassionate man and a former Rhodes Scholar, was the head of this lovely local Anglican Church. Mum liked him. Every Sunday morning from then on Dad would drive me to church for the church service and collect me afterwards. From the age of five, I attended church alone. Mum and Dad never attended the church services, so I had no contact with the children or their families outside church services. My brother was sent to a Church of England school. And later, so was I. Being baptised and regularly attending church, my attending an Anglican school felt perfectly reasonable and normal at the time. Gradually though, this had all sorts of social consequences.

As Mum and Dad couldn't practice being Reform Jews, I didn't understand anything about it. However, it was clear this was an important part of their beliefs and philosophy and they longed to belong to a Reform Jewish congregation.

Was this so different from the other traditional Jewish congregations? I couldn't answer that.

All Mum and Dad's friends were Jewish. The social occasions with them were the highlights of our social life. I enjoyed playing with their friends' children. They were my social peer group. However, as the other children and I grew up together, there was little in their lives that I could be part of or share. I could not go to their schools or to after-school activities or among other things, learn about Jewish history, culture, and songs.

I really appreciated being invited to Bar Mitzvah or wedding ceremonies at the synagogue, and sometimes our Jewish friends invited us for Friday night dinner and prayers. On these occasions, there was candlelight and the dining room table was filled with plates of special food. Before dinner, we would sit with everyone, including the adults, holding hands, saying the prayers in Hebrew and English. The English prayers sounded very similar to the prayers in church. I tried my best to participate. The atmosphere was warm and welcoming; the Bible stories were familiar and their interpretations of them were fascinating, as were the Jewish Hebrew rituals. And I loved listening to the religious debate that would often ensue. I longed to belong. These times were when Mum and Dad were at their happiest. They loved to relax and be with their close friends. I loved those evenings, but no matter how hard I tried, I always felt an outsider.

I once had a strange dream.

It is evening and rapidly getting dark and I am outside a house with all the windows illuminated. I want to join Mum and Dad, who I know are inside the house. I walk around the house trying to enter. The front door is locked. The curtains are open, the lights are on inside, and I hear music and children laughing and happily chatting. The aroma of fresh bread and other food wafts out of the windows. I manage to jump up and hang onto a window sill. I lift myself up, and when I look inside I see Mum and Dad laughing with their happy friends preparing to sit down in the dining room. The beautifully decorated dining table is covered with plates of food. I knock and knock on the window, but no one hears or sees me.

CHAPTER NINE

Holidays, birthdays and boarding school – 1949–54

Our happiest times as a family were when we were on holiday. Mum and Dad loved holidays and we had some interesting trips travelling around Rhodesia, Mozambique, and South Africa. Most memorable though was a holiday for the whole family in England and Europe when I was six years old.

It took us three whole days to fly in a Constellation aeroplane from Salisbury via a hot steamy Cairo to London, England. London was wonderful. It was mid-summer and besides visiting relatives, Mum and Dad took me and my brother to feed the pigeons at Trafalgar Square, then to the Tower of London with the Beefeaters, and finally, of course, we visited Harrods. We also had a rather funny incident that I tell at my expense.

While in London, we stayed in a lovely hotel. Mum and Dad insisted that I go to bed even though the sun was still shining. As far as I was concerned, it was not bedtime. This was not fair! Mum and I must have had words, as I remember being very cross. I wasn't used to going to bed before dark. Shortly afterward, Mum had her usual brandy before going down to dinner. I asked to have a taste, but she refused. Then, she and Dad left. I decided to help myself and taste the brandy. It was awful, but I was angry, so I drank as much of it as I could. Not long after, I was sick and found myself being bathed by my brother. Fortunately, this turned out to be a good lesson and I have never repeated it.

Despite this small interlude, Mum and Dad enjoyed being back with their friends in London. It was a lovely holiday for all of us.

When we returned to Salisbury, I started school at our local state primary school not far from where we lived. At the beginning of the next year, when I was still six, Mum and Dad decided to send me to a private Anglican girls' school called Chisipite Junior School. They took me there with my suitcase. I did not know anybody, but they said I would soon make friends.

I was one of the 'new boarders'. To 'help' new boarders settle in, we were not allowed to see our parents for the first month. After that time, our parents were allowed to take us out one Sunday a month and visit us for two hours on the other Sundays. Many of the other boarders were daughters of farmers or of parents who did a lot of travelling, so this was quite convenient for them. My parents lived half an hour away.

While at boarding school, I made one good friend. We loved to play after school outside in a grassy field. One game I enjoyed playing with her was to gather up piles of grass clippings after the grass had been mown and shape them into the rooms of a house to play in. She was my first real friend.

Birthdays were fun. Garlands of flowers decorated the birthday child's place at the long wooden bench at breakfast and the whole dining room of about 100 boarders sang happy birthday. Later, there would be cake, and sometimes children gave gifts.

Although not sure about the date, I must have mentioned my birthday was coming up. My birthday is in April, but somehow it was decided my birthday was in March. And so, one March morning, I remember feeling joy, uncertainty and acute embarrassment at seeing the garlands of flowers at my place at the table. The whole dining room sang to me and one little girl gave me a pair of scissors that I treasured for years. Later it was discovered that it was not my birthday.

My parents visited me three weeks later, on my real birthday, bringing with them a large doll. That was lovely but there were no flower garlands, or singing happy birthday. I am still perplexed – why did I not know my birth date? I can't remember ever having a birthday party as a child with Mum and Dad and so had probably forgotten when it was.

The terms passed. I quite liked school, but clearly didn't know how to stand up for myself.

One day all the curtain sashes were hooked up and the matron was livid. She made everyone who shared our dormitory line up and then she asked us individually whether we had done it. When she came to me she accused me of doing the devilish deed and made me stand behind her office door for what seemed like a very long time. I wasn't guilty, but there was nothing I could do to make her believe me. When Mum and Dad came to see me, I told them what had happened.

The other girls called me Jane Snail and thought I was a daydreamer. I did not like the name – it haunted me for years. One day though, one of the girls rather enviously told me that I was a 'quick learner' so perhaps I was not a Jane Snail, after all.

I think these incidents had more to do with my own specific circumstances than the school. How could the school know what was going on in my head?

At Christmas, Mum and Dad quizzed me about whether I wanted to return to the school. I said no. They listened. After the school holidays, in February of the next year, when I was seven, I started at a local primary school as a day pupil. I was glad they consulted me and enjoyed school from then on.

I suppose many children have recurring dreams. I had one too, which I have never been able to explain. I do not know how it started or when it happened – but it is an extremely vivid recollection. I was playing in the back garden at home. It was probably over a weekend. A large, shiny black Bentley (it was definitely a Bentley!) with three men in black suits came to visit Mum and Dad. The Bentley was parked in Mum's carport out of sight of anyone passing along the road. This was significant, because it meant that Mum's car had to be parked somewhere else before they arrived. This meant Mum and Dad were expecting the visitors and did not want them to be seen. How strange. When the visitors arrived I was outside near the kitchen. I was told to stay away from the house. Of course, I was curious, wondering why they came. I slipped into the kitchen, walked to the entrance hall to listen to the talking in our living room. Why were they here? I then got the awful feeling that they were coming to take me away! The next thing that happened was that the three men went to their car. I was put into the back right hand seat of the car. They closed the car door, but I screamed, managed to open the door, and ran back into the house. I was terrified. My adoptive parents looked at me, and together with the men, agreed I could stay.

Did this really happen? It is still a mystery. If it did happen, I couldn't explain it, and so later it lived on as a dream.

CHAPTER TEN

Dad and Granddad in Germany, 1876–1933

Once again, I was in Mum's bedroom, sitting happily on my velvet footstool, anticipating a good chat.

Mum began Dad's story by explaining that as Leonhard had been important in Dad's life and had also saved his life, she would talk about Leonhard's life first. I wondered what she meant.

I remember Granddad Leonhard as a portly, well-dressed, distinguished, elderly man who, even in the Rhodesian weather, loved to wear a waistcoat and braces to hold his tailored trousers over his middle. He had a twinkle in his eyes, a smiling face, receding white hair, and seemed to be always smoking a cigar. In the 1950s he visited us in Rhodesia from Israel, where he was living at the time. He was kind and charming, and when I was about nine years old, he sat with me on our veranda doing his best to teach me a few German words. I was fond of him and Mum also had a very 'soft spot' for Leonhard. She considered him a very wise man.

Mum said that Leonhard was born German and Jewish in a small rural village. I found out lately that this was in 1876, near Breslau in Silesia (present-day Wroclaw, Poland). As a small child, his family moved to Breslau, a provincial capital in Germany. Breslau was a prosperous and beautiful town, often called the Venice of Poland. It had a successful, innovative Jewish community, which, I was fascinated to read, combined the Orthodox and Reform Jewish congregations and became a model for other German Jewish communities. By the early 20th century, Breslau's Jews, who made up 4.3 per cent of the population, paid 20.3 per cent of all taxes.

Reform Judaism had begun around the time of the French

Revolution and was influenced by ideas of rationality and egalitarianism. It encouraged secular ideas and values and Jewish assimilation into their communities. In the early 1900s, Jews were accepted as citizens, could settle where they pleased, dress the way they liked, and follow whatever occupations they chose. They went to public schools and universities.[1] Religious services included mixed seating, singing, and were conducted in German (not just Hebrew). For a while, Shabbat was observed on Sunday and services were not dissimilar to those in a Protestant church.

Leonhard and Dad were Reform Jews. Mum and Dad were proud to be Reform Jews, so learning where they first encountered Reform Judaism, and what it stood for was very satisfying.

In the early 1900s, Leonhard moved from Breslau to Berlin, followed by his two brothers and his parents.

The question I wanted to answer was why couldn't Leonhard and his family live peacefully in Silesia? What was it that drove them away from Silesia to Berlin?

It was when I learnt about the fate of the Jews in the Pale of Settlement, less than 50 kilometres away from Breslau on the western border of Russia, that I began to understand why Leonhard and his family fled Silesia. They would have been aware of stories told by poor, often starving, refugees passing through Silesia that the Jews were living with the constant threat of pogroms and sanctions. They would have learnt of the hundred years or more of state-sanctioned restrictions forcing Jews to live in ever more cramped communities and of the government's efforts to convert Jews to Christianity, tax them, steal their property, and subject them to increasingly violent persecution.

In the late 19th century, 4.9 million Jews lived in the Pale of Settlement, half of all the Jews in the world. Then, in 1881, 1891, 1897, 1903, 1906, and 1918, Russian state-sanctioned violence against the Jewish people, their homes, properties, businesses, and religious centres prompted an estimated 3.5 million Jews to leave Russia. They flooded through Germany and the rest of Europe in one of the largest and most tragic mass migrations in recorded history. The US accepted 2 million Jewish refugees.

Those stories would strike fear into anyone's heart and perhaps Leonhard and his family felt that the Pale of Settlement was too close for comfort. Certainly, it would explain Dad's depth of feeling and the fear of the anti-Semitism stemming from the events before and during WWII in Germany.

However, I wish to return to the early 1900s and Leonhard's arrival in Berlin – a vibrant, exciting city where Jews were the most integrated in Europe. Not long after arriving, Leonhard met Esther; they fell in love and married. She was Jewish and also a recent migrant from Silesia. She brought a dowry to the marriage as well, a haberdashery shop.

Hanna was born in 1903 and Dad was born in 1906. In our home in Salisbury, there was an enormous photograph of Dad and his sister that hung on a wood-panelled wall in Dad's study. There were also two beautiful, oil portraits of Leonhard and Esther hanging there. Esther was a beautiful young woman with large brown eyes, an oval face, and a lovely smile. Dad's family had a strong presence in our Rhodesian home.

Even in my home in Australia, I have a beautiful photograph of Esther looking elegant in a long, expensive dress, her hair in a top knot, standing with her two beautifully dressed young children. Unfortunately, Esther died long before I was born, so I never met her.

Esther's haberdashery shop would transform their lives. Up till then, most people wore hand-sewn clothes. However, in the early 19th century, Jewish clothing manufacturing businesses were taking off as Jewish tailors became proficient with Isaac Singer's sewing machines (invented in 1850), which enabled them to mass produce clothes in standardised sizes. At that time, the Jews were migrating in huge numbers from Eastern Europe and Russia to the rest of Europe and America. For Jewish tailors, it must have been like arriving in Silicon Valley in 1986, armed with computer programming skills. In the early 1900s, Jewish families were renowned for being the best in promoting style and elegance, and leading the development of the rag trade and fashions, including producing and designing clothes. The garment industry became a major employer of Jews in Berlin, as in America; where in the early 1900s, sixty per cent of all Jews were employed in the garment industry.

Leonhard and Esther's small haberdashery business soon turned into a thriving women's and children's clothing store – a valuable market for the flourishing Jewish clothing manufacturers. No doubt this was helped by Leonhard's charm and ability to relate to anyone without being conscious of rank. I believe the young family started off living in a Jewish part of eastern Berlin, but as business improved, they moved to the western part of Berlin. As Dad entered his teens, he might well have accompanied Leonhard to work to learn about sales, and relating to customers and staff members. Leonhard would have started grooming his son to eventually take over the business.

I sensed the mixture of manic festivity, creativity, and despair that existed in Berlin after WWI from the way Dad reminisced about his early life in Berlin. All his life Dad loved photography, gadgets, new inventions, motorbikes, cars, cameras, and movie cameras. He loved the silent films, comedy theatre, and the 'singspiel' (song play), i.e. the musicals, as we call them, which Germany introduced to audiences in the 1920s. He certainly was a child of Berlin.

By the mid to late 1920s Dad was a tall, thin, fashionably-dressed, handsome man in his early twenties. He had a lovely mischievous smile, brown eyes, and bushy, unruly eyebrows. He would have been a very eligible bachelor and no doubt he had many girlfriends. Did the fun end for him in 1929, when the US stock market crashed and world depression hit? Unemployment in Germany soared and political instability and poverty followed. Business must have suffered.

In the midst of all this uncertainty, personal tragedy struck the family. Esther discovered she had breast cancer. This must have been a terrible shock for Leonhard and all the family. Caring for her would have become a major preoccupation and a distraction from the deteriorating political situation in Berlin. Then, in the middle of 1932, Esther died.

Leonhard and his family must have been distraught. They all adored Esther. Dad hardly ever talked about his mother; let alone her death. This was his way of coping.

At the time though, there was precious little time for grief. The Nazis were eliminating Jewish businesses by the tens of thousands, selling them below value or forcing the owners to take out high mortgages against their business and give the money to the Nazi party. This drove many businesses into liquidation.

By then, Leonhard's business provided employment for over 200 people. Allegiance to the Nazi movement was growing and perhaps a large percentage of his staff was or would have to have been Nazi supporters. Leonhard may have been compelled to pay taxes to the Nazi movement.

Leonhard must have realised that their lives were at risk and that successful Jewish families were vulnerable to attack. Unfortunately, I know very little about what actually happened to them in their day-to-day life, except that Leonhard started to plan to leave Berlin. Dad was willing to go with his father, but Hanna, Dad's sister, did not feel the same way. She was in love with an SS Nazi officer. Leonhard begged her to leave Germany with them, but she stubbornly refused. She believed her SS boyfriend would protect her. She had found love and she believed she would be safe.

A few months later, after the 30 January 1933, when Hitler became Chancellor of Germany, government-sanctioned attacks and torture of so called 'enemies' of the Nazi Party became common. The first of a raft of laws restricting Jewish involvement in all walks of life and depriving them of rights were enacted. Of relevance to my adoption for example, included the law that Jewish doctors were not able to be reimbursed by the public health insurance company. This caused a significant migration of Jewish doctors, including Dr Davidson, westward to the rest of Europe, the UK, and the US. Jews, Communists, gypsies, and anyone who didn't match up to the ideal of the 'Aryan race' were extremely vulnerable. Many had to pay 'flight tax' before receiving permission to leave.

Then, on the 1st April, Hitler ordered a one-day national boy-cott of Jewish shops and institutions. The Jews' initial response to the Nazi takeover was a substantial wave of emigration (about

37,000 people) to neighbouring European countries, such as France, Belgium or the Netherlands.

So, it was not surprising that later, in 1933, Granddad Leonhard and Dad left their home, all their family, and their business for what the border officials in Netherlands recorded as a 'holiday'. They must have done this with very heavy hearts. I believe they took just one suitcase each. They travelled first to Amsterdam, and then to England as refugees.

Keeping secrets then would have been a vital survival strategy.

For Leonhard and Dad, leaving Berlin when they did was a life-saving decision. This cannot be said for most of the rest of their family. On the website of the Yad Vashem Museum in Jerusalem, which contains a record of Jews murdered in concentration camps, there are scores of people with our family name listed, along with the names of the concentration camps where they were interred and the dates when they were murdered. Out of a total of 160,000 Jews living in Berlin at the start of World War Two (four percent of the Berlin population) 55,000 Jews were killed in concentration camps. Most of those who sought refuge in neighbouring countries were also murdered. After WWII, there were only 8,000 Jews left in Berlin.

Now I understand why Dad was so reluctant to talk about the WWII and the consequences for his family. When I think of Dad's question: 'What is the point of talking about those times?' it seems entirely reasonable. Going back over everything doesn't bring anyone back. Sadly, there would be no answers or resolution. I'm sad I couldn't show him I cared, too.

A unique memorial with eighty signs by artists in the Schoneberg streets (a suburb of Berlin) provides a remarkable record of the German laws starting in early 1933 that led to the systematic dehumanizing, segregation, and slaughter of the Jews, people with disabilities, homosexuals, and gypsies. A permanent exhibition in the Schoneberg Town Hall, called 'Wir Waren Nachbarn' (We Were Neighbours) personalises these events by documenting the fate of more than 160 families, residents of the area, who were deported and murdered in concentration camps. Leonhard's brother, his wife, and their daughter are among those documented who met their fate in concentration camps.

Suddenly, the impact of WWII becomes very personal. It is not remote at all and has shaped the lives of most of the people mentioned in this story.

CHAPTER ELEVEN

Our family secret – 1954

By the time I was seven, I had learnt that what was left unsaid was important.

One morning during the school holidays, Mum asked my nanny to post some letters. This was unusual, because Mum and Dad usually took letters to the business to be posted. She suggested that my nanny take me on a walk to the post office. We were also going to buy some groceries. It was quite a long walk on a dirt road, and then down a narrow, meandering, gravel path in the bush to a few shops and the post office.

At the post office, the nanny let me give the letters to the postman behind the counter. I wanted to practise reading. Curious to see who these letters were for, I asked if I could read the envelopes. To my surprise, one letter was for a 'Jonathan' with our surname and an address in England.

I was very indignant! 'There is no such person,' I told them. 'You do not need to post that!' I insisted, but the postmaster took the letter anyway.

While walking home, I remember wondering who Jonathan was. I asked nanny if she knew who he was. No, Nanny did not know. Later that day, when Mum returned from town, I told her what happened. I asked her why she had written a letter to Jonathan. Who was he? Why had I not heard of him in our family?

Mum looked at me strangely, and then asked me to come upstairs to her bedroom. There, she could speak to me alone without the servants listening. The heavy blue curtains were pulled back and light flooded in. She sat on the stool in front of her dressing table facing me and watched me intently with the blue eyes I knew so well. I wandered around the room. She waited until I had settled on my favourite velvet footstool in front of her. Once there, Mum looked down at me and began her story.

She explained that during WWII, she had tried to get pregnant, and had had two miscarriages. The third time she became pregnant, Jonathan was born. Although Jonathan was their son, he did not live with us. He was born before me, so he was older than me. He was born with Down's syndrome. I had never heard of that before. Mum explained that he had 'Mongoloid' features. I did not know what Mongoloid features meant either, so she explained. She said Jonathan lived in England in a place like a hospital, because he was 'retarded.' That was the first time I had heard that word, too; it did not sound nice. Nobody I knew was retarded. Tearful and distraught, she explained that he would not grow up like other children. He could not speak or dress himself. He needed a lot of help; in fact, he would need to be looked after all his life. She thought he would always behave like a child, even when he was an adult. She then said she and Dad could not give him the kind of care he needed, especially in Rhodesia. He was in a home in England with lovely people, like nuns, who looked after him. They were experienced in looking after children like him. She began to sob. I put my arms around her trying my best to comfort her. She explained that when Jonathan was born, Dad was very distressed about him, and talking about Jonathan or Mum sending letters to him, upset Dad even more. So, this was why she asked the Nanny to post the letter to Jonathan. Then, she sat up and looked straight at me.

'You must promise, Jane, not to talk about Jonathan to anyone. No one in Southern Rhodesia knows about him – none of our friends know about him.' She began to sob again.

I was worried and tried to hug her, but she pulled back; her body stiff. She looked at me through her tears and said, 'If our friends find out about Jonathan, they will ask why Jonathan doesn't live with us at home. Why did we leave him in England? People who haven't had a child like Jonathan, a child with a disability, would find it very hard to understand. They don't know what we have been through and that we made the best decision we could make at the time.'

She paused. 'If you say anything about Jonathan and they find out, we will be extremely angry.'

And just in case I had not understood, Mum's voice changed and with a great sense of urgency, she said, 'Jane! You must not say anything about this to anyone!'

I was startled and did not know what to think. Of course I promised I would say nothing. She must have told Dad I knew about Jonathan, as at a later time, he also said that I must not mention Jonathan to anyone. Again, I promised to keep their secret.

Gradually, as I grew up, I understood better why Mum was so often sad.

Did Jonathan have anything to do with my origins? At that time I had not been told that I was adopted and so had no objective reason to ask questions. But now that I think back, we did have a very strange family ritual.

I suppose most children are teased.

Occasionally, when we were relaxing together or perhaps when we were out at a café, for example, Dad would begin to tease me. Except for one exception, I did not mind. He had a favourite rhyme that he asked me to repeat over and over.

'Was bist du? Du bist eine stupide kind!
Was bist du? Du bist eine dummes kind!'

Translated, it means: 'What are you? You are a stupid child! What are you? You are a dumb child!'

I hated this rhyme. As I became more aware about what it meant, I told him I didn't like it and wanted him to stop saying it. But, he continued. One day, when we were on holiday having a cup of tea at a hotel, he started again, within earshot of other guests. Mum pleaded with Dad, 'Please, don't ask Jane to say that silly poem.'

I was glad she said that, but it made me think. Why did Dad like that rhyme?

Did he honestly think I was a stupid child? And was I stupid?

It was similar to the nickname 'Jane Snail' given to me when I was at boarding school. I also knew Mum and Dad did not have high expectations of me, as far as school was concerned. They seemed to think it was not necessary for girls to be intelligent – just intelligent enough to find a husband. Now I know they were not exceptional in believing this, as it was a common view among their generation.

But that still didn't explain why Dad liked this strange rhyme.

The answer would come to me in a 'light bulb' moment decades later.

CHAPTER TWELVE

Middle childhood – 1955–61

Soon after starting at my new school, I also started ballet classes and piano lessons. Life took on a certain rhythm.

I enjoyed ballet. For years I went to ballet classes in town, near where Mum and Dad worked. At the end of class, I would walk back to their business, and if I did not have any homework, Mum would give me jobs to do in the business to keep me busy. Occasionally, I would sneak upstairs and start reading one of the Famous Five, the Secret Seven or Biggles books, which I loved. Much to Mum's regret, I read few children's classics; although, *Little Women* by Louisa May Alcott was a favourite of mine.

Learning to play the piano was a different story. Twice a week I went to lessons. This meant I was expected to practise on our piano at home for at least half an hour a day. Every day, after Mum returned home from work, she would ask me whether I had practised the piano. If I had not, I would get into trouble. I rebelled against this discipline and twice ran away from my music lessons. My poor teacher, it could not have been pleasant teaching a child who did not want to learn. But Mum was not put off, and twice she insisted that I go back. I accepted my task finally, but it did not stop me getting into mischief when I was bored.

One day when I was tired of practising the piano, I found a way to get under the house and crawled around until I was under the wooden floorboards of the piano room. I knocked on the floorboards, making a loud rat-a-tat-tat noise, just like the knock on our front door. When Geoffrey, our gentle, amiable cook heard the knocking, he went to the front door, opened it, and was astonished to discover no one was there. From under the floorboards, quite far away, I could hear Geoffrey exclaim in surprise, 'Hauw!' After he went a few times to investigate the knocking at the front door, he realised it was me teasing him. He walked into the piano room and stood above where I was hiding, calling to me through the floor-boards. 'Missee Jen, Missee Jen, come out of there! I think you are a Tokoloshe (an evil spirit)!'

Geoffrey was always kind to – though somewhat exasperated by – me! I grew very fond of him and liked the way he called me 'Missee Jen' in his African accent.

Often, over weekends, I would go with Mum and Dad to the business, even when it was closed. As a young child, I began to help with the unpacking of toys and stationery or taking books from their boxes and writing the price on each before putting them on the shelves. Sometimes, we would unpack big boxes of pencils and pack them into tens, with a rubber band around them or unpack boxes of 1,000 rubber bands into boxes of 100 rubber bands. I liked feeling useful.

Dad continued to enjoy taking photographs and movies, especially at home and at public events. For example, he made a movie at a 1953 Rhodesian military parade in Salisbury when Queen Elizabeth II came to visit.

Although Mum and Dad spoke German, they never encouraged James and me to learn German. They did not want us to be teased. But, like most parents, they could not resist speaking German when they did not want me to understand them.

After about five years of living in Southern Rhodesia, we felt more settled. We were all happier and I continued at our local primary school. Initially, Dad drove me to and from school. I arrived early, at about 7am (school started at 8.15am). I was a tomboy, hated dolls, and preferred to play rounders or marbles with the boys, so I liked going to school early. I was very rarely invited to a friend's house after school, as Mum was always at work then, so having time to play in the mornings was lovely. Dad collected me after school each day at about 1.15pm on his way home for lunch. Once he forgot and arrived very late, clearly upset and distraught that he had forgotten. This showed me that I mattered to him and I loved him for it.

Later, at the age of nine, I was allowed to cycle to school on my own. I relished the independence and their trust. Dad could then drive straight home for lunch.

In 1955, we lived on a dirt road two kilometres long. Looking north, on the right hand side, there were grass pavements with hedges or fences separating the road from houses where mostly European 'Rhodesians' lived. On the western side of the road there were no pavements. Instead, the road was lined with beautiful large eucalyptus trees, which Mum said were Sydney blue gums.

Behind the trees was a market garden. Nestled in among the vegetables and almost hidden by the tall corn fields were a couple of small, white-washed, one-room square huts where two African Rhodesian men lived. They were the market gardeners who grew the vegetables. They also grew mealies (corn). One winter's morning I visited them. It was during a school holiday, after Dad had gone to work and before Mum woke up. They were sitting on the ground in the sun with their backs against an east-facing hut wall eating their breakfast. They gave me a broad smile, greeted me in the traditional manner, and offered me some of their food. They ate 'sadza', which is a stiff white corn porridge with tomato and onion relish. They took the porridge with their right hand, kneaded it into a stiff ball of dough, and then dipped it into the gravy before eating it. It was delicious! I enjoyed the snack, thanked them, and then ran back home.

All the time I grew up in Rhodesia, until I left in 1965, the indigenous Africans were friendly and always smiled easily. Geoffrey, our chef and Charles, our gardener, in fact all the Africans who worked with Mum and Dad, were courteous, kind, and friendly to me.

In the mornings during the week, Geoffrey would leave Mum's breakfast tray outside her bedroom door. Mum slept until 8.30 or 9am. I did not see her in the mornings, as I left for school long before she woke up.

My morning routine involved getting up early, having a quick glass of milk with Dad at the breakfast table, and then going out to play, often with a girl who lived next door. Occasionally, if he noticed, I would eat something. Food was not important then. I would come in just as Dad was ready to go and he would take me to school. When I started to cycle to school, I did not need to go so early.

One morning, in my last year at primary school when I was eleven, I slept longer than usual. I woke up in a fright. No one at home had noticed that I was not around for breakfast and that my bike was still there. I dressed quickly, hoping Mum could drive me to school. However, when I emerged from my bedroom, she had already gone to work. I cycled to school, pedalling as fast as I could, only to fall. I arrived at school two hours late, sobbing with a sprained ankle, a grazed knee, and a dirty uniform. This was the first time I was late. Instead of being cross with me, the teacher was sympathetic and for what seemed like an hour, he walked with me around the quadrangle 'til I was composed. I greatly appreciated his kindness. He was the nicest teacher I ever had. I'm not sure Mum and Dad ever knew of this incident and I was hugely relieved not to get into trouble.

Dad owned a number of vehicles for use in his business. Now and then he would bring home his small delivery vehicle, a Vespa van. A nine year old neighbour and I spent many happy hours sitting in it, imagining we were driving.

Just in case I had delusions of grandeur with regard to spending money, Dad and Mum decided I should work for my pocket money. Dad brought home a big box of coloured plastic beads. My task was to pop them together to make necklaces. I worked in Dad's workshop in the garden. It was very boring. Every so often he would bring huge quantities of envelopes, which I packaged into bunches of twelve. Later, I would go with them on a Saturday morning into the business. I started serving both retail and wholesale customers behind the counter. It gave me a buzz to be helpful. I enjoyed chatting to the customers while they bought a book or two, or stationary items. It was also excellent experience for a young person. I began to make sense of Mum and Dad's discussions across the table at lunch or dinner.

On the day after I passed my drivers' licence, at aged sixteen, Dad asked me to drive the van to some customers to show them our new stationery stock and Christmas cards. I was very proud that they trusted me enough to do this.

Mum and Dad enjoyed being with their friends and every now and then invited them home for dinner. I would watch how Mum planned the menu, how she asked Geoffrey to lay the table, and how she asked him to cook the meal. Occasionally, I was her assistant in preparing the entrees, arranging the flowers for the table or greeting their guests before dinner.

Sometimes, if guests came for lunch, I would join them. One day, at the end of the meal, I announced I was full. Mum and Dad scowled at me. After the guests left, Mum told me that in future, if I wanted to leave the table when we had guests, I should say, 'I'm sufficed.' The next time this happened, I could not quite remember the words she asked me to say, so I announced: 'I'm sophisticated!' To my astonishment and embarrassment, everyone burst into laughter, and then I realised my mistake. We all enjoyed that.

One of Dad's favourite jokes used to start with the question: 'How does one make a small fortune?' When there were no replies, he would answer himself with: 'By losing a large one.' And then he would burst into laughter. He enjoyed telling jokes and laughing at his own jokes. Mum and I would only smile, because we had heard them before.

For most of my childhood, I was a tomboy. Clothes did not matter much until I was about fourteen, when I surprised Mum totally and asked to wear dresses. After that, Mum took me shopping for clothes.

The years passed. During the school holidays, James would come home. I was in awe of him. We had a pretty normal sibling relationship. When he was at school, I used to refer to Mum and Dad, as 'my Mum and my Dad'. However, one time I made the mistake of referring to 'my Mum and my Dad' when he was home. He became very angry with me and looked at me in a strange way. I apologised – it was a mistake. They were 'our Mum and our Dad' he insisted – quite rightly. He did not explain why he was so angry though.

Perhaps the fact that I remember this incident meant that it was out of the ordinary. Once again, it was what was not said that was important.

During one of my school holidays, my brother, then aged about 18, introduced me to cigarettes. On one occasion, Dad arrived home unexpectedly and came to the living room door. I was sitting side on to the door in our living room, in one of our green velvet wing-backed lounge chairs. As he came in, I very quickly hung my hand with the smoking cigarette over the arm rest on the far side of the door. I must have looked guilty, because he looked suspiciously at me and asked what I was doing. 'Nothing,' I said, as nonchalantly as I could, only to be betrayed by the tell-tale smoke curling up from the other side of the chair to the ceiling. Dad was very cross with me!

A few days later, I was still curious about why people liked to smoke. Mum and Dad were at work and the servants were at lunch. I knew where there was a packet of cigarettes (Dad smoked) and stole one. I climbed out of my brother's bedroom window and sat on the red roof tiles on the sloping roof. This was about twenty-five feet off the ground. I smoked the cigarette, while surveying the neigh-bourhood. I was anxious, fearing the gardener might look up and see me. I ended up coughing and spluttering and making a hasty retreat through the window back into my bedroom.

In the end, this was a valuable experiment; I did not enjoy smok-ing and never took it up.

I continued with ballet and modern dance lessons, and piano lessons.

One year, Dad gave a Guy Fawkes fireworks party on 5 Novem-ber. They asked some friends with their children to be spectators. It was great fun. We played with sparklers and some children started throwing them about. One sparkler landed in the thatch of our round summerhouse, quickly catching fire. I then marvelled at the presence of mind of Charles, our gardener, as he deftly pulled out each burning strand of grass, saving the whole summerhouse.

Our family holidays continued to stand out as being happy occasions.

In the 1950s and early 1960s we had holidays in Mozambique and in South Africa. Occasionally, in Lorenzo Marques, we would stay in the old Polana Hotel. It's probably a ruin now. Even then, staying there was like stepping back in time. The lift was like a cage that could be stopped anywhere just by opening the concertina wrought-iron doors. And they had fencing championships with uniformed participants, which seemed most out of place in Africa, having emerged from the Middle Ages in Europe when there were knights in shining armour in the age of chivalry. Nevertheless, it was fun to watch.

Another milestone occurred. I began a friendship with a very nice boy called Mike. He would cycle to our home and we enjoyed being together. I was young, only thirteen and it was a very innocent, beautiful friendship.

This clearly caused Mum and Dad to have second thoughts about me being at home alone in the afternoons (with my nanny and our cook and gardener). At the end of that year, they announced that I would be returning to Chisipite Senior School, the Anglican girls' boarding school I had attended at the age of six. That would be the beginning of yet another phase of life.

CHAPTER THIRTEEN

Growing up – 1961–65

I returned to Chisipite Senior School, and this time I really enjoyed it. I was ready for the comparative independence and liked being with girls of my own age. The school provided us with a good all-round education and I continued my piano lessons. The only downside was that I really missed my boyfriend Mike, often feeling isolated and alone.

Practising the piano became an escape. As I was expected to practise for many hours a day to prepare for piano exams, the solitude provided the opportunity to spill many tears. I passed Grade 7 of The Royal Schools of Music; this coincided with leaving school at sixteen. Later, I regretted giving up the piano lessons, as it was clearly a missed opportunity. However, I can still read music and enjoy singing in choirs and going to concerts.

During my two years at Chisipite Senior school, there were some very memorable experiences.

One school holiday, my dear friend Jenifer invited me to go home with her to Zambia. Her parents worked in a community development training centre, training farmers from all over the province in self-sufficiency techniques. Her parents met us at Lusaka airport and then drove across some wide-open African plains to where they lived. It was a wonderful way to spend a school holiday and they all made me feel special. One day, to our surprise, we were invited to play tennis by two Ghanaian students. We were then about fifteen years old. The tennis was energetic and fun. We exchanged addresses.

That was the last I thought of it, until one school day a few months later.

We were back at boarding school and during rest time after lunch

I was called up to see the principal. This was puzzling. What had I done? I walked through the dormitory and past Jenifer. She was sobbing into her pillow. Had she already spoken to the principal? What was in store for me?

At that time 1962 in Rhodesia, Ian Smith was prime minister, heading up a 'white' government. Our school was then an 'all-white' school.

I knocked on the principal's door and she called me in. She then showed me a white envelope addressed to Jane (with no surname) and the school's address. Inside, there was a flattering flowery letter written to me by one of the students from Ghana with whom we had played tennis. Attached to the letter was a photograph of a tall, good-looking black student. You can imagine how this letter was received!

The principal of this all-white private girls' school must have been in a real dilemma and extremely worried about the consequences for the school if the letter became public knowledge. It could have been a real scandal and might have had significant effect on enrolments. In retrospect and from my perspective, although nobody had done anything wrong, I do not think the principal had much choice in how she handled the situation, irrespective of her beliefs.

She kept the letter, and then asked to speak to Jenifer. She phoned Jenifer's parents to find out what had happened. She phoned my parents, too, and told them what had happened, and then told me I would be expelled if it happened again. Jenifer and I were upset and I felt responsible. We knew we had done nothing wrong, except perhaps in telling them which school we went to we had been somewhat naive.

This type of incident looms large in the life of a teenage girl, but it all blew over. Jenifer and I are still good friends, still corresponding some forty-plus years later. Now, thankfully, my old school is one of the premier multi-cultural girls' schools in Zimbabwe.

School holidays must have been a bit of a dilemma for Mum and Dad. They were very busy in the business and decided I needed to be under supervision and away from my boyfriend; so, they booked me into a three-week beachside camp in East London, South Africa.

I was fifteen and was put on a two-day train journey with strangers to this camp. I had little say in the decision, with my parents saying, 'You'll make friends, Jane, do not worry.' I remember feeling as if I was a parcel being sent away. I suppose it taught me independence.

I did not thrive at school academically. I did not know how to study for exams. In the year I turned sixteen, I left school after disappointing 'O' Level grades. A few weeks before our 'O' Level exams, the principal asked to see me. She said that I was an intelligent girl and asked me why I was not studying harder. I could not answer her. For some reason, studying, something that became second nature to me many years later, was a complete mystery. I did not know what help to ask for or why everyone seemed to think I was capable of more.

My parents had left school early, so they did not know how to help me. They had done all that they could do. They rationalised that even if I was not bright, as long as I could make myself attractive I would probably marry young and have children. I think they thought that if I was not able to achieve at school, perhaps it did not really matter. If I put myself in their position, considering the expectations of those times, what else could they have said? At the time though, it left me feeling helpless and responsible for something I did not know how to fix. I guess this happens to a lot of young people.

Not surprisingly, my choices after school were extremely limited: I could either become a nurse or take up secretarial studies. I chose nursing. I liked biology and would enjoy living in the nurses' accommodation away from home. My school friend, Jenifer completed her 'A' Levels at school and went on to university in England. This would later serve as a beacon for me.

At the end of 1963, while still sixteen, I left school, and started a four-year nursing course at the Salisbury General Hospital. I earned the princely sum of seven pounds and 10 shillings a month and enjoyed living in the college attached to the hospital, with the other young nurses. Despite a strict curfew time of 11pm, I soon had a hectic social life, never short of invitations to go out.

The work was immensely satisfying. Being a student nurse working with patients at critical phases of their lives was more rewarding than I could ever have imagined. I also found myself relishing the academic part of the training; though the mostly female hierarchy was a force to be reckoned with. We spent about two months working in a ward before moving on to the next one. However, it was not long before the reality of nursing became evident.

Within three months, I started night duty in a paediatric ward. On my second night shift, I showed the sister on duty that a baby had stopped breathing, and in minutes I was assisting in the preparation of the body for the mortuary.

Given the task of carrying the small bundle alone in the dark, at 4am, to the mortuary building in the hospital grounds, I was stunned, numb, and worried about how his mother would take the news the next day. The mortuary was not a welcoming place; it was grey with a large steel table in the centre of the room and a honeycomb of refrigerated drawers from floor to ceiling in the walls.

In my next ward (the oncology ward), the nurses were high spirited. We sang all the time to cheer up the patients. One elderly lady had a stroke. To cheer her up, I asked her what she would like me to sing for her while changing the sheets on her bed. She answered in a very slurred voice, 'A wong way to Tippewherewee' and her eyes lit up as we sang together. She always greeted me with a broad, lopsided smile.

One of the most inspiring women I met was an attractive, white, middle-aged nurses' aide. Her task was to clean the dirty sheets before sending them to the laundry. I could not imagine anything worse, yet she was always cheerful. After a few weeks, being curious to find out more about her as a person, I asked her how she coped doing this kind of work. She explained that she was caring for her husband at home, who was dying of cancer, and this was what she did for a break! Perhaps this was also a reflection of the work that was available then to middle-aged white women in Zimbabwe. She had a beautiful singing voice and sang a lot while she worked. I sang along with her when I happened to be near.

I do not hear singing in hospitals now.

Another lasting memory was an incident with small boy in the children's ward. He was in severe pain due to kidney problems. The senior nurse asked me to sit by his bed and distract him, so I read to him. When the waves of pain came over him, I suggested that he give his pain to me by squeezing my hand. He liked this idea and squeezed and squeezed my hand before eventually drifting off to sleep. Later that night, one of the nurses from that ward came to my room in the nurses' home to tell me that on the next shift, he asked all the nurses to parade in front of him, because he wanted the nurse back who could take away the pain. This made me realise what a privilege it was to be a nurse and to be valued. I looked for him when I returned to the ward a few days later, but he wasn't there.

The ward with burn patients was the most traumatic. One night, a young newly-pregnant Indian woman was admitted to the ward suffering from terrible burns all over her body. We struggled, doing all that we could, but she screamed intermittently all night. I returned to the ward six months later, just before she gave birth. She was still having operations and skin grafts. I could not imagine anything more awful and heart-rending than what she had gone through. Suffering is not measured out equitably at all!

While there were many tragic experiences during my nursing training, there were also many hilarious times. Life was never dull!

One night, I was to go to a ward on the second floor in a hospital situated alongside a main road in Salisbury. This was a bleak institutional hospital for 'Coloured and Indian' patients, the kind of hospital that had green linoleum on the floors and half way up the walls. It also had large windows with no curtains – anywhere! To say it was bare would have been an understatement. At night, the brightly lit wards were plainly visible to the passing traffic.

On the night in question, I walked up the steps to the ward of about twelve patients to hear a beautiful husky voice singing a lilting love song. As I walked into the ward, I came face-to-face with a beautiful young woman, with a twinkle in her eye, in full view of the traffic, standing on her bed, in her blue and white striped hospital gown pulled in tightly at the waist, rhythmically swinging her hips in time to her song. Competing with this lilting alto melody was an insistent high-pitched quavering raspy voice coming from a middle-aged patient with a broken leg under a frame in the next bed chanting, 'The Lo-o-ord is my she-ep-he-erd, I sha-a-all not wa-a-nt...' The contrast was stunning! The young woman was reputedly a local prostitute. I found it almost impossible to keep a straight face. It took some persuasion to get her into bed.

Part of our training included watching operations. I had the opportunity to watch an operation on a man's eye. Despite being fascinated, I began to feel faint, found the nearest seat and sat down. Later, the senior sisters were extremely cross with me for sitting in front of the doctor. This was not allowed!

Not long after this, I nursed an elegant elderly English woman with long white hair piled on top of her head who had a heart condition. She had a beautiful speaking voice and enjoyed talking about her past. For example, how she played tennis in long white frocks in the early 1900s and the clothes she wore to the glamorous balls she attended in England. She was a real lady and reminded me of Mum. I looked forward to seeing her each day. One day I arrived to find her body on the bed; she had died. She was gone – the reality was stark, hard to accept – more so because I had become fond of her. I was asked to assist the nursing sister to prepare her body for the mortuary. Stunned and sad, this was when I decided nursing was not for me, and I resigned. I was seventeen.

For years afterwards, I missed the strong sense of purpose that nursing provided. It gave me a window into other people's lives and made me realise how fortunate I was.

After I stopped my nurses' training, I moved back home with Mum and Dad. Not surprisingly, I felt constrained. I had lost my independence. My boyfriends had to come in to be introduced and vetted, and I could not stay out later than 10pm. I did not really mind though, as I knew it was for a short time.

One boyfriend came to collect me on his motorbike – bringing an extra crash helmet with him into the house. I did not know him all that well and was surprised when Dad took an instant liking to him. He was fascinated by the motorbike. Much to my surprise, they agreed that I could go out on his motorbike, which was terrific fun! Then I realised that Dad had liked motorbikes when he was young.

It was around this time that boyfriends became an issue with Dad. I went out with a Jewish man about ten years older than me. He belonged to the orthodox Jewish congregation and after a few months the relationship died a natural death.

At this point, Dad decided he had a boy friend solution for me. He said he thought it might be a good idea to arrange a '*shidduch*' for me.

'A what?' I asked.

He explained that it was a regular practice in orthodox Jewish circles, whereby Dad or a trusted friend made inquiries about a pro-spective partner from a 'good' family with the intent of finding out about the person's character, intelligence, level of learning, financial status, family and health status, appearance, and level of religious observance. The goal was to find a possible match for me. Then it would be organised for him and me to date, with a view that if we thought we were a good match, then a marriage could be arranged. He reassured me that many arranged marriages were very successful. Parents could be sure that the prospective partner was from a good Jewish home and that I would marry into a family they would like.

I objected to this vehemently.

Eventually, Mum agreed with me. In any case, as I had grown up attending church schools and had been baptised Christian, it might be difficult to find a good match for me, as I was hardly an ideal Jewess. I found their discussions on the subject bizarre.

Finally, the idea faded. I now know that Dad was well meaning.

Soon after leaving the nursing college, I attended a secretarial college in the city to learn shorthand and typing. What a contrast to nursing! We sat in classrooms all day.

It was during this time that the idea of working in Johannesburg crossed my mind.

I tentatively flagged this idea with Mum one day in April 1965 while in the car on the way home from Secretarial College. I mentioned that there seemed to be a lot of job opportunities in Johannesburg.

Nothing more was said for some months. Then, toward the end of the secretarial course, to my surprise, Mum reminded me of my comment. She encouraged me to think about it more.

Wow! Would they really let me go? For young people, Johannesburg was 'the big smoke' and with the booming gold mining industry was a magnet for many young people from Southern Rhodesia.

It emerged that Mum and Dad were willing to agree that I go to Johannesburg, as long as I lived in the Young Women's Christian Association (YWCA) in Braamfontein, within walking distance of the central business district. I would have my own room; there was a lady concierge and a living room where visitors could wait while you were being called. There was also an 11pm curfew, which especially reassured Mum. She thought that this was a pleasant place for a young woman to start out in a strange, large city in a new country. I happily agreed.

This was at a worrying political time as far as my parents were concerned. Prior to 1964, Southern Rhodesia had been a self-governing colony in the British Empire. Many British colonies in Africa with a substantial population of white settlers were claiming their right to independence. Britain responded by adopting a policy known as No Independence before Majority African Rule; that is, universal suffrage and majority rule. The then- Rhodesian government led by Ian Smith opposed this. Negotiations were long, protracted, and ended with Smith's government declaring the country independent from British government rule on 11 November 1965, a move that Britain saw as illegal. Thereafter, until full independence in 1980, Southern Rhodesia came to be known as plain 'Rhodesia' by the Rhodesians.

This political turmoil in Rhodesia may also have been a factor in Mum and Dad encouraging me to go to South Africa. South Africa was conveniently close and at the time appeared to have a strong, stable (albeit racist) government. This was not the first time political turmoil had caused them to consider uprooting; although at that stage, this was far from their plans for themselves. They had too much at stake in Rhodesia – their friends, their home and business, and some property. There would be little possibility of taking it with them.

As a result, in October 1965, I left Salisbury, Rhodesia for Johannesburg, South Africa. Mum and Dad gave me one hundred Rand (R100) with a strict warning to live within my means, insisting that I promise never to borrow money, not from anybody! The R100 was to last me a month, until I was paid for my first month's work.

The prospect of living independently in a new country was very exciting indeed.

CHAPTER FOURTEEN

Living in Johannesburg
and the summons home

I arrived in Johannesburg in October 1965 and found a secretarial position with a reputable firm of solicitors the following day. Finding employment so soon was a relief. The YWCA was a pleasant spic-and-span place with small, but well-furnished, modern rooms. My room was on the fifth floor with a pleasant outlook over the city. I knew I would appreciate the relative autonomy. Mum and Dad were happy about it too, so I was quite at ease about leaving them.

I listened carefully when Dad warned me not to go into debt or spend beyond my means. Debt was a definite no-no! If I could not manage with the money Dad had given me, I'd have to go back home. This was a powerful incentive. I did not use public transport at all for the first month, walking to work and back every day. At the end of the month, l found I had only spent seven rand on lunches and entertainment. I was immensely relieved. It was going to be possible to live within my means in Johannesburg after all!

I went home for Christmas, returning to Johannesburg quite happily. I made good friends while staying at the YWCA, which I still enjoy. Through them, I met my future husband.

Life continued quite uneventfully until October 1966, when the letter arrived in a brown envelope, Mum and Dad requested I fly home to Salisbury, and my adoption was revealed

CHAPTER FIFTEEN

Adjusting, meeting Rob
and wedding plans

After being told about my adoption, there was very little I could say or do that would help me work through it. Mum and Dad insisted that I must not search for my biological family and that my adoption be kept a secret. They also warned me about the stigma associated with being an illegitimate child and that it was in my interest to be discreet.

I knew no other adopted people, so if I had talked about it, it was so far from most other young people's experiences they probably wouldn't be able to understand.

Fortunately, I was not yet twenty years old and life was filled with work, friends, boyfriends, various courses and lessons, choir, and exploring Johannesburg. Mum and Dad were there in the background, at least in our weekly exchange of letters, and all I really wanted was some peace and to be able to return to my former status quo.

But this was not to be.

Shortly after finding out about my adoption, I dated a young man for a few months before mutually agreeing to end the relationship. A week or so later he phoned me, distraught, saying he had been told that a detective had been hired by my parents to find out all about him. I was stunned and to my absolute surprise, when I inquired about it, Mum and Dad confirmed it was true. Someone had called them from South Africa warning that this boyfriend was not of 'good character.' I was speechless, then very angry. Why did they not speak to me and tell me about what they had been told? I could have reassured them that there was no future in our friendship. They never were able to offer a plausible explanation.

I apologised to him and could not help but wonder about my parent's very strange behaviour and question why any parents would do such a thing.

And also, who was monitoring my relationships? And why?

Sometime later I was between boyfriends, feeling alone and homesick. I wanted to go home and reconnect with Mum and Dad. I wanted also to revisit some of the issues around my adoption. At that particular time they were in New Zealand, so I sent them a telegram asking if I could go back home to live. Perhaps naively, I expected them to say 'yes, of course.' I was not at all prepared for their reply. They sent a telegram and phoned me, insisting I should stay in South Africa and not return to Rhodesia, now known as Zimbabwe. I felt shut out, shed lots of tears and felt terribly alone. They may not have intended it as such, but that was the way I reacted.

Gradually, I realised that Mum and Dad would have found it hard to cope with an adult daughter living at home. Perhaps they thought it was time I left home. Maybe they were concerned about political events. After many months, I felt that it was probably good that I had not returned to Zimbabwe.

Not surprisingly, I felt an outcast. I now had two mothers and two fathers, but felt as if I was nobody's child – orphaned, shut out, alone! There was no one I could talk to openly who would understand. I did not know anyone who was adopted. My experiences were so far removed from anyone I knew; besides, I did not want to sound like a victim or become a burden on my friends. Unlike a death, which is a single, usually public, event mourned openly, the consequences of this were hidden and longstanding.

I found that knowing I was adopted changed the way I related to people. My new identity was not something to be proud of. Mum and Dad had warned me about the stigma attached to being illegitimate and adopted. I was a 'bastard child.' I began to be conscious of social rank.

I worked in a law firm, and when a good-looking young lawyer from a well-known, respected South African family invited me out, I could not bring myself to accept. He was hurt and looked at me very strangely. Socially, I did not want to put myself into a position where I might be hurt or rejected, or where I would hurt or reject someone because I was unable to be open and honest. I felt unequal. This happened a few times.

Not long after this I met Rob, a twenty-three year old South African civil engineering student. He was reserved, but had a twinkle in his eyes. Just a little taller than me, of medium build, with blue eyes and brown hair, he made me feel totally comfortable and safe. This was just three weeks before I turned twenty-one and so, naturally, I invited him to my birthday party.

Shortly after arriving in Johannesburg, over two years earlier, the parents of a boyfriend in Rhodesia befriended me and every week I attended sewing classes with their daughter and her mother at their home. They offered the extraordinary kindness of having a twenty-first birthday party for me in their flat. It was a very memorable night and they made me feel really special. It was also the first birthday party with my friends that I can remember. My birthday present from Mum and Dad was to fly home to see them, which I appreciated.

Rob soon infected me with his love of the Beatles and dancing at parties. He invited me to tag along when he looked at the building of roads and bridges, construction sites, and excavation holes, and he loved to explain the geology of each area.

We liked bush walking and chatting about South African politics. He was the Treasurer for the Student Representative Council and actively involved in anti-apartheid student politics. We would sometimes go together to the university to public lectures about it. He worked part time, which helped to fund a yellow Morris Minor 1000. It was an old car and we called it our 'Yellow Rolls Royce.' It constantly needed attention to fix the brakes!

Rob must have thought I was quite nutty. I was always curious and asked a lot of questions. He was always calm, very patient, and seemed to enjoy answering my questions. His friends idealised him, and this impressed me. He was different to my other boyfriends – we only went out on Saturday evenings, as he studied for the rest of the time. While this was quite frustrating and left me with a lot of free time, I admired his commitment to his studies and his strong sense of self. He was extremely shy and it took quite a long time for him to begin talking about himself and his life and what he hoped for his future.

Gradually, after the initial wonderful phase of mutual attraction, I began to feel this was someone I could really trust. And so, one night around midnight after a party, while parked on Linksfield Ridge in Johannesburg looking at the twinkling lights of the city, I told him my story. He listened quietly and asked sensible questions. It became clear that he did not care at all that I was illegitimate. Much later he told me my adoption was never an issue for him. He accepted me for who I was. I felt safe and I knew he would keep my secret.

I was planning to go on an overseas trip. Rather inexplicably, he encouraged me to go! This was puzzling. While we were very fond of each other, there could be no commitment at that time. We agreed we could continue to go out with others.

My trip included skiing and travelling around Europe and was certainly a wonderful experience. Toward the end of my overseas trip, Rob wrote saying he had been accepted to study at Oxford University and asked if I would like to join him there. This was a very happy surprise! Was this a firm invitation? I could not know until I returned to Johannesburg. Was he genuinely serious about our relationship? Any doubts I had were blown away by his welcome at the airport and my delight at being with him.

Soon after this, we went to meet his family. They beamed and seemed very pleased to meet me. Rob's parents were South African born and spoke Afrikaans and English interchangeably at home. They were thoroughly embedded in South African culture and history, and while ascribing to the ethics of Christianity, were not particularly religious. How different they were to my own family.

Shortly following this visit, we drove many hundreds of miles in our Yellow Rolls Royce to visit my parents in Salisbury, Southern Rhodesia. We were to stay 10 days. Rob was withdrawn. Bridging the cultural gap was no easy task. It was only on the ninth day that he plucked up courage to ask them if we could go together to Oxford while he studied. Having waited so long to speak out meant that my parents did not have much time to talk to him frankly. They agreed that I could go, but only after we were engaged. We were happy about this. We talked about a wedding and they agreed to pay our airfare and bring us back to Salisbury in August the following year. Expense was not an issue for them then. Being able to return to Salisbury for the wedding was perfect, because Rob's family also would be able travel from South Africa to attend.

CHAPTER SIXTEEN

'Please elope'

Soon after we returned to Johannesburg from visiting Mum and Dad in Salisbury, Rob sold his beloved car, our Yellow Rolls Royce, and bought me an engagement ring. After visiting his parents once more, we left for England. He started his studies, took up residence in Holywell Manor attached to Balliol College, and I rented a room with a nice group of girls in the suburbs of Oxford. I accepted a secretarial position with a Professor and two Readers at the Department of Engineering Science in Oxford.

Settling into life at Oxford was awesome – a fairy tale – as anyone who has lived there would know. I will not even try to do justice to this except to say we loved it all – the wonderful old town, the green lawns, the gardens, the history, the beautiful old stone buildings with all their spires, gargoyles, perpendicular Gothic windows, and the lifestyle – not to mention the pubs! We cycled all around the town, including on the towpaths beside the Cherwell. I treasure the memories of the beauty of the countryside, the changing seasons, and especially winter, with snow everywhere and the hoare frost hanging like white lace on fences along the rivers.

As the months passed and our wedding date approached, Mum and Dad became more reticent about having the wedding in Salisbury. We were perplexed. Their letters were tense, sparse, and stilted. In the end, they sent us £50 and told us to get married in England, and that they were not coming.

To say I was hurt and distraught is an understatement.

However, as the weeks passed, we had no choice but to accept it. We were keen to marry and so we arranged a civil ceremony in the local Registry Office in Oxford. We invited Mum and Dad; in fact all my family, including Mum's sister who lived only one hour away in London. I posted a whole lot of invitations to Rhodesia for Mum to give to their friends, but they were never sent on. It was not as if Mum and Dad could not have afforded to come either. They just did not want to.

Again, it was what was not said that was important.

I felt totally rejected. This was very hard to accept! This was never talked about properly. It became an enduring source of hurt that remained unresolved. They were not behaving as if they were my parents. It still distresses me.

Having the wedding in England also meant that Rob's family were not able to be with us. They could have travelled to Rhodesia, but could not at that time afford the expense of bringing their whole family to England. They already had plans to visit us at the end of Rob's university course for his graduation.

We married in late March 1970 in the registry office in Oxford. It was not a pleasant building at all – just a door in the wall of Banbury Road. When we arrived, couples were standing outside waiting their turn to have the ceremony. When our friends discovered our families were not going to attend our wedding, many of them arrived at the registry office. So, in the end, the ceremony took place with our friends standing all around the walls of the small, rather ugly and unremarkable office. There were two formal chairs with armrests and a wooden coffee table between, with a red velvet pillow on which to place the ring. I made my dress for the wedding ceremony and long white velvet culottes for our party that evening in Rob's Holywell Manor college room.

The party was a very happy occasion and some friends took photos, but I don't ever display them. They remind me of Mum and Dad's rejection and the wedding that was planned that never happened.

We console ourselves with the thought it is not the marriage ceremony that is important, but the marriage itself – and we have no complaints about that!

For our honeymoon, we toured England in a trendy MGB GT sports car lent to us by an Oxford don in the Engineering Science

Department where I was working. This was a remarkably generous gesture and we had a marvellous honeymoon driving around the Lake District and Scotland. On our return, we set up home in a suburb of Oxford, within easy cycling distance of the city centre where I worked.

One of the early consequences of marrying Rob was that he inspired me to study and after a year of studying nights after work I had completed two GCE 'A' Level' subjects. This was a significant achievement and I felt that at last I had grown out of being 'Jane Snail' and a *dummes kind*.

After Rob graduated and after having spent two wonderful years in the UK, we returned to South Africa.

The estrangement between us and my parents fortunately did not last. Soon after returning to South Africa, they invited us back to Rhodesia. Although it was never directly addressed, it was clear they felt they needed to reconcile with us about the wedding. They bought a very nice car as a wedding present, but forgot we would have to pay a large duty if we drove it to South Africa. They sold the car and offered us dining room furniture instead. We chose some locally-made oak furniture, which we still have and treasure. Later, they helped us with a down payment on our first home and we were very grateful for their generosity.

More than 40 years later, long after they had both passed away, I began to understand why they told us to marry in Oxford.

Recently, we attended a wonderful Jewish wedding in Sydney, where there were 300 guests. Nothing was spared to make everyone enjoy the wedding. As well as all the material blessings evident at the wedding, the love, the sense of community, the peace and celebration of the two families shone through. I was relating the experience of this wonderful wedding to a friend, who then told me of a Jewish wedding where the opposite was the case. In this wedding, the bride was not Jewish. Although she had done all she could to comply with the expectations of her new Jewish family, there was much celebrating, but little joy. The couple split up within a year.

I then understood why Mum and Dad behaved the way they

did. When we planned our marriage, they were working with several other families helping to start a Reform Jewish congregation. They would have been immensely pleased had Rob been Jewish. But he was not, and we would not have wanted a religious wedding. All their friends were Jewish and our non-religious civil ceremony would have been hard to explain. I would also have been stressed knowing that Mum would have been very tense. With such differing cultures within and between our families, it would have been extraordinarily difficult, perhaps impossible, to have a happy wedding. So after all, 40 years on, I am finally grateful to Mum and Dad for sparing us that pain and angst.

Three years later, they invited us to go with them on holiday to Europe to ski for two weeks. They don't ski, but very much enjoyed the alpine scenery and the lovely hotel. We spent the days on the slopes and they would meet us for lunch half-way up the mountains. Now, we think this was their way of getting to know us and make amends. It was a wonderful holiday, Rob learnt to ski and we remember it fondly.

But aren't families strange? Why couldn't we have talked more about this? Or was I not able to hear what they were saying? Maybe I was too hurt to listen. I'm not sure. I think now Mum would have understood my change of heart. She would have wisely said to me, 'Jane, it's not the wedding day, but the marriage that counts.' She would have been right. Our happy marriage of more than 40 years standing testifies to that.

CHAPTER SEVENTEEN

Rewarding times, challenging times – 1971–87

After we returned to South Africa, Rob worked and supported me for four years while I completed a Bachelor in Social Work degree at the University of the Witwatersrand. This was a generous gesture by Rob and an incredibly liberating experience for me. I found I loved studying.

Our eldest son, Adam, was born within six weeks of me completing my degree. A month or so later, we had a very happy visit to my parents in Zimbabwe. We also enjoyed Rob's parents living nearby. I loved being a mother and often carried my babies the African way, on my back. This always elicited exclamations of surprise and disbelief by black women – 'Hauw' they would say!

A few months after our visit, Mum and Dad came to Johannesburg and we invited them home for dinner. They were relaxed and happy and very complimentary about the roast dinner. They enjoyed seeing Adam, who slept much of the time. I particularly cherished the loving hug Dad gave me at the end of the evening.

That was to be our last hug. The next morning, Dad died from a heart attack on his way to the city to see a philatelist to sell some stamps.

We were all shocked. We helped as much as we could and returned to Salisbury with Mum for the funeral. The rabbi of the newly-established Reform Congregation gave an inspiring, thoughtful, historical review of Dad's life. I felt very proud of Dad and understood more about Jewish history and his place in it.

By then, I was also pregnant with our second son, who was born a few months later in 1977. Rob enrolled to study for a PhD and worked extremely hard for the next three years. Being mother to our two children, while also working part time, meant that our lives were very busy. Rob's parents loved their regular contact with us, especially with our two happy, active little boys. However, the apartheid system troubled us enormously. We knew we did not want to stay in South Africa in the long term.

Mum stayed on in Rhodesia for a couple of years before deciding to leave Rhodesia in 1979. But there is one lovely story that must be told first.

Before she left Rhodesia, Mum came on a holiday with us to a small town south of Durban. We had all been invited for a cup of tea with some friends who had a house nearby. He was a professor at the University of the Witwatersrand in Johannesburg and his wife was also an academic. A few days before, we told them my mother was with us. It is possible we did not fix an arrival time. We arrived at their front door at around 3.30pm on the appointed day, very pleased to have been invited out. Mum stood in front of us, with Rob and I and our two boys just behind her, and she knocked on their heavy wooden front door. The door opened and our friend was standing there, stark naked and smiling. He invited us in. We felt acutely embarrassed for Mum; our children were too young or too preoccupied to notice. Mum surprised us completely. She held her head high and nonchalantly accepted the invitation to sit in the lounge room, as if there was nothing untoward. Eventually, our host went off to put some clothes on, and later we enjoyed a very pleasant cup of tea. It was hilarious, but very embarrassing at the time.

Prior to deciding to leave Rhodesia, Mum talked over her plans with us. This was a huge move for her. She was seventy-three, but fit and healthy. After being in Rhodesia for 40 years she was forced to leave almost everything she owned – her home, her business, and almost all of their money in the bank. She settled in Sydney, Australia. Fortunately, my brother James and his wife, who had been living in Sydney for some time, were marvellous in helping her find and settle into an apartment near where they lived.

With Mum leaving Zimbabwe and Rob completing his PhD in

Management, we decided we should leave South Africa before the boys started school. We hated the apartheid regime and feared for the boys' educational and other opportunities in the long term. With some trepidation we told Rob's parents, and they, rather surprisingly, supported our move to Australia. This would be a real wrench. We knew we would miss them dreadfully, as well as their extended family in South Africa. Leaving our friends also left a huge hole in our lives.

Rob's long held anti-apartheid feelings were affecting his work opportunities. I, on the other hand, found my community development work with people living in black townships exciting and worthwhile. I wrote a book about planning services for urban black elderly people, which was well received. I was asked to be the keynote speaker at the next annual national conference of services for the elderly in South Africa in November 1980. Very reluctantly, I declined – we would already be in Sydney. My boss presented my paper and wrote to me saying it was summarised, disseminated, and used in the planning of services in South Africa.

Another reason for moving to Sydney was that Mum and James with his family were living there. Our families had lived in separate countries for many years. I longed to live closer so that we could strengthen our family relationships.

We arrived in Sydney on 22 July 1980, exhausted, but very pleased to be in our newly-adopted land. Soon we moved into a very small home, close to the city about the same size as a small house in Soweto. Amazingly enough, the only toilet was outside! We soon installed an inside one. We were homesick and missed our family and friends dreadfully, but Sydney was so beautiful and being able to explore the beaches and the sea became a real comfort.

We had no real doubts and were fascinated by the Australians we met. They often made us laugh; we loved the laconic 'no worries' culture in the 'land of the long weekend.' We found Australians to be competent, warm-hearted, and hard-working.

After a few months, both sons started nursery school and I began working. But soon after, we were told something that would change all our lives forever.

We were aware our eldest, Adam, was slow to talk but had been told it was nothing to worry too much about, as there was every possibility that he could 'catch up.' A wonderful early intervention program helped. We were often told Einstein had talked unusually late. Our second son, Sam, was 13½ months younger but he walked, talked, and learnt to read very early. He was always kind and gentle with Adam and a joy to have around.

As part of the process of selecting the best school for Adam, we were advised late in 1981 to take him to be tested by an educational psychologist. To our absolute dismay, he was assessed as having a *moderate* level of learning disability, but with no particular diagnosis. Even though we had known something was not right, we did not expect this.

We consulted a whole range of specialists, but nobody could provide a diagnosis, a course of recommended treatment, or even a reason for his disability. If he had been a child with Down's syndrome, we would have been able to consult and be supported by an association of other parents and access specialists who could offer advice. Adam's situation was unique and we were offered a myriad of tests, training programs, diets and exercise regimes, many of them untested and often costly.

The first question I was always asked was: 'Has anyone else in your family had a disability?' I would then have to explain that I was adopted as a result of my adoptive parents having a child with Down's Syndrome, but that I knew nothing about my biological family. There were no answers and that stopped the questions.

Both our sons were good looking. Adam's appearance belied his diagnosis. He had an attractive, kind, compliant personality to go with his dark brown hair, large dark brown eyes, and lovely impish smile. At age six, he could do most things other four or five year old children could do; certainly he chatted, dressed himself, and all the other normal things one would expect, just at a slightly slower pace.

How could this diagnosis be true? Much of my time in his early years was taken up with extra lessons, visiting early education programs and doctors for diagnostic tests, and doing extra work with him at home.

As I went from test to test with our son and from doctor to doctor, I found myself reliving how I thought my adoptive parents must have felt after Jonathan's initial diagnosis. Was this how Mum felt when she was told about Jonathan? I stubbornly refused to accept it. This was cruel irony!

Irrationally, Dad's nursery rhyme *Was bist du? Du bist ein dummes kind! Was bist du? Du bist ein stupide kind!* ran through my head over and over again. Could it be possible that Adam's delayed learning was a repetition of me being 'Jane Snail'?

Adam lasted less than six months at our local school before the teachers advised us he should be transferred to a 'special school.' If he had a physical disability, it might have been easier to accept, but he did not.

At this stage, Adam began to be sensitive to the developmental gap opening up between him and his younger brother. Once, when he was about six years, he looked up at me and asked, 'Mum, why can't I read?' My heart sank. He understood far more than he could say. I replied something to the effect, 'I'm sure you will in time' and hoped he was reassured. We constantly worried whether we were doing all we could to meet his needs. Everyday events required a steel facade. We saw Mum at least weekly and she watched how we were coping, which must have been heartbreaking for her.

Despite everything, we did our best to be as light-hearted as possible. Adam helped by giving us some very funny moments – and he loved us to laugh with him.

One weekend, some close friends offered to have our two boys stay with them for two nights enabling Rob and me, for the first time in many years, to have a weekend to ourselves. We went to a hotel in Bondi.

On the boys' first evening the bath was filled with warm water and they were invited to 'jump into the bath.' Adam, keen to do as he was told, did just that – he jumped into the bath enthusiastically – drenching everything in sight! Our friends collapsed with laughter. We never lived this down. It was fodder for stories for years.

Our younger son, Nick grew up being gentle, wise beyond his

years, and always considerate of others. I began to long for a baby, so that Adam would enjoy being at home with me. Nick could then feel free to take up his own sporting and extramural activities, without feeling guilty his brother couldn't come along. So in 1986, when the two boys were ten and nine our daughter, Kathryn, was born. This was wonderful turning point; a happy time for the whole family!

Adam continued to entertain us. On one occasion our family was invited to some dear friends for lunch, delicious takeaway pizzas around a table on a patio on the first floor overlooking a neighbour's property. Everyone was happily chatting when Adam picked up his pizza and threw it into the neighbour's garden like a frisbee. It was one of those unbelievable moments: the pizza spun past our faces, with Nick and Kathryn and our friends doing their best to keep a straight face. Their visitors from overseas, who did not know Adam, looked on in absolute astonishment. It was hilarious and surreal, but no one could laugh. As a rule, we tried to ignore inappropriate behaviour so as to not encourage it. We continued chatting and replaced the food on Adam's plate as if nothing had happened. Later, we chuckled and I do not think Adam minded.

Around this time, new disability legislation, the Disability Services Act 1986, was introduced encouraging people with disabilities to live more valued, socially-inclusive lives in normal suburban homes. This was a generational change. No longer was it acceptable to have one solution to fit all; no longer were people with disabilities to be cared for in a custodial manner, institutionalised and excluded. Care was to be tailored to meet an individual's specific needs, encouraging more learning and greater independence with more opportunities to make friends and work.

This was a very welcome change.

Following these values two others and I, working in a voluntary capacity, submitted a funding application to the Australian Commonwealth Government for a desperately needed supported-accommodation service for our local community.

In 1986 The Housing Connection began, and now provides individually tailored support so that adults with a disability living in our local geographical area can lead independent quality lives while staying in their own homes.

One of the many innovations included an unusual clause in the constitution limiting the length of time board members could serve to five years. We hoped this would encourage regular regeneration and renewal of board members and leadership, while also making the building up of vested interests less likely. I chaired The Housing Connection for the first four years and then resigned. Twenty-five years on, due to an amazing commitment by everyone involved, it is a thriving community and supports more than sixty people.

The philosophy of the Disability Services Act 1986 was amazingly liberating and healing on a personal level; both in our relationship with Adam and also in my attitude towards Jonathan. It meant that when we needed to advocate for Adam it was not from a position of weakness, as recipients of charity, because I was not coping; but from the perspective of what would be best for Adam's short- and long-term learning and development. No longer was it a shame to have a child with a disability, like Jonathan or Adam; nor should they have fewer opportunities or be hidden away and kept secret. This made Adam's place in our family all the more poignant and valued and our attempts to lobby and advocate on his behalf all the more determined.

Moreover, I could not help noticing parallels in the changing social values and legislation relating to adoptions. The social stigma of adoption remains, but hopefully, this is becoming much less. Being considered illegitimate and somehow less deserving or even a bastard, as I have been called, is thankfully now more a reflection of the prejudices and outdated values of the person making the statement than adopted people themselves.

However, my heart goes out to adoptive families who in the past received their adopted child on condition they maintain the secret that their child is adopted, and where access to information about that child's biological parents is blocked; while at the same time attempting to value and love their adopted child and provide them with a home and family in an unfettered way. With the benefit of hindsight, this is a tragic and self-defeating situation to be put into. Now, I believe, in

Australia at least, when a child is adopted, they become a full member of that family with all the same rights as any other children.

Mum (Elizabeth)

For her first few years in Sydney, Mum thrived particularly after joining the Sydney Bridge Club. This provided balance and structure to her life. After ten years, she very much appreciated the recognition of her considerable skill when she became a Grand Master. We saw her regularly, often for Sunday lunch and Christmas lunch became a ritual for our family. It was around this time Mum gave me some lovely recipe books I still treasure. We also enjoyed swapping recipes. One I loved was her delicious low-fat Boston Bread recipe.

Boston bread recipe
Combine:
2   *cups boiling water*
1⅓ *cups chopped dates (250g)*
½   *cup raisins or sultanas (100g)*
1½ *cup brown or raw sugar (250g)*
2   *teaspoons holsum (oil, or butter) (10g)*
2   *teaspoons bicarbonate of soda (10g)*

Add:
2 *well-beaten eggs*
3 *cups flour*

Pour into 2 large (or 4 small) well-greased and floured loaf tins. Bake at 170 degrees Celcius for 1 hour and 15 minutes (or until a skewer comes out clean).

A few years later, Mum was diagnosed with cancer and we did our best to support her. During her last few weeks, she stayed in a hospice. One day, shortly before she died, I was pushing her around the garden in a wheelchair. She asked to stop and I sat down next to her on a bench. We chatted for a while, and then she looked at me and said, 'Jane, if I could have my life over, I would have done things differently.' I sensed she was referring to my adoption and Jonathan. At that time, I was still loyal to the promise I had given her not to search for my biological family. This meant she could not talk about it either – and the barrier had to stay. It was not possible to reverse what had happened.

I loved her dearly for saying that. I knew too that beliefs and knowledge in the 1940s were so different from today and it was not fair to judge decisions made in the 20th century by the beliefs, values, and standards of the 21st century. In the two weeks before she died, she asked me to 'look after' Jonathan and keep in contact with the people who cared for him. I accepted gladly. Adam had taught me what I needed to know.

Shortly after this, the hospital called to ask me to be with her. As I arrived, her words to me were 'They won't operate.' This was terribly confronting. She clearly wanted to continue living. All I could do was check with the hospice staff, who said nothing further could be done. She knew. I do not know how to describe how I felt. I had to be outwardly strong for her, but inside, things were very different.

She was brave, but frail and weak. She indicated she was glad to have me there. I asked her if she needed any pain relief; she nodded and I organised it for her. Slowly, her ability to move or express herself ebbed away. I stroked her hands. She looked wooden, slightly anxious, and pale. Strangely, an hour later, she raised her head, turned, looked past me and the expression in her eyes and face changed to one of relief – almost as if to say 'Oh, if that is where I am going, it will be okay - it will be fine.' Then, she was silent. She had gone. Her body was there, lifeless, chilled and white, but she was totally absent! How strange! I was stunned – and desperately alone, but extraordinarily grateful to have been with her for those last two hours. I treasure this memory. Fortunately, my brother arrived soon after and I was relieved when he took charge.

It was late 1987; now both Mum and Dad had passed away. I was very sad for a long time and missed them both.

PART TWO
Introducing Phyllis

CHAPTER EIGHTEEN

The search begins

After both my adoptive parents died, a niggling thought began to worry me. Adam's behaviour started to become more and more unpredictable and I began to wonder what the likelihood was for our son or daughter to give birth to a child with a disability. Further consultations with a specialist geneticist confirmed the necessity to clarify my genetic history.

Although I still had strong feelings of guilt about breaking my promise never to search for my biological parents, no longer was this just a selfish pursuit of my identity or the resolving of personal curiosity. It had a direct bearing on the future health of our whole family.

This led to the exchange of correspondence between an adoption and reunion organisation in England called NORCAP (National Organisation for Counselling Adoptees and Parents) who allocated a wonderful researcher, Pam, to my case. She supplied a number of birth and death certificates, with lots of names and dates.

It was Pam who first introduced me to my mother, Phyllis Margaret.

To be clear at the outset, it is worth explaining the various names mother was known by. Up until the end of her first marriage in 1938, Mother was known as Phyllis. After this, for reasons that will become obvious later, she was known by her second name, Margaret. I will call her Phyllis for now.

Pam posted me the marriage certificate of Phyllis to Jim Whicker, as well as a birth certificate for a son, Paul, from that marriage. I was aching to find a family I belonged to, and to find a brother, son to my biological mother, was wonderful and very exciting. I was exhilarated for days, but then in her next letter, Pam advised me not to contact Paul until I was certain my mother was no longer alive. This was because my birth might have been a secret and Phyllis might not have wanted Paul to know about me.

Pam's next letter sent two further marriage certificates to John Kleyn and Alan MacRobert.

It was so strange finding out about my family like this.

So, Phyllis had been married three times. I didn't know what to think. What had happened to her first and second marriages? If only I could have spoken with her. I wrote to Pam a number of times asking her to find out whether Mother was still alive. Pam did her best, but to no avail. Just as my curiosity was at its height, the research hit a dead end, as in August 1992, Pam resigned from her post.

I was so disappointed! She had done so much to provide me with documentation about my family. Although another researcher was allocated, nothing else was done, and then she resigned, too.

Then Adam's health tragically deteriorated. We watched as he found everyday living skills more and more difficult to do. We were in crisis and our family issues naturally took precedence, so I gave up my search.

I still did not know whether my biological mother was alive or dead, and now had lost hope of ever finding her. Maybe this was the end of my search. Adam was now fourteen and needed constant support for all his daily living skills. With both Rob and me working, our lives were too busy to take on anything else.

At the end of 1992 we were lucky enough to be able to organise respite care for Adam in Australia, so that we could attend an important family event in South Africa. We decided, as part of the same trip to visit Jonathan, my adoptive brother with Down's syndrome, for the first time in Worcester, England.

This was for me an incredibly poignant time. Jonathan, now forty-six years, had spent forty-five years of his life in an institution. Just twelve months before we met him, he had been moved into a purpose-built, very comfortable house in a suburb of Worcester. He was living with four other people – all with high support needs. We were invited to meet Jonathan at his home over afternoon tea.

Jonathan was an endearing, short, portly, grey-haired man with a toothless happy grin. It was easy to warm to him, but the legacy of being in an institution for most of his forty-six years was all too clear. During our visit he seemed very happy to have visitors, communicating in grunts and gestures, and was very affectionate.

I found our meeting extraordinarily poignant and surreal. We sat with Jonathan in his comfortable living room, smiling and talking to him and his caregivers. Our lives were uniquely connected. If he had not been born, my fate might have been quite different. I felt uncomfortable and partly responsible for his life, and yet helpless. I do not have the words to describe my situation. In defence of Mum and Dad (Elizabeth and Benjamin), I know that times were different then and that they made their decisions in good faith and based on the best advice they had at the time.

We could not help but feel extraordinarily sad.

We met Jonathan's caregivers at each visit over the years and I was greatly reassured by the quality of the care he received. They treated our visits with extraordinary sensitivity and kindness. For years afterwards until Jonathan died, we were given regular updates and kept informed with letters, postcards, and videos of his activities, holidays, and health checks. The quality of the care he received gave me a yardstick to measure how services could be provided. Meeting Jonathan strengthened my determination to lobby harder for more community-based services in Australia.

Services for people with disabilities in Australia were grossly inadequate given the level of need. So in the early 1990s, we participated in the lobbying efforts for more services. It was hard to understand why such misery caused by this lack of services was allowed to continue. It felt to us as a family, that we were living in a third-world country as far as the availability of support for people with disabilities. And we knew many other families in the same situation. I joined in the lobbying and the demonstrations. On one occasion, my daughter and I camped out in Sydney's Hyde Park with several hundred other families while Rob stayed home with Adam. It was hilarious, cars hooted their support and that night the automatic sprinklers turned on at 3am, drenching us all. This demonstration, together with many years of intense lobbying and marches to Parliament, was remarkably successful and day services for all school leavers with disabilities were finally started. Fortunately, this occurred just as Adam left school. A few more supported living places were released, but nowhere near enough.

Around this time, Adam's care needs escalated sharply and the story about how he eventually secured supported accommodation in a home in the community is a story for another time. This was an extremely difficult time for all the family. He was seventeen when he left home and is now happily settled, sharing a house with people close to his age. His caregivers are committed to doing everything possible to ensure he is content and happy, and most have known him for years. We applaud the quality of care he is receiving. Both Rob and I take an active role in his life, see him regularly, bring him home, and continue to be involved in the life of the organisation that supports him – The Housing Connection.

Some years later, in 2002, Rob was invited to work in London. This was an opportunity too good to refuse. Our daughter, who was seventeen years old at the time, chose to attend boarding school in Sydney. Our sons were twenty-seven and twenty-eight years. After a lot of thought and a heavy heart about leaving the children, as well as putting a whole range of support in place for Adam, we moved temporarily to England. Our other two children promised to visit their older brother regularly and to support him while we were away. A close friend kindly agreed to act as a guardian in case of emergency and the organisation that cared for him sent us regular emails.

We looked forward to living in London and relished the opportunity to enjoy the beautiful scenery, wonderful architecture steeped in history, beautiful gardens, and the theatre. Although wary of what I might find, I hoped also to use the opportunity to find out more about my biological mother and her family.

CHAPTER NINETEEN

London – 2002

It was 6am and dark when our plane touched bumpily down onto the shiny wet tarmac at Heathrow airport. The yellow and white lights from the terminal reflected off the black surface, becoming dim in the grey of the emerging dawn. As the fog of weariness and jetlag lifted, I could hardly contain my joy – we had looked forward to this trip for so long. It was November 2002, winter was approaching, and we had arrived in London.

This city held a very special magic for me. It was where I was born. I also could not help but be infected with some of Mum's nostalgia for London in those early years in Rhodesia. I returned twice as a child on family holidays, in my early twenties to explore, and with Rob to Oxford where we married.

Now there was an extra special reason for returning – to search for Phyllis, my biological mother. I could not suppress the butterflies when I thought of this upcoming adventure. The exhilaration and anticipation, with more than a twinge of trepidation, was amplified by my not knowing what might transpire.

The planeload of passengers waited silently, but rather impatiently, for the doors to open, as I wondered what might be ahead of me.

Whimsically, I thought about Phyllis growing up in London in the early 20th century. How different it must have been. I wondered when she first listened to BBC on her own wireless, or what music she liked. What did she think of the smash hits at the time, like *Happy Days Are Here Again* or *Ain't She Sweet*? Were those songs that typified the 'Roaring Twenties' for her?

I was jolted out of my reveries when the aeroplane doors were opened and we were disembarking at last.

We were delighted to be in London, despite the weather. Our first day was wet, grey, cold, and windy. The wind was so strong it turned our umbrellas inside out. The air was icy. The days became even shorter. While Rob spent his days at work, I walked long distances exploring London, entranced by the beautiful Christmas lights. In the darkness, at 5pm one evening, I walked from the Victoria and Albert Museum towards Harrods, attracted by little white twinkling fairy lights outlining the buildings against the black sky. It was magical, easily compensating for the loss of daylight.

The next few months were spent finding a home, as well as renewing old friendships. We went to see Jonathan, my brother. Every few months we arranged to meet him – often at pubs for lunch or at a café for coffee and cake or in parks on warm sunny days. His caregivers were wonderful. Nothing was too hard or difficult; they were always light-hearted in their interaction with Jonathan and Jonathan himself was always cheerful and smiling. We were glad to participate, even at a peripheral level, in Jonathan's life. We also attended his yearly planning meeting. These were happy times. I always took photographs and here is one I love.

Jonathan and the author enjoying some time together, 2003

A few months passed. With Rob at work during the week, the opportunity for me to also work became rather attractive. I wanted to become involved in English life and not just be a spectator. So, for almost two years I worked as a social worker at a disability team in one of London's Councils, working with families caring for their children. The work was demanding and often emotionally challenging. Nevertheless, I never lost sight of the privilege it is to be involved in the lives of other families and become acquainted with such a rich tapestry of cultures.

A year, and then two years, passed and already it was time to start planning to return to Australia. Suddenly, I realised I had waited too long and the urgency to resume the task of finding by biological family became all too apparent. Part of my hesitation had been because, frankly, I was fearful of the outcome and facing the disappointment that had ended all my previous searches.

The most important question to resolve was whether Phyllis was still alive. Finding her death notice had eluded the researchers in the 1990s. It was now highly unlikely that she was still alive, but I couldn't stop hoping. So, early one Saturday morning in August, we visited the Family Records Centre in Holborn, London.

Once there, I felt very awkward and vulnerable, unsure of how to search the records. Knowing one's mother is something most people take for granted, whereas I had no idea whether mine was alive or dead.

It felt odd in another way, too. I was resuming the search after a ten-year break. All the old feelings returned, especially guilt at the betrayal of the promise made to my adoptive parents that I would never search for her. Yet, denying my own needs to find her felt like a leaden weight. I knew this was the right thing to do for my family, but still could not squash the rising tide of disquiet and uneasiness. As I stood hesitating in front of the Centre, Rob sensed my internal struggle and squeezed my hand.

Gradually, we understood why it had been such a daunting task to my previous researchers. After entering the building, we passed through a series of security checks before walking into a large, cavernous room that was segmented by rows and rows of tall, open, dark wood bookcases. The printed death notices were bound in thick, dark brown leather-bound books, with faded gold letters stamped on their spines. Each quarter year was split into four books, labelled A to E, F to J, and so on. There were sixteen books for each year and all were packed tightly in the shelves. Between each row of bookcases were waist-high wooden tables running the length of the bookcases.

Usually people know the approximate or exact date of death of the person they are looking for, so searching for a death notice is a fairly straightforward process. In our case, this was not so. We stood throughout the search, as there were no chairs provided. Each heavy book had to be lifted from the bookshelf, placed on the table, and then the list of names, in alphabetical order, checked. If the entry you need is not found, the heavy book is replaced in the bookcase and the next book is removed and checked – a tiring, tedious process.

We searched for Phyllis' last name, MacRobert, and then for her first name. That afternoon, we decided to start with the four books from each quarter containing the letter M in 2004, and then work backwards through each year to 2000. That would be twenty weighty books. When we finished searching the last book for the year 2000, Phyllis' name had not been found and our excitement rose. Could she still be alive?

We continued searching each volume, back through ten more years to 1990, then through the 1980s, and finally the 1970s. We became more hopeful as we travelled backward. We knew Phyllis was born in 1906. I hoped that by not finding her name, Phyllis just might be still alive.

Two hours later, our backs were seriously hurting and we were exhausted, but that was immaterial. Had we missed her? That became our nagging concern as we searched.

It was Rob who eventually found her name. We double checked. Yes, it undoubtedly was Phyllis. We had not missed her: she died on 3 January 1963!

I was in shock. In 1963, I was only fifteen years old. This was four years before I was told I was adopted. I felt cheated and extremely disappointed. Why, oh why, did it have to be this way?

Feeling exhausted, flat, and sore from standing so long, we ordered her Death Certificate. It was too much to absorb all at once. Mother died so young – she was only fifty-six. The possibility of meeting her, hugging her, or hearing her call my name was now totally gone. I felt forlorn and miserable. Was this really worth the heartache?

As we walked slowly away from the building, Rob gently took my hand. We were silent, still absorbing the information. The thuds of our footsteps on the hard pavement echoed discordantly against the buildings. Disappointed, defeated, and upset, it was better just to be quiet. There was nothing more to say. Across the street was a pavement café. We sat down thankfully at a table in the sunshine and broke the silence only to order something to eat and drink. We rested in the quiet between us. I wondered how many other people had used this café to sit and ponder their discoveries made at the Family Records Centre.

The waitress brought the coffee and sandwiches. Slowly we returned to reality and began to work through what we knew. While sitting there, resting and sipping our coffee in the sunshine, we were all too aware that this was yet another turning point; that there was no way of preparing for what lay ahead. There was no choice now but to reach beyond our own nuclear family. For decades, the issue of my biological family had been mine and mine alone. From now on, the search had to involve others outside our immediate family and this made me feel extremely vulnerable. I really was in unchartered waters.

An image of Victoria Falls in Zimbabwe flashed through my mind – I felt as if I were canoeing silently along a creek meandering through the bush unaware of the waterfall that lay ahead. Could I control the outcome?

Why was I so apprehensive and uneasy? Did I want to continue? One part of me wanted to withdraw and hide. I was scared of the unknown. But we were leaving England in the near future – this would be the last opportunity to pursue my heritage. There was little choice. I had to go on.

CHAPTER TWENTY

Finding Paul, Phyllis' son

After the fateful discovery in August 2004 that Phyllis was no longer alive, our lives became frantically busy. The opportunity to continue with my search did not present itself until just before Easter 2005. We had only six months left in England.

I had stopped work temporarily to have some minor shoulder surgery and found myself at home alone with time on my hands. In the quiet of our apartment on Tuesday in the week before Easter, I reviewed what I already knew.

I knew Mother was born Phyllis Hogg, that she married Jim Whicker, and that in 1932 she gave birth to a son, Paul. I put his full name, Paul Whicker, into Google and pressed the search button. Nothing came up. I tried again. Pages of irrelevant information came up, but nothing referring to him. Then, I tried searching for Eileen, Paul's wife, and this time I was successful – I found her. I knew from their marriage certificate that she had been a nurse. There was a short biography of her, stating that she had a nursing qualification and now was a psychotherapist. It was some years old, but it gave an address and a telephone number. This was a break-through, but I very much wanted to find information on Paul.

I tried his name again. Different pages of information came up; I examined them systematically and yes, there he was! His name and phone number was among a list of bridge teachers on the English Bridge Union website.

Like me, he played bridge. This was the first of what would evolve into quite a long list of shared skills and interests. Although rationally this was to be expected, he and I were brother and sister after all, I still found it amazing and confirming.

I now had a decision to make. What was the best way to approach him? The warnings from the adoption literature were clear. It was important to have an intermediary make the first contact. It was not as confronting for the person being contacted and it was possible to offer the person being contacted a choice about whether to meet or not, how best to do it, and their preferred timing.

Certainly, I did not want to phone Paul. I would find that far too confronting and hardly an optimal way to begin a relationship.

What would I say? 'Hello, am I speaking to Paul?'

If he answered, I would need to ask his full name, his date of birth, and his mother's full name and date of birth. It would not be surprising if he resented this intrusion into his privacy. And imagine his reaction if I then said I thought I was his sister.

But how else could I do it? I tried to contact the local authority working with adoption issues and was told appointments were difficult to obtain. I had a couple of helpful conversations with social workers, but we had recently moved council areas and knew it would take months to obtain an interview with a social worker in the local adoption team. We just did not have the time. Was not there a better way?

I wondered how much Paul knew – did he know he had a half-sister? He had not been adopted and was fifteen years older than me. Would he have had a reason to go to the Family Records Centre to search for birth records? I doubted it. It was possible that if I phoned him directly and confronted him with the fact that I was his half-sister, it would come as a huge shock. This would be difficult for me, too. I feared the emotional turmoil this might cause him and did not know how he would react.

It was now the Wednesday before Easter.

I decided to ask Mary for advice. She was a dear friend whom we had known for more than 30 years. She was an experienced professional in the medical field and I had enormous respect for her integrity, clarity of thought, and strong sense of ethics. She also knew of my adoption. I contacted her and explained that I had found the phone number of my half-brother Paul and was wondering what would be the best way to contact him. We discussed many ways to minimise the impact, in case it was a shock for him. Eventually, I asked whether she would be prepared to phone him on my behalf. She thought about it for a moment, asked some questions and then consented. I was thrilled. I had complete confidence she would do this with sensitivity, and kindness. She confessed she had not done anything quite like this before, but that did not trouble her. We agreed I would email her all the details about Paul and Phyllis, including Paul's full name and date of birth, as well as Phyllis' names and date of birth, the full name of his father, and the names of Phyllis' two subsequent husbands.

Mary and I agreed that it was important to check out whether he really was Phyllis' son, then to gently let him know of my existence, and finally to let him know I would love to meet him if he was agreeable. I asked if she could also mention that I would love to find out more about Phyllis and other family members to clarify our family's genetic history for my children. Mary would also invite Paul to contact me, if he wished. I explained that we were going away to Cornwall for Easter and that if Paul wanted to phone me to please do so on that next Tuesday. We were planning to arrive home quite late in the evening of Easter Monday. I thanked her for her willingness to phone Paul for me.

At last, I was getting somewhere. 'What will be, will be,' I thought. I had set things in motion and was no longer in control of the outcome. A new phase in the journey had begun and once again I did not know where it would lead.

CHAPTER TWENTY-ONE

Contact with Paul – Easter 2005

It was a relief to be going away for the Easter Holiday. This would provide a much needed break from the intense emotions the search for my family was generating.

The process was now extending beyond our family and in large measure was out of our control. I struggled to be centred, certain of my purpose, and tolerant of the uncertainty and ambiguity. There could be so many possible outcomes. Could I cope with being disappointed again? What if Paul did not believe Mary and did not want contact with me? I could not bear to think about it. What would he look like? I knew he was fifteen years older, so I knew I had to be prepared for possible health issues. How would I cope with that? And what about his family? Would I like them? What would they think of me? Would they be inquisitive about my family? Usually families live and grow together and I wondered what it would be like to meet close family members as adults. How different would the relationships be because of that?

Cornwall was green and beautiful and peaceful. It was wonderful just to be us, just Rob and me. We were aware that this was a brief and very precious interlude, and for this long weekend, we put everything aside. We drove to St Ives, meandered through the art galleries and explored the nearby Eden Project and the Lost Gardens of Heligan. We also walked, scrambled, and clambered along the wild, rocky coast west of St Ives with the fresh sea breezes in our faces.

After a long day of challenging driving and unbelievable traffic, we arrived back at our apartment. It was 7pm on Easter Monday. While wheeling my suitcase to the bedroom, the small yellow light on the answering phone caught my attention. There were two messages waiting to be heard. I came back to reality with a jolt and sat down suddenly in our little alcove. My heart thumped.

I hesitantly pressed the button on the answering machine.

The first message was from Mary. She spoke with a strong, clear, authoritative voice.

'Hello Jane. I hope you enjoyed your weekend. I phoned Paul and he was thrilled to discover he had a sister. It came as a complete surprise. He was astonished, as he knew nothing about you. He wants to contact you, so I gave him your number. I told Paul that you were going away for the weekend and would only come back on Monday evening. He sounds an extremely nice man and asked all the questions one would expect from someone in his situation. He phoned me twice during the weekend to talk things over and to ask questions. I told him that he could not have a nicer sister. Please, do let me know how things go.'

There was no time to think as the answering machine automatically went on to the second message. A deep male voice resonated from the machine's small speaker.

'Hello Jane. This is a message from your new half-brother, Paul. I received a call from your great friend, Dr Mary, who told me that you are my sister. What a huge surprise.'

Then he said emphatically, impetuously. 'I am delighted to know I have a sister. She did say you would be away until after Easter, but I thought I would phone to let you know my telephone number. I am intrigued. I would love to meet you both, you and Rob. So I will phone again after Easter.'

Click. That was the end of the message.

I felt as if I had just been hit in the pit of my stomach. Could this actually be happening? Fortunately, I was sitting down. I could not believe what I had just heard – yet there was a welling up of excitement and of sheer joy. This, at last, was a tangible outcome to my years and years of searching.

I sat there, pressing the button, listening again and again to the two telephone messages. Time seemed to stand still; my whole life flashed before me. Other than the voices on the answering machine, the apartment was totally silent. I felt cocooned in space. In that suspended second, I thought back to when all this started thirty-nine years earlier, as a result of another phone call, when Dad called asking me to fly to Salisbury.

While I was deep in thought, the door handle turned and Rob came into the apartment carrying the rest of the luggage. I told him about the phone calls. He knew what this meant to me. In one of those long moments, he smiled and then gave me a hug.

Suddenly the phone rang, demanding attention, intruding into the silence and interrupting our long, quiet hug. I gasped, startled, picked up the phone, and attempted to say in my usual voice: 'Jane speaking.'

'Hello Jane. This is your half-brother speaking.' I recognised his voice – the same as the message left in the answering machine. It was Paul. Blood rushed to my head.

I giggled nervously.

'Hello Paul, I have just listened to your message. We returned a few minutes ago,' I said, very aware of my Zimbabwean accent.

He laughed nervously, too; then it was if he had prepared a little speech. 'I am delighted to know I have a half-sister. Your great friend, Mary phoned me and told me about you. I *would* like to meet you. I did not know anything about you.'

Before I could say anything more, he asked, 'Could we please meet soon? I'm not good at waiting.'

I mentioned that Rob would like to meet him, too, and asked whether we could meet in five days, over the next weekend.

'Please, could we meet sooner?' he said urgently. 'I can hardly wait. I am very impatient.' There was a bit of a silence. Then he said with a slight giggle, 'It runs in the family.'

I laughed – and agreed. Yes, it would be lovely if we could meet sooner. We agreed to meet in two days' time, Wednesday, 30 March 2005 at lunchtime at Canary Wharf. This was where Rob worked, so he could also be there. Rob would choose the venue and phone him back.

I made a note of these conversations in a little notebook, writing: 'I feel much more at peace now. He sounded extremely pleased to discover I existed and thrilled he had a sister. He seemed also to be a real gentleman, courteous and kind. That was immensely reassuring.'

Canary Wharf would be a convenient place to meet and Rob said he would try to find a quiet place to have lunch together where we could talk. When he came home the next evening, he told me he had chosen a pizza restaurant. All that was left for me to do was to phone Paul that evening, which I did and discovered that he was out playing bridge.

Eileen, his wife answered and was very friendly. That was such a relief. She said he would be looking forward to meeting us; that he would be easy to talk to. He had white hair and would be watching out for me. She mentioned also that they had a cousin who was looking forward to meeting us. Eileen told me that Paul had been phoning his friends saying: 'my sister and I'. She said that she was happy for him to meet Rob and me on our own and was looking forward to meeting us very soon after this.

Eileen put me at ease; I was almost bubbling over with anticipation.

CHAPTER TWENTY-TWO

Face to face with Paul – 30 March 2005

The next day on my way to Canary Wharf, I was conscious that it was a two-hour trip for Paul to come into London. Canary Wharf has one of the most modern of the tube stations – a vast, but light, bright cavernous space with marble and stone surfaces. Rob found me and went to check whether Paul was waiting near the other ticket booths.

Then I saw him.

He was quite far away, at the distant end of the concourse. He beamed, obviously recognising me, and approached us – a man of seventy-three with a portly upright stature and a confident walk. He was of medium height, with lots of white hair and wore a black leather jacket. His lovely smile welcomed us; then he greeted us. He had an authoritative voice with a beautiful English accent. He shook Rob's hand, then kissed me on both cheeks and gave me a hug. I was a little apprehensive and taken aback by this spontaneous intimacy, but I liked it. I appreciated him wanting to be welcoming; he was my brother, after all.

We walked away from the Canary Wharf tube station along the granite pavements towards the restaurant. It was noon, but it felt like dusk and more like London in winter than in spring. Dense clouds covered the sky staining the light dark grey. Our three pairs of footsteps echoed loudly, discordantly, against the tall concrete and glass building. The canals between the buildings and the regularly-spaced green topiary trees provided visual relief. To my surprise though, the canal water was like charcoal-coloured glass between the hard angular reflections of the tall grey skyscrapers and the darker grey sky. I was still feeling apprehensive and this environment did nothing to relieve it. I hoped that the outcome of the impending new experience would not be as dark and ominous as these surroundings.

The sound of our steps on the concrete pavement echoed back at us, dissecting time. We were in step now. Perhaps our meeting would go well, after all.

As we walked towards the pizza restaurant, we did not speak and the time it took to reach there seemed to stretch endlessly. I was longing to get started and felt very impatient. Rob led the way. I snuck a glance at Paul and sensed that he was feeling the same way. His head was down as he walked along determinedly. I hoped that the restaurant would be quiet enough and that we could chat comfortably for as long as we wished.

We arrived and sat down at a table set for four. I looked around. It was busy, but not too noisy. This was my first time there and it seemed fine for our purpose. Canary Wharf was a busy place.

I could hardly wait to start chatting with Paul and felt he was just as eager. I remember feeling extraordinarily irritated when Rob presented me with the menu, consulted Paul, and gave our pizza choices to the waiter.

Paul sat opposite me, appearing exuberant, and smiling broadly. I could not help but gaze at him, a stranger still, and yet my half-brother, a portly man with a friendly face, tanned skin, and a shock of white hair. How strange.

His brown eyes returned my gaze, while he continued to smile. He too was quiet, just looking. Then, his mood changed. He had all the cards – he was the one with the knowledge about our mother. He had a kind look on his face.

'Jane, have you seen a photo of our mother?' he asked gently. Shaking my head, I gulped, unable to speak. Paul bent down, opened his briefcase, took out a buff-coloured envelope and handed it to me. He looked at me again, expectantly. I opened the envelope and there she was.

Initially, I could not focus. I did my best to control the tears, cross with myself for not having anticipated them. Feelings welled up.

Phyllis Margaret and Paul, 1938

This was such a surreal experience – seeing Phyllis for the first time at my stage of life. I was 58. Suddenly, the immensity of the loss of not knowing her hit me in the pit of my stomach. Now I knew she was real and no longer a forbidden ghost haunting me in the back of my mind.

Paul saw I was overwhelmed and beamed – delighted to be able to offer me this wonderful gift. I felt immensely grateful to him. Rob put his arm around my shoulders.

Coming face to face with Phyllis was almost too much to bear. She was there – right in that photograph. But as I looked, gradually the strangeness of the photograph became all too clear.

She was well dressed and holding Paul's hand, then a boy of around eight. Initially, I thought she seemed to be smiling, but as I looked closer it was clear she was defiant, looking straight at the camera and only half-smiling. Her left hand was curled into an angry clench while she held Paul's hand with her right hand. There was a whole world of hurt and anger in her eyes. She did not want to be there. Paul seemed to also just manage a half smile. Phyllis' body language oozed passive aggression; she seemed to be saying 'Don't you dare.' If only she was still here and could explain the circumstances in which the photo was taken.

I was oblivious to the chatter of voices all around us as I gazed at her photograph. I vividly remember thinking: we do not look alike at all – not at all. I was so disappointed. All my life, I had longed to belong, to resemble a member of my family.

I looked at Paul and Rob, and said, 'I don't look like Mother. I must look like my father.' Paul acknowledged what I had said and told me right away that he did not know who my father was.

From here, we took turns talking. When one of us tired, the other would take over. We had a whole life time to catch up on.

At one point, when he realised I knew so little about Phyllis, Paul paused, and with his eyes shining, looked at me carefully.

'Mother was a spy, Jane. She was asked by Dutch Intelligence to go to Arnhem. She found the 9th and 10th German Panzer Division there and returned to warn the British. And just after WWII,

Mother introduced me to a Dutch General – perhaps someone who she worked with during WWII.'

I let his statement hang. I could not accept it. This was too much to believe.

He understood and didn't press me further. I liked him for not expecting me to accept everything straight away.

Our conversation moved on. Much of what I discovered about Phyllis comes from the family stories that Paul told me that day and at our subsequent meetings, which led to further research. But that day in March 2005 was amazing; the beginning of a warm, vibrant relationship. It was the first of many happy days we spent with Paul and his friendly wife, Eileen.

Quite fortuitously, soon after that fateful meeting at Canary Wharf, Paul and Eileen's daughter and her husband invited us to attend the baptism of their first-born baby son. On that day, we met all their family. I now had a new brother, sister-in-law, niece and her husband and baby boy, as new close relatives. Rob and I found ourselves to be instantaneously an uncle and aunt, as well as great uncle and great aunt.

The whole family welcomed us warmly, including our two cousins, Jeremy and Brian, sons of Phyllis's sister, and Brian's wife. We were entertained by many fascinating stories and a remarkable birthday party (Jeremy's). We are very fond of them and enjoy a happy bantering friendship when we are together.

Brian and his wife invited us on a number of occasions to lunch at their home in England, and twice to his large, beautiful, thatched African holiday home in Kenya. Their delightful residence was just one hour from Nairobi in Kenya, where wild animals roamed freely through their property in the African veldt. Curiously, Brian was the only family member who knew about Phyllis' pregnancy and my birth. He was told about me many years ago by his mother, my aunt, Phyllis' sister. Unfortunately, she is no longer living.

There is, however, one more crucial story to tell from that incredible first meeting with Paul.

Toward the end of our meeting, Paul made a curious and totally unexpected statement that made me sit bolt upright.

To my absolute amazement, Paul said, 'I think you got the better deal, Jane.'

We both laughed – but it was no laughing matter. His comment came totally out of the blue, causing me to reflect. Thinking about my adoption still caused searing hurt. I felt very sad that I had been prevented by my adoptive parents from knowing about my origins. I resented the secrets and the lack of honesty in our family relationships. My childhood felt bleak and lonely – I knew nobody who had been adopted. So, to see my situation as being the 'better deal' was a huge surprise.

But, in reality, I had been spared the ramifications of WWII and repeated abandonment by Phyllis. After listening to the stories Paul told us about his childhood, it did not take long for me to agree with him. Yes, I did have the 'better deal.'

Both he and I had felt the chasm of despair and loneliness, but we were not going to wallow in it. We resolved there and then to be positive, to have lots of fun, to enjoy our time together, and to make the most of the rest of our lives as brother and sister.

I need not have worried beforehand about the meeting with Paul. We felt an immediate synergy and warmth toward one another. I cannot think of enough adjectives to describe our meeting: it was poignant, wonderful, and astonishing. Moreover, my world view changed altogether, as I gained an entirely new family who could not have been more welcoming or kinder.

We had a remarkable journey ahead of us.

CHAPTER TWENTY-THREE

Resolving the question 'Who am I?'

I cannot imagine what it must be like to grow up with one's own mother and father, and those who have cannot imagine what it is like not to.

Sometimes it may not be possible for children to stay with their parents, and then adoptions can be a very good solution.

However, adoption is an artificial social construct, governed by laws and social institutions imposed on families, set so that society has a process of finding homes for children who would otherwise be homeless. Most adopted children now grow up knowing they are adopted from an early age (these are called 'open' as opposed to 'closed' adoptions), and now, of course, at least in Australia, where it is possible and feasible for the child's sake, regular contact between the adoptive and birth families is encouraged. The balance now is shifting more towards meeting the needs of the child.

Whether one likes it or not, everyone's identity is inextricably linked with one's genetic and social inheritance. Just not knowing that is one big difference – and it matters. Why, I'm not able to answer fully.

The secrecy involved in my own adoption means that this information has been elusive, often out of reach, requiring an act of courage to search for it. I feel as if I am climbing a steep hill that never seems to end. I have questions that need to be answered. I hate not knowing and find it demeaning having to ask others to help me with something that normally would be taken for granted. But, that is how it is.

Where there is contact between adopted people and their biological families, in a majority of situations, it is a positive experience. In a reunion, it is much easier when there is a skilled intermediary who

The author and her half-brother, Paul

can sensitively explain the motivations of the persons concerned, and soften the shock.

That was why I asked Mary to contact Paul and tell him about me.

Fortunately, my new half-brother and I felt an immediate affinity and this was truly wonderful for both of us. However, he often mentioned how amazed and shocked he was initially, and how for a few days the news made him feel completely disoriented.

Despite this, very soon and at every opportunity, we were asking and answering questions about each other's lives; sometimes on the phone or at a café or in our apartment. Rob and I invited Paul and Eileen to come to London and stay for a few days. Despite some initial apprehension (probably on both sides) and to our delight, we thoroughly enjoyed being together. We laughed and laughed and talked late into the evenings.

'So, when did you decide to start searching for Mother, Jane?'

asked Paul, soon after our meeting at Canary Wharf. Fortunately, he was a wonderful listener. The fact that he was so much older than me somehow seemed to make things easier.

'We were in Sydney when Mum died, in the late 1980s. After that, I began to reflect on our situation. Rob was working hard, our two sons were fourteen and thirteen, and our daughter was three and a half years old.'

Paul nodded.

'Adam's behaviour was starting to become more and more unpredictable and the question arose: Was there anything more we could do to help him and prevent this happening again?

'I began to worry about whether there were any genetic consequences relating to Adam. Consultations with a specialist geneticist advised us to do whatever we could to clarify my genetic history. Gradually, I accepted that if I wanted peace of mind, everything possible had been done to ensure this would not happen again. There was little choice but to search out my biological family.'

Paul nodded again.

'This was not a sudden decision. Even though now it was far more than a self-centred search for identity, I could not help but feel strong feelings of guilt. I was torn between wanting to be loyal to my adoptive parents and keep the promise I made to them and doing what was right for our own family. My adoptive parents were both dead; the search for my biological parents could not hurt them any longer. Moreover, the secrets about Jonathan and the fact that I was adopted no longer needed to be kept confidential.'

Paul's eyes widened.

'It was then that I again began asking the question, 'Who am I?' I found myself working out all the positive reasons to start searching. The idea of finding out about my biological mother and father intrigued me. Did I have any siblings? How wonderful that would be.'

Paul grinned. Oh, I loved those grins.

I continued. 'I also wanted to know more about who my grandparents and my extended family were. Where did they come from originally? And the thought crossed our minds that our children might eventually find this interesting, because it was a vital part of their heritage, too.'

'Of course,' Paul said. 'But weren't you also curious?'

'Yes. I was. But the curiosity wasn't there initially. Paul, can you understand? I had had to dam up my thoughts and feelings for so long. I hadn't allowed myself the luxury of asking the obvious things. And then when I started, it was like the dam wall had broken. I was very interested to find out more. I knew Mother's name, but nothing more. She was on my birth certificate, but my father's name was left blank. The secrecy about his identity continues.'

Paul's eyes grew wider.

'Gosh, I was angry about that. I felt it was a real cop out and not fair, not fair at all. The focus was clearly on the needs of parents with little regard to needs of the child, and this deliberate absence of information perpetuated the secrecy and deceit.'

'But that was the way they did things in those days,' he remarked. 'So, when did you start your search?'

'Mum died in late 1987 and I started writing letters to the UK in 1990.'

'And so, how did that go?'

I really liked Paul for being gentle and not hurrying me. I was feeling amazingly raw.

'I received the information in fits and starts. Being so far away from England did not help at all. NORCAP, a British adoption support organisation, was very helpful and provided a researcher to correspond with named Pam. At first I asked if information about Phyllis could be found, for example, where and when she was born, if she married, and whether she was still alive. Writing the letters was fine, but I found it very hard waiting for the replies. It took six whole weeks for the first letter to arrive in our post box. When I saw it there, my heart jumped and my hands shook. I was extremely nervous each time a letter arrived. These were major events.'

'So, what did you find out, Jane?' Paul asked.

'Paul, I'm sure you will be able to explain a lot and put all I know in context.'

Paul smiled. 'I know, and I will when you want me to – but please, carry on. I'm very interested.'

'In 1990 in Australia, I knew my birth name – Jane Kleyn – because it was in my original birth certificate, the one given to me when I was told I was adopted. Mother's name was recorded as Phyllis Kleyn. I asked for Phyllis' birth certificate and her marriage certificate to Johannes Leonardus Kleyn and discovered they married on 24 November 1937, ten years before I was born. I was astonished – elated – for days. Every little detail fascinated me.'

Paul's eyes lit up. 'I knew Mr Kleyn. I met him and called him 'Jopie', which is Dutch for John.'

'So, Jopie was Dutch. That's interesting.'

'Yes, Jane he was, although he liked to be known as John Leonard Kleyn in England.'

'The most surprising thing for me, Paul, was to discover their ages. John Leonard Kleyn was forty-four when he married Phyllis, so he must have been born in 1893, and Phyllis was thirty-one. She was born in 1906. He was thirteen years older than Phyllis.'

'Yes, that's correct,' said Paul.

'Also, recorded on her marriage certificate with John Kleyn, was that this was Phyllis' second marriage and that her first marriage had been to a Herbert James Whicker.'

'Yes, he was my father.'

'Aha,' I said, while thinking about this. 'The next surprise was that the marriage certificate stated that John Kleyn was the divorced husband of Phyllis Violet Kleyn. I was really confused about this. Another Phyllis Kleyn – the same name as John Kleyn's previous wife? How awkward! And what did Phyllis do about this?'

'I can answer that,' Paul said, beaming and as pleased as punch. 'Mother was originally known as Phyllis, but after she married John, she used her second name and was known as 'Margaret Kleyn.'

'That makes sense! I would have changed my name too in those circumstances.'

I continued. 'Pam wondered whether John Kleyn adopted you, Paul – but he did not. That was curious.'

'She was correct. John did not adopt me because I didn't live with them – but that is a story for later.'

'So, how did you find out about me, Jane?' Paul was being impetuous.

I smiled back. 'Be patient. I'm almost there. I then asked for Phyllis' marriage certificate to Herbert James Whicker, and it was then that Pam searched for children from this marriage and found you, and that Phyllis gave birth to you in 1932. Pam also discovered you married Eileen and that you had a daughter, Karen.'

'Yes.' Again, Paul beamed. 'So why didn't you try and contact me then, Jane?'

'In retrospect, I wish I had, but while living in Sydney, so far away, I was guided by Pam, my researcher. She even found your address, but everything was happening through her and she warned me not to contact you, but rather to try and contact Phyllis first. At that stage, we did not know Phyllis was already dead.'

I continued. 'Pam also discovered that John Kleyn married again, to Diana, and together they had a son called Peter, born in 1949, two years after me.'

Paul's eyes widened. Clearly this was news to him – he did not know about John's subsequent marriage to Diana or about the existence of Peter.

'Is that so? Another secret. Mother told me as a child that Jopie died. Perhaps she did not want me to contact him. I was really sad, because he took me to see the Arsenal football team playing a game one Saturday afternoon when I visited Mother. I liked him. I knew she sometimes told me porkies!' Paul looked quite distressed.

I waited a few seconds, but he indicated that I should go on. He wanted to hear me out first before telling me his story.

'Pam also checked whether Phyllis had any other children besides you and me, but she found none.'

Paul looked astonished. 'No, I don't think so – but then I might not have known, Jane. I became aware that Mother kept many secrets.'

'Coming back to John Kleyn, I was given his name at birth, and so naturally wondered whether he was my father. Could he have still been married to Phyllis when I was conceived in 1946 and born in 1947? But, Pam was not able to resolve this. Amazingly, Pam then discovered that Phyllis married again, after the marriage to John Kleyn failed, this time to Alan MacRobert in November 1949.'

I continued.

'Realizing that Phyllis would be about 84 years old if she was still alive, I asked Pam to persevere in her search of the death certificates. The burning question about whether Phyllis had died was not answered until last year. If Pam had found Phyllis' death certificate back then it would have saved fourteen years – and would have given us fourteen more years to know each other.'

This was sad, but was not worth dwelling on.

I also shared with Paul other information contained in Phyllis' marriage certificates and the subtle hints that they revealed about her life. I felt as if I were an observer of Phyllis' life, despite her no longer being alive. She seemed to be slowly becoming part of me, part of my own identity. I was slipping into a rather uncomfortable role of being my mother's daughter and I was not sure I liked it!

Paul laughed when I told him about this. To help me clarify everything I knew then, we went over the factual information as told by the birth and marriage certificates.

Phyllis was born Phyllis Hogg; she became Mrs Whicker, then Mrs Kleyn, and then Mrs MacRobert.

Her three marriages raised many questions, such as how did she cope with the tumultuous emotions that would have been involved marrying and divorcing in the 1930s and 1940s, an already chaotic and turbulent time. Paul was not able to help with this.

I was also fascinated by how her names changed in each marriage certificate. She signed herself as Phyllis Hogg in her first marriage certificate, when she was twenty-one. On her marriage to John Kleyn; she signed herself as PM Whicker, and then as Margaret Kleyn in her third marriage to Alan MacRobert.

Her residential address is recorded in each marriage certificate as well. Phyllis left her family home in 3 Whitworth Road, South

Norwood, South London for her first marriage; moved to Brighton, East Sussex, prior to her second marriage; and to Evington Hotel, Cadogan Road in Cromer, Norfolk, for her third marriage.

In her last marriage certificate, Phyllis recorded her career as manageress of a hotel. That was curious. We were never able to find out anything more about this. On her third marriage certificate, she recorded her age as forty-two when she was forty-three. That was interesting. Was it just a mistake or a little vanity showing through?

I was also curious about her description of Owen, her father and my grandfather. In her first two marriages, Phyllis refers to him as Augustus Owen Hogg; and then, in her third marriage as Owen Fitch Hogg. Phyllis seemed to have a mischievous sense of humour. It was good to see how Owen Hogg's career progressed from marriage to marriage. He went from being a clerk in a bank in her first marriage in 1927 to being of independent means in her second marriage in 1937 to being a bank manager in Lloyds Bank in her third marriage in 1949. Clearly, he had a successful career and must have been well respected. I wondered how Phyllis related to her father.

Most of all, I could not suppress my curiosity about Phyllis; as a young person growing up in London, a person who married three times, and who would also have been buffeted by the impact of WWII and the consequent social upheavals.

But first, what was life like in the early 1900s and what were the context, the events and experiences that would have shaped her upbringing and opportunities? Phyllis surely would have had legitimate reasons to make the decisions she did at the time. There was much to explore and understand.

CHAPTER TWENTY-FOUR

The Hogg family,
London – From July 1906

Phyllis was born more than a century ago, so in trying to imagine life in London in the early 1900s I relied initially on the memories and stories told to me by Mum, who was born only a year before Phyllis.

I will now call Elizabeth my adoptive mum, Mum, and my biological mother, Phyllis, to avoid confusion about which mother I am referring to. Elizabeth's descriptions and interpretations of British attitudes of child rearing, family life, politics, and world events at the time proved to be very useful when thinking about how Phyllis might have lived her life.

Soon after my first meeting with Paul, my new half-brother, we had another very memorable meeting – an invitation to lunch to meet my new cousin Jeremy at his Earls Court apartment in London. Much of my information about Phyllis and her family came from his wonderful, funny recollections.

I could hardly wait for the day of our lunch visit to arrive and when it did, Rob and I met Paul just outside Jeremy's apartment. I rang the doorbell and the front door clicked open to reveal an entrance hall. As we stepped into the hall, a deep male voice called down from the top of the staircase in an impeccable English accent: 'Is this my new first cousin?'

I chuckled, feeling slightly embarrassed, and called out in reply, 'Yes, it is!'

'All these years I thought I had only one cousin, and now I have *two*!' Jeremy exclaimed, as he walked down the stairs to welcome us. He was casually dressed, of medium height and build; twinkling brown eyes, brown hair, and a short brown beard. He had a huge smile on his face.

Jeremy was the younger of our two cousins (my aunt's younger son). We had no idea what to expect, but it soon became very clear there would be no awkward moments. Jeremy was very outgoing. Almost immediately both Jeremy and Paul launched into the task of welcoming us. Many stories later – sometimes humorous, sometimes poignant and sad, and other times astonishing – we were introduced to the personalities, the history, and atmosphere of my brand new family. They told us about Phyllis's early life, her three marriages, how she abandoned Paul and, very significantly, that she was a secret agent for the Allies in WWII. They also described how Phyllis died a cold, lonely death with just her Dalmatians hovering near her.

My inner turmoil was in full swing and I was grappling with the inevitable crumbling of the ghost of my mother, the one in my imagination for the better part of four decades. Astonished and over-whelmed, all I could do was listen and suspend judgement. Applying 21st century values would misinterpret all that my parents' genera-tion lived, fought, and died for – the challenge now was to attempt to understand their lives within their own historical cultural and social context.

It was enormously reassuring to watch Paul so enjoying having a sister, his new sibling – a feeling very much reciprocated. Jeremy was enthusiastic, gracious, and generous with his invitations. Together, over many lunches and glasses of wine, in Jeremy's apartment, our apartment or Paul and Eileen's comfortable terrace home in Port-smouth, we heard tale after tale about Phyllis and her family. Although Jeremy did not often see Phyllis, his mother Barbara (Phyllis' sister) talked about her, and from this he was able to offer a completely dif-ferent perspective on her life.

I was the newcomer, doing my best to find common ground and integrate into my new, ready-made family. I felt like a sponge, listen-ing intently, trying to catch up on our parallel life stories and col-lapse the years we had been apart.

In less than a month in 2005, I found I was a member of a much expanded family. I had become a sister to Paul, a sister-in-law to Paul's wife, Eileen, an aunt to my niece (Paul's daughter), and a cousin to Jeremy and Brian. To describe this in a different way, in theory and in fact, I have two mothers, two fathers, eight grand-parents, and possibly many more than the three siblings and two cousins I know about.

For a few months after meeting Paul, their memories were all I had to go on. But one day at the National Archives, it was suggested to me that I should apply for Phyllis' army record.[2] This turned out to be by far the best written account of her life.

Fortunately, much about Phyllis' life is compelling and poign-ant, and it is not hard to imagine the key themes influencing the atmosphere in which she grew up. Nevertheless, I was curious about the world she was born into and grew up in. I also longed to know more about her as a person – her likes and dislikes. There was no shortcut in finding out – I had to do some reading.

Some of the flavour of the early 1900s is very well described in a few news items from around the world, including New Zealand and Australia. In January 1906, the New Zealand All Blacks thrashed the French team in Paris, 38:3. Of interest to every householder around the world in February 1906 was that the new motorised fire engine in Melbourne beat the horse-drawn vehicle, changing the way fire fighting was done for all time. The New Zealand Premier, Mr Sedding, stressed the need for 'purity of race.' And in Melbourne, the Salvation Army condemned dancing as a sin. An inquiry revealed that slavery of women and children in Sydney industries was endemic. 1906 was also a year of tumultuous earthquakes and environmental disasters, including a typhoon in Tahiti and earth-quakes in San Francisco and Valparaiso. Political disasters were present, too. Russian officials in June admitted they planned the massacre of hundreds of Jews at Bielostok.

England must have seemed a wonderful safe haven by compari-son. Britain was riding high in pride and patriotism; and no doubt, the Hogg family would have felt part of this.

In March 1906, the Census of the British Empire completed in

1901 announced that the growth of the British Empire, unparalleled in world history, now occupied one-fifth of the globe, incorporating 400 million people. King Edward reigned. Rule Britannia would have been sung everywhere.

Also in 1906, the Olympic spirit was rekindled after the success of the first (and only) Intercalated Games in Athens; and at short notice, London generously agreed to stage the 1908 Olympic Games. London must have been abuzz with activity.

Ethel and Owen Hogg (Phyllis' parents), with their much adored three-year old daughter Barbara, would have been relieved to be living in Croydon, Surrey. Theirs was a world apart and their interest and focus would have been much closer to home. Heavily pregnant, Ethel would have heard of the London County Council's warnings that tuberculosis was being spread through infected milk, and no doubt, would have taken great care to boil theirs.

Hot air balloons were quite often seen above London in the skies, but in early July, there was another reason for an air of excitement around London. They were soon to witness the technological spectacle of London's first hot-air balloon race high in the sky. The family might have seen the seven balloons racing without even leaving their home.

Croydon also happened to have an important railway junction, which would have made it possible for Owen to commute to Threadneedle Street, where the headquarters of Lloyds bank[3] was located in the City of London.

Phyllis' birth

Phyllis was born on 18 July 1906. She was the second daughter, three years younger than her big sister, Barbara, and became the middle child three years later when her much-adored brother, Boy, was born. In 1906 the young Hogg family lived in a semi-detached house in Chalfont Street, South Norwood, close to Norwood train station, and just one stop away from Croydon.

While they all no doubt loved each other, the Hogg family, like all families, also had their quirks and foibles, and their share of happy and sad times.

With most newborn babies, there is a lot of rejoicing in the family. According to Jeremy, this certainly was not the case with Phyllis' birth. For Ethel Hogg, then aged thirty-six, this was a pregnancy she would rather not have had.

We know Ethel had a very close relationship with her daughter, Barbara, and often used to confide in her. Many years later, Barbara told Jeremy that when Big Granny (Ethel) was pregnant with Phyllis, she did not want the baby, and tried to abort the baby by swallowing castor oil and having hot baths. One wonders why? She must have had good reason to go to such lengths, but whatever it was, we shall never know.

I recoiled in horror when Jeremy told us this and when I looked at Paul, he nodded his head, supporting what had just been said. I became very sad for Phyllis. I knew of research that showed that unborn babies are sensitive to their mother's attitudes and feelings[4] and that carrying an unwanted child might well have been a barrier for Phyllis's mother in bonding with Phyllis.

Jeremy explained that Big Granny used to repeatedly tell his mother that 'Phyllis is a difficult girl.' and 'I'm being punished by God because I tried to abort her.'

Jeremy repeated this story many times over the first few months, adding that he thought his grandmother had been unkind to Phyllis and felt guilty about it. He was convinced Phyllis would have been aware of her mother's animosity.

Curiously, he also said, 'There was one other thing I did not think was good in my mother. There was this rivalry between the sisters.'

He thought awhile, and then continued. 'Phyllis seemed to be rather unbending, I'm afraid.'

So, Phyllis had not been an easy child. I wanted to understand more.

Jeremy gave me a wonderful surprise one day – a photograph of the family – an unimaginable gift. It remains the only photo I have of my extended family, and the family of Phyllis.

Hogg family, 1932 - the author's extended family

After not being part of my biological family for most of my life, I can hardly believe that they are my relatives and that I am their relative, too. This gives me the strangest feeling.

Photographs can be an insightful window into family dynamics and this photograph is no exception. It shows my great grandmother, my grandparents, Ethel (Big Granny) and 'Grandfather Owen', my great aunt and great uncle, and my Aunt Barbara, Phyllis' sister. Her first-born son, my elder cousin Brian, is a baby and sits on my great grandmother's lap. The photo may have been taken at a special occasion, perhaps a birthday, but where were Phyllis and Boy?

Paul referred to Phyllis' mother as 'Big Granny' and this photograph revealed the obvious reason – she was tall and buxom. She also had a reputation for being rather formidable and forbidding; although Paul said she had been really good to him. She stands erect and rather stiffly in this photo, with a fixed smile on her face.

Big Granny's sister, Great Aunt Vie, stands a little apart, almost seeming to be appraising the situation. Phyllis' father, Owen, and Barbara are standing close to each other looking relaxed and happy. Did Barbara feel closer to her father than to her mother? Aunt Barbara is a very attractive woman with a lovely open face.

This made me wonder what Phyllis looked like at that age. Did Phyllis also feel closer to her father?

Grandfather Owen was born in 1872, the middle of seven children. They were considered comfortable financially. They were members of the Church of England, attending church nearby. He was a gentle, quiet man who had an excellent career, eventually becoming a bank manager in Lloyds Bank.

So, was Big Granny the dominant person in her family?

It would seem so. She was the youngest of three children; she had a brother, Thomas, and a sister, Alice, who is great aunt Vie in the photograph. They were a comfortable middle-class family; oddly though, the 1901 census records her father's career as domestic gardener. This fits with a family story about them.

In 1873, when Big Granny was born, her family lived in a big house and they were considered by the neighbours as being a 'high degree' upper-middle-class family. Her father was a civil archaeologist who discovered a horde of Roman coins during a 'dig'. The coins disappeared. Then one day, her father came home and said to his wife, Big Granny's mother, "My dear, I think we are ruined. We will not be able to stay in this house and town any longer." They moved to a villa down by the sea, eventually recovered, and moved back to Croydon.

In the early 1900s, and even today, class plays a prominent role in English life. British-born people are acutely aware and motivated by their sense of place in their community and where they are aspiring to be. Paul and Jeremy believed Big Granny and Barbara were more concerned about social appearances than they should have been. Could this also be a legacy of Big Granny's family's experience of 'being ruined' and their changed social status? Jeremy qualified this by saying his mother 'never looked down on people, but she liked to look up. She was not the kind of snob that looks down on people — that's the wicked snob.' He said this a few times.

One of the most apparent markers of class in Britain is how one speaks. I was struck when first meeting Paul by how well he spoke and what an impeccable, well-modulated English accent he had;

as did Jeremy and Brian, as far as my colonial ear could tell. This reminded me of conversations I had had with my adoptive mother, Elizabeth, who also spoke beautifully – the Queen's English – she was always quick to tell me, and I grew up wishing I could change my Rhodesian accent. Accent is a very powerful discriminator. To some extent – through growing up in Zimbabwe, discovering I was 'illegitimate' and moving to another social situation altogether in South Africa – belonging to a particular class and having a certain status largely passed me by. This matters much less than it might have. I largely escaped; although, I would love to speak like Elizabeth and Paul, and even perhaps like Phyllis.

However, no doubt these issues and attitudes would have been around Phyllis as she grew up. She would have been acutely aware of this and I suspect she spoke beautifully.

There was one particular family story about speech and pronunciation that caused a lot of mirth: it relates to their surname, 'Hogg.'

When Big Granny married, her name changed from Whybrow to Hogg. Whatever it was that attracted her to Owen, it was not his name. Jeremy and Paul laughed when they reminisced about this. Big Granny hated answering the question, 'What's your name?' One can imagine how often she was asked that. In response to the question, she began to talk as if she had a hot potato in her mouth. When she introduced herself, she would say she was 'Mrs Ho' with a staccato 'ho' sound, without pronouncing the 'g'. Often people just accepted this, but frequently people wanted to clarify what she was saying or would ridicule her and ask the question again. To which she would again reply: 'Mrs Ho.' Sometimes, this happened two or three times. She just hated having to say 'Mrs Hogg.' Fortunately for Big Granny, there were two famous Oxbridge members of the Hogg family in the Houses of Parliament. She was very relieved to be able to refer to them and believed their family was related to them – though we never did find evidence of this.

Their name became a laughing matter at school, too. Aunt Barbara told Jeremy that in her class at school they were often teased because of their name, especially when two other children, with the surnames Bacon and Trotter, were around.

The surname Hogg first appeared in the ancient, medieval records in Durham. Their ancestors can be traced back to Scotland in the 11th or 12th centuries. The name comes from an old English word, 'Hoga', which means a prudent person. Interesting!

Big Granny died of liver cancer when she was seventy in 1943. Barbara cared for her at home, while also caring for her invalid husband and two sons. It was war time.

Jeremy said again his mother had told him that Phyllis was an unwanted baby and that she became a 'difficult' child. His mother had confessed to him that Big Granny had been unkind to Phyllis and had felt guilty. Jeremy then added, 'I'm afraid Barbara felt that Phyllis had "lost the plot" though that expression was not current in her day.'

This was a real indictment of Phyllis and it was hard listening to these stories. I did so want a mother I could identify with – and this knowledge certainly did not help.

Jeremy said he had thought carefully before telling Paul this particular story and only did so because it might help to explain Phyllis' relationship with her family. It might even help to explain what subsequently happened to Paul and perhaps make him more sympathetic to her. Paul confirmed this, agreeing that it was better to know the truth.

I was indebted to Jeremy for being frank. I wondered how best to understand it and what affect this would have had on Phyllis. At the very least, it would have made it difficult for her to feel close to her mother and I wonder what her mother felt about her. Did Phyllis become the scapegoat of the family? It is possible that having a harmonious relationship with her family as a child would have been an ongoing struggle for her?

I wondered what her relationship was like with her father. Did she feel closer to her father? Could this have contributed to her growing up not afraid to be independent-minded? That quality may have been very useful to her later in WWII.

CHAPTER TWENTY-FIVE

What is it like to be a bastard?

I became extremely fond of Jeremy and welcomed his lunch invitations. His generous, enthusiastic, and engaging manner with his wonderful story-telling ability made these occasions very special.

Not long after our first meeting, he invited us to his birthday party. We were delighted. When we arrived his apartment was crowded with his friends happily drinking and chatting. He enthusiastically introduced me to his friends as his 'new first cousin' and it was lovely to be so embraced into his circle of friends.

It was then that I had the strangest of experiences.

A woman's voice softly said, *'What is it like to be a bastard? What is it like to be an illegitimate child?'*

The voice was so soft at first that I did not really hear it. The room was buzzing; people were laughing, drinking, and chatting loudly. I was happily chatting to a tall, attractive friend of my cousin, Jenny, on my left. I had to concentrate and try to lip read, because I could only just hear what she was saying.

There it was again. I remember feeling slightly irritated; I was engrossed in conversation with Jenny not wanting to be disturbed. We discovered we worked in similar areas and were exploring our common ground as one does at cocktail parties. But this time the voice was louder and more insistent. It was very noisy in the room; then, all of a sudden, there was a hush.

'So, what is it like to be a bastard – what is it like to be an illegitimate child?' Her voice was clear and now insistent in tone.

This time, I knew the voice was directed at me. I turned my head to face a small woman with large brown eyes, looking to be in her early seventies, standing next to Jeremy. He was smiling broadly at me, eager to introduce me to his famous friend.

'This is my new first cousin, Beryl,' he said loudly with an impish smile on his face. 'Jane, I would like you to meet Beryl, Beryl Bainbridge.' I smiled, bent forward, and said hello. I did not know who she was at that time.

Then, she asked me yet again. 'Your cousin has told me a little of your story. What is it like to be a bastard – an illegitimate child?'

I looked at her in disbelief, not able to speak. This was the first time anyone had spoken to me like that. While I was genuinely curious about her, I was not prepared for my own reaction: I felt as if I had been dumped and her words cut into me, unexpectedly piercing old wounds. She stared intently at me, clearly fascinated by how I might be feeling. I felt as if I were outside myself, watching myself in a movie.

A few seconds later, there was an urgent but gentle prod into my left arm just above the elbow. Jenny was speaking to me, urgently but quietly. 'Did you mind her calling you that? Are you OK? Are you willing for her to speak of you like that?'

Jenny was clearly taken aback too. That was reassuring – I was not being overly sensitive.

Keeping myself in check, with my emotions securely latched and contained, I responded by laughing and reassuring her that I was fine.

But, oh my God, I *did* mind. I was not fine. Nevertheless, I could deal with that later.

Beryl still had a smile on her face. She was being purposefully confronting, hoping to catch a glimpse of the depth or strength of my feelings. Now I understand. I was fodder for her curiosity, her creativity. As an author, she was curious – curious about my unusual situation and my life story.

I suppose I should have expected to be a bit of an oddity, an object to examine or interrogate. It felt like I was a fish in a fishbowl. It was a response to which I eventually grew accustomed. In the beginning, I did not mind too much, because when I told my story I was experimenting with how to tell it. As my research was only just starting, this often resulted in people volunteering new and occasionally valuable information. Perhaps I would gain a new insight. Each fragment of new information felt like a jewel or a treasured gift. I was always pleased to discover more.

Now I think about Beryl's question with a smile. People respond to my story in many ways, often due to their own cultural and family situations. Sometimes being able to watch their reactions is helpful; for it not only provides insight into how they see their world, but it also helps me to understand and come to terms with my own.

While I would be loath to repeat it, Beryl's confrontation and interrogation of me was not the first or the last, but was the most useful. Since it happened soon after I met Paul and Jeremy, and soon after I had started the long process of working through my emotions about being adopted, I was thankful to her for her piercing clarity.

Recently, Jeremy wrote to me, saying: 'About Beryl Bainbridge – I was not standing by when she said those things to you – I would have objected to her doing so at once! She was very silly and tactless in saying what she said, but as I have told you (I was not aware of this) her youngest child was born out of wedlock...But of course, she should have told you this at the time. She was a much loved woman...I do not think she meant it maliciously at all. She was being her usual forthright self, with a novelist's curiosity. Anyhow, in the Bohemian circles in which she and I move, it would be seen as rather romantic, being a love child.'

Sadly, Dame Beryl Bainbridge died in July 2010. Jeremy sent me a copy of a short talk he gave about her at a memorial party on 11 November 2011. Her children asked him to make it short and humorous and he invited me to add some of this to my account of the incident, if I thought it appropriate. I offer a slightly abbreviated version not only because it describes Beryl, but because it also gives a wonderful insight into Jeremy and the perceptive and sociable person he is.

I first met Beryl at a little party (in 1973), but we did not get engaged till a few years after this. She always used to hail me at parties with 'There's my fiancé,' and she even referred to it in her column in The Evening

Standard. When asked why we did not get around to tying the knot, I would say that every time I managed to drag her to the altar she'd suddenly have an idea for another novel, say 'I must have a ciggie, darling,' and disappear in a cloud of cigarette smoke.

When I first went to her house in Albert Street I remember having to wriggle past Eric, the stuffed buffalo gazing grimly at one in the hallway. He took up so much of the hallway that either one had to be quite extraordinarily emaciated or else one crawled underneath. On sitting down at a table in the living room there was a stranger sitting opposite, curiously stiff, unblinking and uncommunicative, which I soon learnt was a waxwork known as Neville, after Neville Chamberlain. It was early February and Beryl took me to the back of the house to show me the garden. Opening the back door there was a tree covered in brilliant blossom that on closer inspection consisted of daffodils and tulips hanging in the branches. On even closer inspection these turned out to be made of plastic, Beryl had bought at a local street market, loftily regardless of the season.

Beryl was one of the most delightfully eccentric people I have ever met. She came to a lot of my parties where she always claimed the music I put on consisted either of 'Oh, Oh, Oh What a Lovely War' or else 'Non, Je Ne Regrette Rien'. We used to dance wildly to these tunes, and certainly I regretted nothing about her. She was full of fun and laughter and I never in almost 40 years heard her say a nasty thing about anyone – not even about Eric and Neville. She was a brilliant novelist and it now turns out she was an original extremely talented painter. I was extremely fond of her and miss her terribly. If only she was with us still. Here's to Beryl.

The Times newspaper included Beryl in their list of 'The 50 greatest British writers since 1945' and aside from winning a number of other literary awards, she was also nominated five times for the Man Booker Prize. She clearly was an exceptionally talented writer.

And she certainly gave me cause for thought.

CHAPTER TWENTY-SIX

Phyllis' childhood – 1906–18

The Hogg family's modest attached terrace home in Croydon, South London was very conveniently located being only a few minutes from the local shops. It was also just a ten minute walk to Norwood station, which is only one stop from East Croydon, a major railway junction in the train journey between Brighton and Victoria in London. Living near East Croydon must have been very useful for Owen, as he would have commuted regularly by train to the bank where he worked in central London.

In the early 1900s, the trains were pulled by puffing steam engines and Owen Hogg would have been fascinated by the rapid modernisation and expansion of the London transport system. This continues today, a century later! Even now, just as then, new deep-level tubes are being added to the network.

Closer to home, Owen and his family would have already been introduced to the electric tram along the high street. In 1901 Croydon was lucky enough to have the first fully operational tram service in the outer London area where the power was delivered from overhead wires. This replaced the horse-drawn trams and would have been a cleaner, quieter way to travel. Seeing the horses and hearing them clip-clopping in the street would fast become a fading memory. One can imagine the family and others in their local community watching the experiments with petrol engine buses with perhaps wonder and a twinge of sadness and regret. The trials in central London were so successful that very quickly from late 1911, over only 2–3 years, the horse-drawn cabs and buses were replaced by the now much-loved and very familiar London red buses.

The Hogg home would still have been heated by the coal-fired kitchen range and they would have used candles and gas for lighting.

I wonder if this meant that when they did stay up after dark, they would stay together in the dining room or lounge indulging in games or talk.

Their most accessible and comprehensive news source would probably have been the daily newspaper, such as *The Daily Mirror*, *The Evening News*, *The Times*, and perhaps some local newspapers, too. They might have had the newspaper delivered, like the milk, or perhaps Owen bought one in the morning at the station prior to commuting to central London. The corner shop, less than five minutes away, might also have sold the newspaper. Ethel might have had time to glance at the newspaper after the children were in bed.

Owen and Ethel would have read about the new technological inventions, the latest musical hits, the popular artistic and cultural events – for example, the new ballet in Paris – and the gathering pace of the military build-up.

Living in Croydon meant that the Hogg family was never short of places to visit, both on a local level in or near Croydon, and in outer London itself.

If Owen was a fan of British rugby, he would be been very disappointed in the British team late in 1908 when the Wallabies, on their first tour of Britain, won twenty-five out of thirty-one games.

In the summer of 1908, when Phyllis was only two, London hosted the Olympic Games, and what a spectacle it was. It was the greatest sporting festival in the British Isles, providing a fitting climax to two years of planning and building. Most impressive was the new White City stadium. I wonder whether Owen and Ethel were able to see any of the events. Perhaps their grandparents might have looked after the two small girls for the day. It would have been a wonderful opportunity to attend the Olympic Games.

Amazingly, many of the iconic buildings in London that I loved in 2003 Phyllis could also have enjoyed. For example, I wonder what she thought of the Victoria and Albert Museum, the National Gallery, the Royal Academy, Big Ben, the Tower of London, Hampton Court, and of course, Westminster Abbey. It is pleasing to see that the much-loved Australian artists, Arthur Streeton, Tom Roberts, and

GW Lambert succeeded in showing their work at the Royal Academy in April 1910. Harrods was even then a prestigious department store and Ethel Hogg would have liked Selfridges when it opened in 1909, promising 'all your shopping under one roof'.

In October 1908 in Britain, the Parliament approved a means-tested old age pension, and in February 1909, a Royal Commission slammed the poor laws saying conditions in London produce a 'degenerate race, morally and physically enfeebled'. This was followed by the *National Insurance Act 1911*, which provided a contributory scheme of health insurance for the employed and a rudimentary unemployment fund. This, of course, was the beginning of the welfare state.

In 1909 significant topics for discussion about events around the world might have been the terrifying earthquake killing tens of thousands at Messina in Sicily and the aborted attempt by Shackleton to reach the South Pole.

Back in Britain in May 1910, King Edward VII died, and his funeral brought together all the royalty of Europe for the last time before World War I (WWI) broke out in 1914. In June 1911, King George V was crowned at Westminster Abbey in a seven hour ceremony, as the King of the United Kingdom of Great Britain and Ireland and of the British Dominions beyond the seas, Defender of the Faith, Emperor of India.

In January 1912 China became a republic and the revolutionary flag was raised in February in Shanghai; in March, martial law was declared.

More poignantly, on 15 April 1912, 1,503 people died when the 'practically unsinkable' White star liner *Titanic* collided with an iceberg and sank within hours on her maiden voyage from Southampton to New York. She was the largest vessel in the world at the time of her launch, but was equipped with enough lifeboats to save only about half the number of passengers and crew on board. Three months later Captain Smith was found guilty of negligence. This was a terrible tragedy that shocked England.

In August 1912 there was severe embarrassment at the Louvre

Museum in Paris as the Mona Lisa was stolen in the dead of night. Fortunately, the painting was recovered and returned to the Louvre on 12 December 1913 and three people were arrested for the theft.

Technological developments came thick and fast in the early 1900s: in 1908, the gramophone was invented, and on 24 February 1909 colour films were shown for the first time in public in Brighton. In March 1910 the first movie in Hollywood was produced. Only a few months later, Thomas Edison was able to add sound to his motion pictures. Charlie Chaplin, on 30 November 1913, makes his film debut in Mack Sennett's *Making a Living*.

I wonder when the Hogg family bought their first gramophone and when they did, what music they liked. Did they like the 1908 hit 'Shine on Harvest Moon' or did they prefer 1909 hit 'I Wonder Who's Kissing Her Now' or perhaps they liked the hit of 1913 'You Made Me Love You'?

In those early years, Ethel and Owen would have extremely busy with their small children. Owen would then have become more established at the bank and perhaps could afford to provide Ethel some 'help' at home. Ethel seemed close to her sister, Alice, in the photograph; so perhaps she saw quite a lot of her. And as she was aunt to their children, Barbara, Phyllis, and Boy, perhaps she might have taken an active interest in their growth and development. Having the two small girls together, Ethel and Owen would have had a lot of fun being their 'audience' when they, as most little girls do, perform their latest dance or gymnastics. Perhaps it was this that gave Ethel the idea to find a ballet teacher and join the latest craze all the rage in France – ballet!

Ethel was very much ahead of the times when she arranged for Barbara to take ballet lessons. Phyllis also studied ballet. Amazingly, this was confirmed in Phyllis' army record, where she stated she studied ballet with Judith Espinosa. Clearly an important pastime in her childhood, this became one of the most valuable pieces of information in helping me understand Phyllis.

While ballet until 1920 was not an established art form and profession in Britain, it was already very fashionable in France. England then was considered to be a place where foreign dancers performed, not a place where ballet was taught and developed. After the newspapers in England began writing about the ballet in France, this changed. For example, in December 1909 the Russian ballet, and especially Anna Pavlova, electrified French audiences with their transformational and revolutionary dance. In Paris in June 1912, the French Ballets Russes presented the first complete performance of Ravel's ballet *Daphnis et Chloé* to much acclaim. And again in Paris in May 1913, uproar greeted the premiere of the ballet *The Rite of Spring* by Stravinsky.

The fostering of ballet as an art form in Britain began in the 1920s when Eduoard Espinosa and Philip Richardson founded the Association of Operatic Dancing, later to be known as the Academy of Dancing. I was delighted to find a photograph of Judith Espinosa with her brother Edouard on the front page of the History of the Royal Academy of Dance website. Later, to my great joy, further research unearthed reports that Judith Espinosa was a very well-known West End ballerina in her time, and in 1928 was considered to be the best ballet teacher in all England. Not only did her students top the competitions; she taught some especially prominent dancers. I was delighted to discover that one such dancer, Anne Woolliams (1926–99), produced *Swan Lake* in 1977 for the Australian Ballet.

I wish it were possible to know more about Ethel's efforts in finding Judith Espinosa to teach Barbara and Phyllis. Barbara and Phyllis were clearly at the beginning of this ballet movement. Both Jeremy and Paul told me that Aunt Barbara was an excellent ballet student and that she and Big Granny were extremely disappointed when her height became the limiting factor to her continuing her ballet career. Barbara would have loved to have been a professional ballerina. This was not mentioned in relation to Phyllis.

A family story I love is one Barbara told to Jeremy. Like any mother, Big Granny particularly enjoyed going to ballet performances in which Barbara was performing. At the end of the dance, after Barbara curtseyed, everyone would clap. But, as Barbara told her son Jeremy, Big Granny would clap the loudest and the longest.

She would continue clapping long after everyone else had stopped clapping.

'My mother used to be so embarrassed by this,' Jeremy said.

Big Granny clearly cherished these moments – and who would not be proud of seeing one's daughter achieve? It is one of the joys of being a parent. Big Granny came across as a woman committed to her children in this story.

Barbara and Phyllis were clearly among the early ballet students and this would have set them apart from their peers. Ballet is extraordinarily good for teaching good posture, coordination, and musical appreciation. It also provided an introduction to French terminology, useful for learning French. Ballet also teaches a love of music, costume design, performance, rhythm, grace, poise, acting, and performance. In the early 1900s it provided a unique blend of skills valued by women and society at that time and so it was, I believe, a really significant part of Phyllis' education.

Barbara and Phyllis could well have been taken to ballet performances, not just by other students, but perhaps by professionals in central London. Did she also see Anna Pavlova? Could this have been the genesis of Phyllis' love of dance, performance, theatre, and acting?

It is certainly possible that Phyllis also knew and trained with ballerinas that subsequently became famous. Barbara's two sons, my new cousins, continue to love ballet and I had the great pleasure to accompany the eldest of my two cousins to the Sydney Opera House to see a modern ballet choreographed by Graeme Murphy. It was wonderful.

Interestingly, the mention of Judith Espinosa and her significance in the ballet world became part of a pattern, and from this example, I realised Phyllis never mentioned the name of a person, whether to Paul or in her army record, if it was not someone who was very significant in their profession.

Intriguing.

CHAPTER TWENTY-SEVEN

Was Phyllis a product of her time?

It is somewhat shocking now to read about the child-rearing practices of the early 20th century. The belief that women were inferior to men seemed to be pervasive and evident in all their major social institutions. I wonder how this influenced Ethel and Owen, and of course, Phyllis?

Then, boys were believed to be the 'superior sex'[5] and this justified giving them access to better quality education and university. Men were expected to pursue careers and earn income, and were, of course, able to inherit property. The establishment of 'gentlemen's clubs' in London, where membership would be restricted to men only, followed quite naturally.

In contrast, education for girls was aimed to facilitate a smooth passage from the care for their fathers to caring for their husband and children. Women were not permitted to inherit 'real' property until 1925. Quality education for daughters was considered a waste of time – nothing could be worse than an 'intelligent girl' to put off a prospective suitor. Education was aimed to equip girls to become 'gentlewomen' and tended to focus on languages and the arts.[6] Before WWI, aspiring to a career or any type of paid work was frowned upon.

At that time, children were to be seen and not heard and parents were to be respected and obeyed. Physical affection between parents and children was discouraged. Children were expected to be good losers, to offer a stiff upper lip, and of course, to never cry. Opinions could only be expressed if they were positive. Punctuality, discipline, good table manners, and other forms of 'proper conduct' were considered essential attributes of well-behaved children.

Can I dare suggest that these rather rigid ideas continued well past the middle of the 20th century in Great Britain and its colonies, too? Of course they did.

I wonder how Phyllis coped with all the rules. If she was regarded as a difficult child, often 'unbending', it would be reasonable to assume her parents might have been more positively inclined towards her siblings, Barbara the eldest, and Boy the much anticipated son. How might this have influenced Phyllis, not only in her attitudes towards her siblings and parents, but also in her expectations of her son Paul, and children generally? I can only speculate, but Paul confirmed that his mother did not tolerate emotional expression or frippery, and that he was expected to be seen and not heard. He found Phyllis to be brusque and self-controlled.

Another major theme of the early 1900s was the military build-up by Germany, France, and Britain. It was probably not all that obvious in the early days of the 1900s and a young couple like Owen and Ethel, in love and in the midst of planning a family, might have been cocooned somewhat from these insidious developments.

But the signs were there and regularly reported in the press.

In 1908, Britain made defence service compulsory for single men aged between 12 and 26, with older men required to join the Army Reserve. Churchill confirmed the British Navy aimed to maintain its superiority over the German fleet.

On 5 December 1912, Germany, Austria, and Italy renewed their Triple Alliance for six more years, as Britain strengthened relations with France and the US.

In March 1913, France introduced three-year national service, and in November of the same year, the US ordered the mobilisation of men (500,000) – a first during peacetime.

Amazingly, life continued on with lighter moments in the rest of the world.

In Western Australia in April 1913, fourteen women were fined seven shillings for wearing unsheathed hatpins in the street and on Christmas day in 1913 in New York, a couple was arrested for kissing in the street and fined $15.

But in Europe, the drumbeat of war was increasing, with too few foreseeing the consequences.

It's not clear how WWI affected Owen and Ethel and their three small children, aged five, eight, and eleven. Did they stay in London during the War or might they have stayed with their grandparents? Phyllis was eight years old at the start of the War and the next four years would have been hard for all the family. Living through the Zeppelin raids would have been frightening. War would play a dominant role throughout her life.

Alongside the military build-up leading to WWI, the struggle for democracy was hotting up and the suffragette movement gathering pace.

I'm interested in this because the movement towards enfranchisement and gender equality may have caused debate within the Hogg family. Initially, it may have been between Ethel and Owen, and perhaps later with Barbara and Phyllis getting involved. This may have influenced Phyllis to become the person she was. From the perspective of the 21st century, it is amazing that the UK survived politically as such an undemocratic country. For example, in 1780 only 3 per cent of the total population in the United Kingdom was eligible to vote, and they were all men. Large industrial cities like Leeds, Birmingham, and Manchester did not have a single MP between them; while Dunwich in Suffolk, with a population of thirty-two had two MPs in parliament. The electorate was increased from 366,000 in England and Wales in 1831 to about 8 million in 1885 – that is, only men who were house owners. So, political power was still left in the hands of men in the numerically small aristocracy and middle class.

In the 19th century and the beginning of the 20th century, women had no involvement in national politics. It was assumed women did not need the vote because their husbands would take this responsibility. Their role was child-rearing and caring for the home.

In 1913, Sir Almroth Wright published a book, *The Unexpurgated Case against Woman Suffrage*, vehemently arguing women were inferior to men. This view was still prevalent, despite the fact that the campaign for universal suffrage (the right to vote) was launched in 1865 by John Stuart Mill. Although this was rejected by parliament at that time, by the end of the century the issue of the vote became the focus of women's struggle for equality. Millicent Fawcett started the movement in 1897, when Ethel Hogg was 24 years. She argued that if women could hold responsible posts, such as sitting on a school board, and if women worked and paid taxes like men do that they should have the same rights as men. Fawcett's progress was very slow, as most men believed that women should be excluded from the vote because they would not understand how parliament worked. This made many women extremely angry.

In 1903, when the suffragettes initiated their campaign, it was intended to be peaceful. However, in 1912 they were not taken seriously, and they became progressively more militant – eventually interrupting public meetings, chaining themselves to railings, and setting fire to mailbox contents. After the Church of England campaigned against them, they burnt down churches. In May 1913 a suffragette bomb was found in St Paul's Cathedral. Some suffragettes refused to pay taxes and some politicians were attacked and their homes bombed. Men ridiculed and slandered the suffragettes. They were mostly women from upper and middle class backgrounds who were intensely frustrated at still being regarded as second-class, inferior beings who could not be trusted in positions of power; unless this power was inherited, e.g. Queen Victoria.

This was a long and, at times, extremely bitter campaign in the UK. Interestingly, it had more success in the US, where some states gave women over 21 the right to vote in 1869, as well as New Zealand in 1893 and parts of Australia in 1894.

When WWI was declared in August 1914, the British suffragette movement suspended its activities and around a million women took on men's jobs, as the men went off to fight the war. Some say that it was the role that women took on during the war that helped to turn around attitudes towards the participation of women in the workforce and parliament. After WWI in the UK, in November 1918, 30 year old women owning property were given the vote. 8.5 million women voted in the General Election of 1918. In July 1928, all women over the age of twenty-one were given the right to vote.

This is a very brief overview of the campaign – how it actually played out was much more complex than can be described here. There is no doubt that the suffragette movement brought the issue of the inequitable political and economic situation of women to the nation's attention, and kept it there; and that this was very significant in the eventual enfranchisement of women.

It is highly likely that the Hogg family would have been well aware of all these events and that their beliefs and values would have been influenced by them.

CHAPTER TWENTY-EIGHT

Growing up in England during WWI – 1914–18

At the start of WWI, Phyllis was just eight and would have been attending school with her older sister Barbara, who was eleven years old. Once the war started, their home would have been prepared for blackouts. The Croydon special constabulary enforced the blackout and manned observation points, so there was no choice – everyone had to ensure their home conformed.

The German Zeppelins started dropping bombs. Living in South Norwood meant they were close to Beddington airport, which was created in May 1915 to try to defend against the Zeppelin raids.

Croydon was bombed by Zeppelins in October 1915 and again in 1916. Although the casualty rate was small (9 civilians died in 1915), the effect on civilians was devastating. This was the first time British civilians had been military targets.

The economic impact of the war meant there were shortages of all products, most importantly food. In 1918, sugar, meat, butter, and cheese were all rationed. Living standards plummeted, but it could be that Ethel and Owen and their family were better off than most. Owen was too old to join the army – he just missed the upper age limit when forced conscription for single men between 26 and 41 was introduced in January 1916. The fact that Ethel was married and a mother probably meant that she could continue a near normal life; though, she might have found a way to volunteer when the children were in school.

For other women, this was not the case. The serious shortage of able-bodied men meant that women were required to take on male roles, particularly in the area of arms manufacture, agriculture, and in the civil service. As the war progressed, many women joined the army, becoming cooks and nurses.

Everyone watched as the Royal Family battled through their dilemmas. They renounced their German roots and became the 'House of Windsor.' King George V was first cousin to German Kaiser Wilhelm II who, for the British public, symbolised all the horrors of the war.

Interestingly, Britain recognised the need to counter German propaganda and maintain the public's morale early in the war. Popular writers such as Conan Doyle, Rudyard Kipling, and HG Wells, as well as the newspapers were asked to contribute to the propaganda campaign. Despite newspapers operating ruthless self-censorship, the public demand for news dramatically increased. *The Times* was often sold out by 9.15am. The propaganda appeared to be very effective and the public was led to believe that everything was going well, when in reality enormous numbers of people were dying.

Britain suffered over three million casualties, two million wounded and just under a million killed. Psychologically, the impact was incalculable. Hospitals were full to overflowing. Almost every family was affected, including the Hogg family. This was illustrated when we accompanied Paul to France to pay our respects at the grave of an uncle from his father's side of the family who died during WWI.

To exacerbate the situation in 1918, immediately after the war, there was an epidemic of Spanish Flu and the number of deaths, after one year, was on the same scale as the number of deaths from the 'Black death' epidemic in the middle ages.

The role men and women performed in the war helped Britain accept universal franchise. However, WWI was the cause of a major British economic catastrophe that saw Britain fall from being the world's largest overseas investor to its biggest debtor, with interest payments covering 40 per cent of the budget. With this devastating circumstance also came rapidly rising inflation and a depreciating pound sterling.

Phyllis would have been a young teenager just after the war

ended, and may well have been argumentative and stubborn. Barbara might have started to date, and I wonder what Phyllis might have thought about that. She was intelligent and probably had some definite ideas about a lot of socio-political issues.

For everyone in the United Kingdom, the time after WWI was filled with social turmoil, fatherless broken families, mourning, rebuilding, economic hardship, and rising unemployment; hardly a calm environment in which to rear children. Phyllis, at this time, was sent away from home to a finishing school in Belgium. However, no one in the family can remember if Barbara went there also. Might Owen and Ethel have sent Phyllis to bring some peace into their home while Barbara went about the important business of finding a suitable husband without the interference that sibling rivalry would bring? Would sending Phyllis to a boarding school in Belgium remove her from the social turmoil in Britain and be in her best interests as well? There she would lead a sheltered life governed by nuns and structured around her studies to prepare her for the destiny every parent at the time would have wished for their daughter: a good marriage.

CHAPTER TWENTY-NINE

Phyllis and her introduction
to Dalmatians – 1918–27

I believe this was one of the most rewarding phases of her life. Phyllis, between the ages of 12 and 18, began to really blossom. She was sent to finishing school in Belgium and came home for school holidays to her family. She learnt to play bridge, loved amateur acting, became a gourmet cook and was taught how to care for and breed Dalmatians. Also during this time, the family took enjoyable family holidays in the south of France.

Following our memorable first meeting with Paul after Easter, and our subsequent visit to Jeremy, Paul drove me around London for two days visiting all the places of significance to Phyllis; interrupted, of course, by traditional English lunches at local pubs. Paul was able to tell me amazing family stories while I shared quite different information gleaned from my research. We laughed a lot, enjoyed getting to know each other, and certainly deepened our understanding of our enigmatic elusive mother.

We visited two homes in South Norwood, the first where she was born and grew up in Chalfont Street; the second, a much larger detached house in Whitworth Road, where she stayed with her family, from 1919 until her marriage in 1927; and the third in Matlock Road in Caterham, where she lived when she was first married. Clearly, Owen, her father, had done well enough at the bank to send one of his daughters to a finishing school and to afford their larger Whitworth Road home.

Phyllis and her family would have settled into a rhythm after WWI ended, with Owen travelling to and from Lloyd's Bank in Threadneedle Street every day, while Big Granny, Barbara, and Boy stayed at home, with Phyllis coming home for school holidays.

From the fragments of personal information and newspaper articles, it's fun trying to imagine how they spent their leisure time. After the war ended in November 1918, the musical hits voted best for the year were 'If You Could Care for Me', 'After You're Gone', and 'Till We Meet Again.' Television and computers had not yet been invented and families frequently made their own evening entertainment. This could include reading or music, with one or more members of a family playing a musical instrument, or charades or word games or amateur theatre.

However, the Hogg family had another hobby: Royal Auction Bridge, later to be known as Auction Bridge. Auction bridge, a derivative of whist, became popular from 1904, and because of its complexity, required instructors who, as a professional group of people, served to market the game widely. At the time, there was a rapid growth of the 'leisured classes' and this game became a very desirable way to entertain guests. Church opposition to the playing of card games relaxed and this served to make the game even more popular. By 1910, Auction bridge was almost the only card game played by fashionable society. It was a game most often played without stakes, and never for high stakes.

Both Paul and Jeremy enthusiastically mentioned that Ethel and Owen loved the game and as soon as Phyllis was old enough to learn, she was asked to play as a fourth player. Could this be the genesis of the spirit of rivalry between the sisters that Jeremy had mentioned? Perhaps. We do know she played bridge regularly for the rest of her life, progressing from her familial home to the local bridge club. Eventually, family stories confirmed she began to play bridge regularly at Crockfords (also called Crockford's club) a sumptuously decorated club that became increasingly popular with the rich and famous.

It is interesting to note that both Paul and I learnt to play bridge quite independently of her and each other, and that it was through Paul being registered as a bridge teacher that I found his contact details.

Although Phyllis' early education remains somewhat of a

puzzle, she wrote in her army record that she attended *Le Couvent des Ursulines* in Verviers in Belgium. This supported a story told by Jeremy that Phyllis attended a finishing school. Paul thinks that she could have attended the convent soon after WWI ended, possibly staying until 1924.

This was fascinating; though for a long time it could not be substantiated.

However, a friend whose native language was Dutch found a reference in a Dutch website to *Le Couvent des Ursulines* in Verviers. In 1904, the Ursulines Sisters sought asylum from Bourges in Belgium, where they set up school for English girls as boarders for the purpose of studying French (and possibly other languages) prior to passing to Oxford. Clearly, *Le Couvent des Ursulines* was aimed at providing the most desirable education possible for the daughters of the British upper classes, in accordance with the social needs of the times. At this finishing school, it was reasonable to assume that Phyllis would be taught cultural and social skills such as languages, etiquette, grooming, how to entertain, and gourmet cooking – all the skills needed for girls to marry well. This was a real find and seems to support other information we have about Phyllis, such as her being an excellent cook. Could this be a skill Ethel started teaching Barbara and Phyllis at home?

I also wonder whether the convent nurtured her acting, ballet, and dramatic skills, and whether she took part in plays there.

We later discovered why it was so difficult to trace the convent. In 1940, there was a terrible railway accident in which a large number of the Sisters were killed. The Convent was subsequently passed to the Sisters of Charity, becoming known as the Saint-Francois-Xavier Institute (Verviers).

Dalmatians also played an important part in Phyllis's life. When Paul first told me about this, I was astonished. I had never imagined this about my mother. We wondered how best to explore this interest of hers further. Was it worth contacting the British Dalmatian Club?

I decided it was and phoned them. I spoke to the Honorary Secretary, Shelagh Stevenson and told her about my first meeting with

Paul and that I was trying to discover information about my mother, Phyllis, who apparently had bred Dalmatians from the 1930s to 1950s. She was charming and most helpful. After a long conversation, Shelagh said she would put a notice in the fortnightly online newsletter explaining our circumstances and asking if any members knew Phyllis. I was very curious to see what would come of this. During our conversation, she asked if I had ever been to a Dalmatian dog show. I confessed my ignorance and said I knew nothing about Dalmatians. To my amazement, she then invited me to the upcoming Windsor Championship Dog Show where Dalmatians, along with other breeds, were being shown. She was encouraging and said that this would be an excellent way to see what was involved in breeding and showing Dalmatians.

On the appointed day of the show, I caught a train to Windsor from London and was greeted at the Home Park exhibition grounds by ushers who wore long black morning coats and top hats! They certainly set the tone and atmosphere.

The Dalmatians and their owners were mingling around a large open shed and as I drew near, I asked to see Shelagh. One of the participants pointed her out to me – a lady of medium height, with sandy-coloured hair and light-coloured eyes. Unlike the men in long black morning coats, she and all the other participants were relaxed. Wearing beige slacks and a long shirt, she was gazing into the distance. I approached her, not wanting to intrude.

'Hello. Are you Shelagh?' I said rather hesitantly. She turned around and smiled. 'I am Jane.'

She immediately recognised my name. 'Oh, Jane, I was just talking about you. I was wondering if you were going to come here today.'

'I hope I am not too late,' I said.

'Oh no, you can see what we are doing. The dogs are still being judged.' She then showed me the dog she had entered into the competition, a year old puppy. She talked about the people there, and then her eyes lit up.

'I have an idea, Jane. There are quite a number of people who knew your mother. Many of them have died, but I will give you a list

of names of people who knew your mother or had something to do
with her dogs.'

I was delighted. 'Thank you so much. That would be lovely.'

Then, Shelagh introduced me to a woman 'of a certain age' who
knew Phyllis. She was sitting comfortably on a chair watching the
arena. She had curly white hair and was in a grey dress with small
white patterns. She was obviously at home, observing and soaking
up the atmosphere. I squatted rather uncomfortably on my haunches
alongside her to chat. I explained who I was and she immediately
she said she knew Phyllis, but not well, as she only met her at events
like this one. She recalled that Phyllis used to sit next to her sometimes and they would chat about their dogs.

'Oh, I rather liked her,' she said, giggling to herself at the memory.
'She had some interesting ideas.'

How curious. 'What interesting ideas?' I asked.

'Oh, she talked about using natural feed for her dogs,' she replied
and then talked about this for a little while.

'What did she look like?' I asked, hoping for a first-hand description of Phyllis.

'Oh, she was good looking.'

'What colour hair did she have?' I asked.

To my surprise, she laughed and said, 'She had black hair! But,
it may have been coloured.'

At the show, I met another Dalmatian enthusiast who asked
me whether I was enjoying the show. After listening to my story, he
started to chat about the distinctive qualities that made a Dalmatian dog attractive as a family pet. I listened, fascinated, and resolved
there and then to find out more about the social qualities of Dalmatians and their role in society. What was the appeal of these dogs that
attracted Phyllis, making this her lifelong hobby? What magic did
the history of the Dalmatian breed have for her?

I thoroughly enjoyed the Windsor Championship Dog Show that
day in August 2005. Shelagh and all the people I met were friendly
and willing to chat. The atmosphere was focused but relaxed and I
could easily imagine Phyllis enjoying herself in that situation. After

HANBOOK 1956.

DALS SHOULD BE BOLD   DALS SHOULD BE GAY

BELLET

As a child I helped Addy and Lucy Parson's kennelman during my holidays. When I left school I picked my first Dal from Desdemon's litter, who was

BANDOL BEAUTY,

C.C. Richmond 1929, four firsts, Best of Breed, Redhill, beating her half brother, Ch. Bookham Swell. Taken to South of France 1930. Shot with five others, one a lovely daughter of Ch. Lucky James, in 1939.

THE COMET,

Four firsts, Best of Breed, Met. and Essex, 1930. Sold to G. A. C. Bury in 1930 when I left England. Sire and grand-sire of many champions.

I returned to England in 1939 and found a bitch of my breeding. All my stock are descended from her, carefully line bred for the correct Dal type, taught me by Mrs. Kemp, who had asked me to judge at the Autumn Committee Meeting of the S.D. Club in 1929.

AT STUD:

THE BLACK PRINCE,

Home Bred   -   Fee 8 gns.

Best puppy in show Brit. Breeds. Junior Warrant at nine months, 2 C.Cs., 5 Reserve C.C.s. Perfect temperament. Born November 3, 1953. Not yet at his prime

BROOD BITCHES.—The Begum of Bellet, The Black Velvet of Bellet, The Black Queen.

Watch for Black Beauty, Black Empress, and Black Emperor.

* * *

Mrs. Alan MacRobert
BELLET : BARFORD : NORWICH
BARNHAM BROOM 288

Advertisement in the Kennel Club Catalogue, 1956

chatting awhile with various attendees, I wandered back to Shelagh and thanked her for the invitation and her help thus far. She gave me some names of people to phone and ask if they had known Phyllis.

A week or two later, Shelagh contacted me again to say Sally Ann (of Puech de Barrayre Dalmatians), who breeds Dalmatians and lives in France, saw the notice and took a keen interest in our story.

Sally Ann found an advertisement Phyllis placed in the 1956 Kennel Club Catalogue advertising her stud dog, The Black Prince of Bellet. This was a real breakthrough and I was elated for days. It was the first written proof I had found to substantiate Paul's stories about Mother and her Dalmatians.

Moreover, Phyllis describes in the advertisement how during her school holidays (from 1918 to 1924) as a child, she helped Addy and Lucy Parson's kennelman, and that when she left school she picked her first Dal from Desdemon's litter. This must have been in 1925. She also mentioned that Mrs Kemp taught her how to breed for the 'correct dal type' and later asked her to judge at the Autumn Committee Meeting of the Southern Dalmatian Club in 1929. Mrs Kemp was married to Mr Fred Kemp, who was the first President of the British Dalmatian Club (BDC). Lucy Parsons and Mrs Kemp were listed as honorary members of the club, so they were also recognised and significant in the world of Dalmatians and influential in establishing Dalmatians as a desirable breed. The Southern Dalmatian Club started in 1925, just after Phyllis left school, and the BDC was formed in 1930; so Phyllis was involved from the very beginning as a young breeder.

Dalmatians have always occupied a special place in Britain as a working dog and a desirable pet. Like zebras, giraffe, and many other animals with markings, each dog has spots that are specific to that particular dog. I understand that the best dogs have well-defined jet black or deep brown spots. They also have the most exquisite body made for running long distances. Watching a Dalmatian in motion is beautiful – they have a graceful gait and will keep going happily for miles and miles. It is for this quality that they were chosen as guard dogs to follow coaches from Brighton to London.

Besides knowing them as carriage dogs following coaches, Phyllis would have been familiar with the rest of their fascinating history. Dalmatians have a long aristocratic heritage; Egyptian tombs show Dalmatians running behind Roman chariots. Because of their natural affinity for horses and their impressive endurance at running, they became popular with European aristocrats. Some would say that Dalmatians still have 'aristocratic' personalities due to their long stint in high society.

Coaches driven by horses in the early 20th century were not such a distant memory for Phyllis. Dalmatians love horses and most will fall in behind a horse and cart, a wheelbarrow, a bicycle, or just run along, beside or behind a horse. They had quite a lot of nicknames besides the English coach dog, such as the fire house dog, the carriage dog, and of course, Spotted Dick! Before motorised fire engines, there were horse-drawn fire wagons and Dalmatians used to run in front, clearing the path for the horses pulling the fire wagons. They also calmed the horses in the confusion of fire. Dalmatians have other endearing attributes and make wonderful pets. They are a gentle, loyal dog and occasionally are referred to in England as a 'real Englishman' or a 'quiet chap.' Also considered wonderful guard dogs, Dalmatians have a strong attachment to their master and remain loyal and willing all their lives. They are sensible and dependable. They are courteous with strangers and even have a smile! When defending their owner or property they can nip and when they bark it is easy to tell the difference between barking for fun and barking for a purpose.

From a breeder's point of view, they are easy to groom because of their short coats. Unlike most other dog breeds, all they need to prepare them for a show is a wash and a brush. However, to keep them in peak condition they need lots of exercise.

I understand a little about Phyllis' passion for her dogs. Years ago, my daughter and I had a beautiful pedigree Bichon Frise dog called Chloe who had two litters of puppies. Chloe was a wonderfully happy companion and when she died, we missed her dreadfully. But, interestingly, as I came to appreciate the effort and costs associated with breeding, such as dog and puppy registrations, vet fees, dog-sitting fees, monitoring the newborn puppies, let alone the show fees and travel expenses that Mother would have had to bear, it is clear that Mother must have been totally committed.

Phyllis' skill and knowledge about Dalmatians learnt during her school holidays stood her in good stead for the rest of her life, providing an ongoing interest and a 'career' from which she gained considerable recognition among like-minded people. It also gave me a rare and wonderful insight into Phyllis' personality, as well as her resourcefulness and imagination.

CHAPTER THIRTY

Phyllis' marriage to Jim – 1927

Phyllis was just sixteen years old in 1922 when she met Jim
Whicker. They fell madly in love. Jim was four years older; a
sporty, handsome young man over six feet tall. He loved to swim and
play golf, and played chess and bridge very well. He was kind and
gentle, and never seemed to get angry. He went to Dulwich College,
a school with an excellent reputation, not far from where Phyllis
lived in South Norwood. Paul thought the school might have had
an association with the Bank of England, as some of the old boys
became senior executives and one became a Governor.

Jim was an outstanding student and towards the end of his
schooling, the school supported his application for a position at the
Bank of England as a bank clerk. Jim was immensely proud of this
at the time. He started working at the Bank of England in 1923 and
only retired from there in 1957. The Bank of England was to be his
only employer.

Phyllis joined the Bank of England in 1924 on her return from
Le Couvent des Ursulines. She was eighteen years old.

Was it usual for the bank to employ women at that time?

With Jim and Phyllis working for the same organisation, their
relationship may well have blossomed. She did not stay there long –
only two years – and one wonders why she left. Might it have been
bank policy not to employ married women? That was common in
those days.

Phyllis and Jim married in the local Catholic Church in Croydon on 1 October 1927, five years after they met. Jim's family were
Catholic, while Phyllis' family were members of the Church of England. Phyllis was twenty-one and Jim was twenty-five.

Paul said that Phyllis and Jim took their honeymoon in the
south of France near a place called Bandol. This must have been a

happy time, because when they bought their first home, a bungalow in Matlock Road, Caterham, they named it 'Bandol'. Names were always significant for Phyllis.

We know that while they lived there they enjoyed going to the horse races in the evenings or over the weekends. Sometimes Phyllis would phone Jim at work to let him know there was a race on. 'Let's meet at Hurst Park at Hampton Court,' she would say, and this was what they would do. Jim also loved vintage cars and owned one later in life.

After Phyllis married Jim and was no longer working at the Bank of England, she started breeding Dalmatians. She mentions this in her 1956 advertisement for her stud dog, The Black Prince.

Phyllis was always dedicated to breeding her dogs – was it because they were loyal, loving companions, or could they also have provided her with much-needed income? Paul said that Phyllis always tried to own three bitches and one stud dog.

Another pastime was playing bridge. Jim and Phyllis joined the local bridge club, where they met Phyllis and Johannes (John) Kleyn, who had a son called Howard. (John would later become Mother's second husband.) The two couples often played bridge, and according to family stories, the two men talked about moving to Nice in the south of France to grow carnations and how they could make a fortune on the stock market. This must have been before the stock market crash in 1932.

It was around this time I suspect that Phyllis started playing bridge at Crockfords. While Jim worked she was not expected to work, so she might well have had free time. Crockfords was a prestigious, magnificently furnished club located at No. 16 Carlton House Terrace, close to St James's Park and Pall Mall, an exclusive part of London. In the 1930s the club was a magnet for the well-to-do and other celebrities. The famous gambling club was originally started by William Crockford, with the sponsorship of the Duke of Wellington, in 1793. It was very popular in the 19th and early 20th century, employing famous chefs, such as Louis Eustache Ude, known for his description of the sandwich in his book, *French Cook* (1818).

Phyllis told Paul a curious story that one of her bridge partners was Iain Macleod, a future Chancellor of the Exchequer, who before WWII lived off his Crockford's bridge winnings. Another story involves Phyllis playing bridge for serious money after the war.

It could well be that Phyllis went to play bridge in Crockford with John Kleyn. Jim might not have been happy about this relationship if he could have foreseen what was going to happen.

Paul was born on 13 April 1932, four and a half years after they married. This was to be a happy occasion, for they had waited a long time, but something went terribly wrong.

When Paul was two months old, Jim returned to his home one evening to find Paul alone with a warm bottle of milk and a note from Phyllis saying: 'I can't cope. Please do not look for me.' This shocked Jim. They had known each other for ten years by this time. He was dreadfully upset and very concerned about the possibility of losing his position at the Bank. It was June 1932 – the stock market had tanked and the UK was rapidly approaching a depression. Jobs were extremely scarce. Jim immediately took Paul to his mother's home for her to look after him. There seemed to be no doubt that Jim would keep custody of Paul. Phyllis had vanished. This must have been a very difficult time for them all – Jim, Paul, and Phyllis.

Three years later they tried to get back together – but this failed. (This will be told in the next chapter as part of Paul's life story.) Their marriage ended and divorce proceedings were started.

Jim was a Catholic and honestly did not want a divorce. Divorce was not common and considered a social disgrace in the 1930s. English law at that time did not allow for divorce by mutual consent, one party had to provide proof of adultery or violence.

Three years later, in 1937, their divorce came through. This time must have been a real emotional roller coaster for Phyllis.

Both Jim and Paul were already living with Jim's mother, Maud, who owned a hotel called Splash Point House, in Worthing. Jim commuted between London and Worthing every day during the week. When the divorce papers came through they cited Phyllis as being the respondent who was guilty of adultery with John Kleyn, their former bridge partner. Soon after this, Jim married Caroline, one of the guests in his mother's hotel, and Phyllis married John Kleyn.

I wondered why Phyllis abandoned Paul – it was a tragic outcome for them all. Were her intense feelings and impetuousness caused by post-natal depression? Was she sick or anaemic or depressed? Could it be that the way she was cared for by her own mother as a baby influenced her own ability to parent?

I will never really know – and am sorry I will never know Phyllis' own perspective on what happened.

We do know that Big Granny did not want to be pregnant with her and tried to abort the unwanted pregnancy and later pronounced her to be a 'difficult' child. The fact that this story was so well known by Phyllis' sister adds weight to the idea that it could have contributed to her ambivalence toward Paul and motherhood in general.

Perhaps her relationship with her mother and sister at the time was not good enough for her to ask for help without the fear of being blamed or scolded. She was known to be 'unbending' and difficult. Sometimes people make it difficult for others to offer advice and help. I wonder who supported her and how long it took for her to recover.

Paul often wondered where she went and thought that perhaps she stayed with her brother, Boy, in Brighton.

As I grew to know my new family better, new stories emerged that added insight into other factors that might have contributed to Phyllis leaving Jim.

After reading my manuscript, Jeremy, my frank and forthright first cousin, wrote to me saying Phyllis had told Big Granny and her sister, Barbara (Jeremy's mother), that she and Jim had encountered issues with their sex life. He wrote: 'She would not have told her mother if it had not been hugely significant.' This was confirmed by Paul, who said Jim in his later life had said as much. When they married, this would have been something Phyllis could never have anticipated. How sad.

Jeremy continued: 'I understand Phyllis did try to get Paul back and there was a custody battle, which she lost.'[7] So, if this is to be believed, Phyllis *did* want to mother Paul and have him back. How damaging this whole experience must have been for her.

What happened to Phyllis after she gave birth to me? Did she suffer from postnatal depression then as well? And how did she feel after my adoption? If she had been depressed, members of her family knew nothing of it. Her relationships with her mother and father and sister were never straightforward. Her unhappy experiences with Paul may have been one of the factors influencing her to give me away.

CHAPTER THIRTY-ONE

Paul's story

Meeting Paul was the breakthrough in my search for my mother; and so, at our first meeting at Canary Wharf, when Rob returned to work, we were not at all ready to leave. We had a lifetime to catch up on and as we talked we both were astonished by the other's life stories. It felt unreal, as if we were living in a movie. As far as I was concerned, it was also a realisation of a long-held dream. We ordered coffee after coffee and continued chatting until we were exhausted and could not absorb anything more. We left the café around 4.30pm.

So, what happened to Paul at such a tender age, just two months after he was born?

I can picture him in a pram or bassinette, perhaps with a warm bottle of milk next to him, ready for Jim to feed him as soon as he came home. At two months, he would not have been able to hold the bottle and feed himself. Phyllis must have waited until she thought Jim was almost home before dashing out the door.

Paul struggled with this for the rest of his life and often wondered where she went. He said his father was appalled and amazed that she had left him. Immediately, he took Paul to his mother, Paul's paternal grandmother, who managed a hotel. During the week, Jim left early in the mornings and returned late at night, and so a nanny was employed to care for Paul. Paul bonded with his nanny.

In 1935, when Paul was three years old, Phyllis and Jim tried to repair their broken marriage and moved back into their bungalow at Caterham. Paul's life was turned upside down. His nanny in Worthing was asked to leave and he was very upset. When he moved with his father back into their home, he did not realise this stranger was his mother. She was firm with him and not nearly as nurturing or forgiving as his nanny had been. He also shared his mother with her Dalmatians. Single women in England were not eligible for any significant welfare payment, so breeding Dalmatians might have provided an opportunity to make ends meet. There were costs associated with their breeding, so she would not have wanted to give the dogs away. As luck would have it, one of the bitches gave birth to a litter of puppies soon after they moved back together. Not suprisingly, and sadly, Phyllis became distracted soon after the puppies were born — making sure each puppy had its fair share of milk. This required her constant attention and very soon Paul was forgotten.

Phyllis did not know Paul and would not have had the usual affectionate bond between mother and child. She also clearly did not realise how attentive she needed to be with him. He was a curious, resourceful little boy; he remembers seeing Phyllis' bag on the bed, found her purse, opened it, and found some money. I can imagine Paul, as a three year old little boy, relishing the thought of buying a sweet or some chocolates. He promptly walked out of the house and crossed a number of roads to the nearby neighbourhood shop to buy sweets.

Not long after this, Jim returned home and looked for Paul. He was nowhere to be found. Jim asked Phyllis, who thought he was at home and was extremely surprised to find Paul missing. They searched the house, found Phyllis' bag and purse open and the front door open. In the meantime, Paul was enjoying himself in the shop choosing sweets. They found him at the shop and took him home. Not surprisingly, Jim was very angry with Phyllis and this incident proved to be the end of their fragile attempt at reconciliation. Paul was taken back to his grandmother and his nanny, where he stayed until he was five years old.

Paul felt for a long time that he was to blame for what had happened and for Phyllis leaving. These feelings were also mixed up with having to say goodbye to his nanny and his ambivalence towards Phyllis; she was a stranger to him. He listened to the emotional tone of the conversations around him and felt guilty about having these mixed feelings. He felt responsible and yet could not understand what was actually happening.

It did not help when his father would not talk about this time; Jim was always upset about it. Later, after Paul had re-established contact with Phyllis, she would not talk about it either. Paul said this made it doubly difficult for him to come to terms with his mother leaving.

In 1936, Paul's Aunt Barbara returned to London with her baby son for a quick visit. Barbara normally lived in North West India with her husband, who was a Colonel in the Ghurkha Regiment in the British Indian Army. Phyllis asked Jim if she could have access to Paul, then came and collected him, and took him with her to see her sister, Barbara.

Paul remembered Phyllis taking him, aged four, with Aunt Barbara to an Army Tattoo in Earls Court. However, before they met up with Barbara, Phyllis told Paul not to say anything about his life or her life. Paul thought that his aunt did not yet know that Phyllis had separated from Jim. This could not have made Paul's relationship with Phyllis any easier.

In 1937 Phyllis and Jim divorced; shortly afterwards, Jim married Caroline. Paul said he was never close to Caroline. It was about this time, when he was five years old, that he was sent to board at Chawton's School, Rustington, Sussex. Paul said that it must have been fine, as he did not have any negative memories of it.

Paul rarely saw Phyllis and said that he remembered a discussion about her wanting to see him. He understood later that she was prevented from doing so because Paul's father thought Paul was disturbed by seeing Phyllis and found it hard to readjust afterwards.

Apparently, there were always questions about who Paul would stay with for his school holidays. Sometimes Paul went to stay with his father and Caroline in Worthing, and occasionally, he would stay with Big Granny, Ethel Hogg, who was then living in Ventnor Villas, Hove, in Brighton. Sometimes Paul would go to stay with Phyllis over Easter. Eventually, this became a reasonably regular event.

One year, Ethel Hogg bought a rabbit for Paul and he was as pleased as punch about this. When he went to stay with her, he had this pet rabbit to play with. However, he was most put out during the early part of WWII when food rationing started, as Big Granny took the rabbit to the butcher to be killed when they were short of food. Paul remembers a song, that was written by Noel Gay and Ralph Butler in 1939 and sung by Bud Flanagan:

Run, rabbit, run, rabbit, run, run, run
Run, rabbit, run, rabbit, run, run, run
Bang, bang, bang, bang! goes the farmer's gun
Run, rabbit, run, rabbit, run, run, run

He often thought, 'my poor little rabbit' when he heard the song.

As WWII with Germany drew near, Paul said that the Bank of England wanted his father to move closer to London to make commuting easier. Consequently, Jim and Caroline took out a loan and bought an apartment overlooking Croydon Air Field.

Paul meets John Leonard Kleyn (John) – Easter 1940

Paul had clear memories of staying with Phyllis and John, Phyllis' second husband, in their small one bedroom flat in Tottenham, in North London. John was kind to Paul and Paul liked him a lot. John took him to see a football game in which the Arsenal team were playing; and so for all his childhood, Paul supported and identified with the Arsenal football team. During that visit, Paul said the Germans invaded Norway and John was extremely worried and tense. Phyllis was also tense and warned Paul to behave himself because John did not like children. Paul did not have this impression.

Paul's narrow escape

On one of Jim's trips away from home, Paul, aged eight, was home from school for his summer holidays. It was 7pm on Thursday,

15 August 1940, and Paul's stepmother, Caroline, and he were together in their apartment. They heard the deafening sound of fifteen German Messerschmitt 110 planes and two engine bombers flying low overhead from south to north. It was the Luftwaffe and they had been sent to bomb the RAF Hurricane fighter base at Croydon airfield close to where they lived. Fortunately, most or all of the British fighter planes had taken off.

The German planes flew over from the south looking for the airbase. They did not bomb the airport then, but the air raid siren went off anyway. Caroline told Paul to go downstairs to the basement, where the boiler was but he was reluctant to do so. Then they started to hear the drone of German aircraft returning. Paul was dressed in his 'jimjams', that is, his pyjamas, dressing gown, and slippers, and he held his little toy car, which he had been playing with. He refused to go down to the basement. He vividly remembers not wanting to run away – all he wanted to do was to fight the Germans! His stepmother grabbed his arms and began to push him downstairs. She wanted Paul out of danger. Paul vividly remembers shouting to her: 'Don't do that to me. I don't want to go downstairs.' She continued to push him down the stairs and as they were going through the doorway, one of the bombs fell on the apartment building. There was a massive explosion and the blast hurled Paul against the opposite wall of the room where his head hit the wall.

He must have been concussed, because when he woke up it was dark, quiet, and dusty. He was covered with bits of rubble that smelt of burning rubber. Both he and his stepmother were trapped in the rubble of their home. She was lying nearby, sobbing. Paul asked, 'Are you alright?' He thought she was hurt. 'Oh, you silly boy, don't you realise we do not have a home any longer – go back to sleep.' His stepmother realised they had lost everything. Paul was not aware of anyone nearby.

The British Hurricanes flew at about 10,000 feet above sea level, but the German Messerschmitt planes were flying at about 1000 feet. The Hurricanes came down and attacked the planes. Because of the intervention of the nine Hurricanes, many of the bombs fell wide outside the airfield's perimeter and onto the surrounding private houses that abounded in this area. Some seventy people were killed and many more were injured.

The next morning, Friday, 16 August, they were rescued and helped out of the building rubble. That night, Caroline and Paul went to stay with a friend called Aunt Jane. They slept another night there as well.

On that particular Friday, while the two adult women were talking at the kitchen table over a cup of tea, Paul was playing under the table with his one now very precious toy car. While playing, he overheard Caroline and Jane talking. Jane asked where they were going to stay and what would be happening to Paul. Paul's stepmother said that she had asked Phyllis if she could care for Paul, and Phyllis had said no, because she had joined the Army. She then said that since they had nowhere to stay, Paul would probably be evacuated.

Paul remembers wondering what the word 'evacuated' meant, not liking the sound of it. He became quite fearful of what was being planned for him.

Soon after this, Paul's stepmother took him to some nearby shops and used all her clothing coupons to buy him a new set of clothes. He was given one of everything; one pair of shorts, socks, and shoes, as well as one shirt and a pullover.

On Saturday morning they went to Paddington station where a whole trainload of children were being evacuated. Paul remembers saying goodbye to his stepmother and specifically remembers her putting her arms around him and kissing him. This was to be the last hug he had for years. He then climbed onto the train. Paul thought he was going to be a lucky little boy, as she had told him not to worry. 'You will be given a nice family,' she said. The journey was about three hours and they stopped somewhere in Devon.

Paul was a late addition to the children that left London on Saturday, 17 August 1940 and there had not been enough time to arrange for him to be billeted. All but three of the children on the train were billeted. Paul was given the number ENNL 3051517 and he remembers many different adults at the station coming to ask him for his number. When he told them they would turn aside, as he was not their assigned child. The children had been given numbers so that boys and girls could be allocated fairly. The reason for this was because, in the past, when children were billeted and families were given a choice, they asked for girls, and boys were left without families.

When all the other children were collected, a police officer took the three children, including Paul, home for the night. The next day they were taken to a local Barnardo's Children's Home.

Although at the start, there were not many children at the home, soon it was full. All the beds in the large bedrooms were crammed together with no spaces between. The children had to climb over other children's beds to get to their own.

One can only imagine what it must have been like to live in that crowded dormitory. All the children had been separated from their families. Night times must have been quite traumatic and in the mornings there would have been many wet beds.

Initially, the children helped in the home and in the garden. Paul remembers growing some of the vegetables. 'I was in charge of planting and tending the onions, leeks, and shallots. We all had to dig and plant the vegetables. We always had nice vegetables and the food was decent for the war time. We also had chickens and eggs.'

Paul did not like the children's home. One day, he fell down some stairs and the woman who cared for 50–60 children gave him a hug. She thought someone had pushed him and he reassured her that he had fallen by himself. She then slapped him across the back of his head. Paul said that what had amazed him was how much comfort he had taken from the hug and how much he had missed physical contact. That was the only embrace he had during all the time he was at the children's home. He was there for four years, from when he was eight to twelve years old.

Paul's stepmother was in the Women's Land Army. This was fortunate for him, as she worked on a farm near Whitchurch and arranged for him to go to a local family for a holiday once a year. Due to the shortage of accommodation in the area, Paul's father and stepmother lived in a small caravan. The only way he could stay near them was to find a local family who would have him to stay.

Jim had an allotment as part of the 'Dig for Victory' campaign. He grew potatoes and vegetables. Paul remembers eating meals with them and thinking how delicious their vegetables were. Any time away from the children's home was an absolute treat.

Phyllis' visit

Phyllis visited Paul only once while he was living at the Barnardo's children's home. Paul had been living in there since 1940. Phyllis arrived in style, coming by taxi one Friday evening, very smartly dressed in an Army uniform. She collected Paul from the institution and whisked him away to stay together at a pub at nearby Taunton for the weekend. This was an immensely enjoyable and memorable weekend for Paul. They wandered in the nearby forest and Phyllis taught Paul how to recognise edible mushrooms. They picked berries together and he was immensely proud of being with her. This was his mother! In the evening he enjoyed listening to the stories she told to the other 'patrons' who were also staying at the pub. During this visit, Paul and Phyllis really connected. How sad that they could not have seen each other more regularly.

While Paul was still at the children's home, Jim arranged for Paul to sit an entrance examination for a public school, Churcher's College in Petersfield, Hampshire. Paul was thrilled to discover he was successful and he started at his new school in late September 1944. By this time, his father and stepmother lived in a flat in Whitchurch and every school holiday he would go and stay with them. They had another son by this time and Paul found that when he visited he was a bit of an outsider in the family. Paul remembers his father fondly – always calm and fair, a sporting man who enjoyed swimming in the sea. Life for Paul began to be more normal and he enjoyed both the school and the holidays and did well.

One particularly memorable visit with Phyllis happened after

WWII when Paul was 14. Phyllis was staying at 5 Little Chester Street, Belgravia, and while Paul was staying with her, she introduced him to a Dutch General. This charming story is relevant to both Phyllis's wartime activities and my adoption.

After Paul left school, he joined the Royal Air Force and trained to be a jet pilot. After some years, he went on to become an electronics engineer and worked for a large Dutch company. Like his father, he had a stable working career.

Paul lost touch with Phyllis. She left her third husband without telling him where she went. Paul was going out with Eileen and wanted to invite Phyllis to his wedding, but very sadly, he could not find her. He married Eileen and they had a daughter, Karen, who now lives near us in Sydney, Australia.

I cannot help but reflect back to that first afternoon at Canary Wharf, London, when Paul first told me the bare bones of his story. I am particularly grateful to Paul for having such an excellent memory and providing me with these rare glimpses of Phyllis. We found ourselves, sometimes together, exploring her life in the most amazing places in London, southern England, in the south of France, and in the Netherlands.

Out of our sharing came such joy and a whole new family.

CHAPTER THIRTY-TWO

Phyllis and John Leonard Kleyn
in Europe – 1937–39

Phyllis was thirty-one when she married John Leonard Kleyn in Holborn on 24 November 1937. He was forty-four at the time. Phyllis registered me as Jane Kleyn on my birth certificate – so I was keen to discover whether John was my father. And what was it that attracted her to John?

Further questions came to mind as well.

Dr Davidson assured my adoptive parents that my biological parents also provided 'mixed' parenthood. Benjamin, my adoptive father, was German and Jewish, and Elizabeth, my adoptive mum, was English. Was John also German and Jewish like my adoptive father? This is not far-fetched. In 1947 in South Africa, and probably in the Netherlands too, Kleyn was a common name among Jewish families.

John Leonard Kleyn, Phyllis Margaret's second husband.

Paul's information about John Leonard Kleyn

Paul stayed with Phyllis and John in 1940. He learnt that John was born in Leiden, in the Netherlands, and that during WWII John was involved in the Secret Service.

This was intriguing and became another piece of information I endeavoured to substantiate.

Sadly, although Paul liked John, he never saw him again. The next time he stayed with Phyllis was in 1946 after the war. When he asked her about John, to his surprise she told him that 'John' had died! He did not believe her and perhaps she did not want to let him know they were divorced. Perhaps she was concerned that Paul might try to contact John and she wanted to prevent this from happening.

At our first meeting, I was able to show Paul Phyllis' marriage certificate to John and John's will, giving his date of death not as 1946, but 3 October 1970. Paul's eyes grew wide when he read the will – John also had a son named Peter. He was a new stepbrother! We resolved to contact him, too.

From his reaction I realised that Paul had also grown up in an environment where there were lots of secrets. And while I became gradually aware that Paul had an excellent memory, he met Phyllis so seldom that there were still many unanswered questions.

Was Phyllis still married to John when I was conceived and born? What was the date of their divorce and John's next marriage? This would surely help answer the question about the likelihood that John was my father.

A further visit to the Family Records Centre in Holborn, London was called for.

Family Records Centre

This was my first time back to the Family Records Centre since August 2004 when we searched for Phyllis' death certificate. I found

John Kleyn's marriage certificate to his next wife, Diana, and Peter Kleyn's birth certificate. John married again on 27 November 1944, about 19 months before I was conceived. So, it was not likely that he was my father.

I was so disappointed. I wanted so badly to find out who my father was and it now seemed unlikely that it was to be John Kleyn. I had become accustomed to thinking he might be. Feeling stranded and adrift again with no clear answers and with the prospect of the search continuing into the ether, I decided to try to find out as much information as I could about Phyllis. Perhaps she would lead me to my father.

John had changed his occupation and rank. In November 1944, he declared on his marriage certificate he was a 'Capt. Intelligence Corps and a Company Director.' It was really good to see Paul's story of John working in Intelligence during WWII being substantiated.

The next step would be to contact Peter, our new step brother, but I hesitated. I felt vulnerable. My story is hard to believe at the best of times, especially for people who do not have any connections to it. I could imagine his response to a phone call from a stranger saying something like, 'I think we might be related. I share your name and may be your step-sister.' A reasonable response would be one of disbelief, discomfort at the confrontation, and annoyance at the invasion of privacy. What is this person trying to say? What are they inferring regarding the fidelity of his father? And if his father did have a daughter, why did he not know about it? Were there issues about his father that he was not aware of? This was hardly the best way to start a relationship with a step-brother.

I discussed this with Paul and Eileen. Eileen, knowing how I felt, offered to make the first phone call to Peter, Paul's new step brother. I happily accepted her offer.

Eileen phoned me the next day. She said his response was at once welcoming and open. He spoke kindly to Eileen and confirmed Paul's story that the Kleyn family came from Leiden in the Netherlands. John had three brothers, who had all died, and he had had four marriages!

Peter explained that John Kleyn's first marriage was to a young woman with leukaemia in The Netherlands who died a few months later. After this, John moved to England and married his second wife, Phyllis Violet, and had a son called Howard. Then in 1937, he married Phyllis (my mother) who became known as Margaret Kleyn. And in 1944, he married again and Peter was the result of that marriage (John's fourth marriage).

The biggest surprise was that John had another son, Howard, when he was married to Phyllis Violet, before his marriage to my mother. Peter gave us Howard's phone number and said he would let him know about me. He had only recently discovered Howard – about two years previously.

Two new step-brothers?

So, I was not the first secret in his family. This was a huge relief. The next step was to meet Howard and Peter. I decided to initially meet them separately, so that they could tell me their stories independently.

Meeting Howard Kleyn (John Kleyn's eldest son) – 9 July 2005

Our first appointment was for Saturday lunch at a lovely old pub in Cambridgeshire, close to where they lived. Howard arrived with his wife Margaret. Another Margaret – and another Margaret Kleyn – this was too much!

Howard came well-prepared with an A3 size family tree and albums of photographs. He was also delighted, almost gleeful, that we had met on his birthday! I was his birthday gift and a most unusual one at that! Howard was a tall, well-built man in his late seventies, with a shock of white hair and playful, expressive eyes. He had been a director of a major telecommunications company and now was a published writer, a lover of Shakespeare, keen bridge player, and gardener. He embraced computer technology and had an extremely alert and active mind!

He was also a mine of information about his father, John Kleyn. He confirmed John came from Holland. John's parents, his grand-parents, lived at Plantsoen, Leiden; later moving to Dunklerstraat's-Gravenhage, where they died in their late seventies within a few months of each other in the spring of 1941.

Howard was born in 1927 in London and a few years later his father and second wife, Phyllis Violet, moved to a large house that they built in Caterham. This was close to where Mother lived with Jim Whicker.

John worked for Royal Dutch Shell, but left in 1931. How he made a living after that was uncertain. John and his wife played bridge with Phyllis and Jim Whicker as two couples and that was how they met.

When Howard mentioned that John stopped being employed in 1931, I wondered if it could have been that Phyllis was struggling with her relationship with Jim Whicker at that time. And perhaps Phyllis found his charm difficult to resist and their relationship developed from there?

Howard confirmed that John Kleyn tried to set up a carnation farm in the south of France, but this effort failed. He confirmed that in WWII John joined the British Army, and then British Intelligence, probably because he spoke English, Dutch, and French.

This was as much as he knew about his father's wartime career.

Howard talked of his father with some bitterness. At one point, he exclaimed, 'He was a man of considerable charm, but few morals!' He was clearly upset that his father abandoned him and his own mother, Phyllis Violet. I felt sad for him and had a strange sense of feeling responsible for my mother's actions. I felt very uncomfort-able for something that was clearly out of my control.

After a very pleasant lunch in the pub, Howard and Margaret invited us to their home, about half an hour's drive through the Fens. It was on the drive to Howard's home that he said with pride that they were going to celebrate their 50th wedding anniversary the following year. This was in direct contrast to his father who had four wives and Howard clearly was aware of the irony.

We sat and drank tea in their beautiful, lush green garden.

Howard brought out more photo albums and they were fun to see. John looked really dapper in the photos, with his dark brown hair plastered flat on his head in a dashing side-part. He wore plus fours with 'presence' or 'attitude'. He had such a handsome open face, the sort of face one could trust! Or so it seemed.

Howard showed me photographs of himself with his mother and other photos of John playing golf, going shooting with horses and dogs, with expensive cars, and in the south of France. Clearly, they had an active family life. Did Phyllis and John also have this kind of lifestyle?

The lifestyle in the photos was about to end though. Howard's mother, Phyllis Violet, discovered some letters from my mother addressed to John while they were living in the south of France. John left the marriage, and presumably continued seeing Phyllis. Understandably, Howard was very disappointed his father left and broke up his family.

Just before we left Howard, he described how one day he plucked up courage to go and visit his father at Cadogan Square in London. Cadogan Square was a prestigious location in an expensive part of London. This was obviously in stark contrast to how Howard lived as a child; growing up alone with his mother after his father left. Howard said his father gave him an icy reception, not talking much, and so after a time he just left. That was the last he saw of his father.

Howard's description of this was sad and poignant and highlights the lifelong, ongoing trauma he and Paul felt because of their parents abandoning them and their broken marriages. Both had to make huge life adjustments.

DNA test with Howard Kleyn

The question of whether John Kleyn was my father and whether Howard and Peter were my half-brothers or step-brothers still needed to be resolved.

Howard very kindly agreed to do a DNA test with me the next time I was in London. The results proved that we were not blood related – Howard was my step-brother. I think he was quite disappointed, as was I.

This answered once and for all whether John Kleyn was my father. I was born Jane Kleyn, but John Kleyn was definitely not my father. I was very sad not to have this question resolved.

Howard and Margaret invited me to their 50th wedding anniversary and I travelled to England alone to stay as a houseguest and attend their celebrations, meeting and being introduced to all the family as Howard's sister and aunt to his children. A year later, we were able to reciprocate: Howard and Margaret stayed a whole month with us in Australia. This was a very precious time. We introduced them to our friends and family and Howard, just like his father, charmed everyone! Margaret was wonderfully warm with her quick wit and the gleam in her eye. Rob and I treasured this experience.

Sadly, Howard died suddenly and peacefully in his chair at home three months later.

Meeting Peter Kleyn (John Kleyn's youngest son)

After our wonderful get-together with Howard and Margaret in July 2005, we looked forward to Peter and his wife coming for dinner with Paul and Eileen. It was fortunate they did not live too far away from us. What an evening! We all enjoyed it, laughed a lot, and gained further insight into our family.

In stark contrast to Howard's experience of his father abandoning his family, Peter found his father to be loyal and loving, and his parents' marriage was a happy one. Peter confirmed that John Kleyn was charming, with a great sense of humour. He was comfortable mixing socially with all classes and was always impeccably dressed. He ruefully admitted that his father was embarrassed that he had been married so many times. He did not divulge his previous marriages to his wife's family for a long time. He only told Peter when he was nineteen about the other marriages and about Howard being born.

Once again, having secrets seems to be a theme shared by all our families.

Peter was able to add new information about John. For example, he was musical, played the cello, and particularly enjoyed sport. At one time, he and his wife formed a company making toys for Harrods, hence his title, Company Director, on his marriage certificate. He was also the Secretary of the local Hunt Club in the 1960s. He played chess and bridge very well. John smoked a lot and eventually died of emphysema in October 1970.

In a letter to me, after I gave him the text about his father to read, Peter said, 'I was just twenty when he died. I just remember him as charming, optimistic, and concentrating more on the future than the past. He and my mother did without a lot to send me to boarding schools. He confirmed Howard did come to visit his parents, just after he was born. Apparently, he came asking for money. My father did give him some, but not as much as he requested, so that may be why he got an icy reception.'

Peter goes on to say, 'I got on really well with Howard, he reminded me much of my father both in looks and charm. However, we agreed to disagree about my father's personality. For me, my father was always so affectionate to my mother and loyal. He told me about his previous marriages when I was nineteen, and that was quite a surprise.'

Peter expanded our knowledge of John's wartime role and how he met his mother.

It was wonderful meeting both Howard and Peter, and after we returned to Australia, with their support, I applied for John's War Record; something they had not asked for prior to this. They were delighted. I had already received Phyllis' army record and being able to cross-check both their army records added significantly to the information we had about them and their wartime roles.

Phyllis' life with John – 1937–39

Phyllis and John married just after their respective divorces, both leaving behind a young child and a spouse. The stigma and repercussions of this for Phyllis must have been very significant, especially in her relationship with her mother, father, and sister, and the rest of the family. It was no wonder that escaping to Europe was very attractive to Phyllis and John at the time. Howard said that they stayed at St Roman de Bellet in the south of France. He suggested that John loved the highlife and being a playboy.

Marrying John in November 1937 must have given Phyllis a whole new identity. As John' previous wife was called Phyllis, she chose to be known as Margaret Kleyn.[8] Moreover, in her army record, she states her nationality as 'Dutch by marriage although British born.' She wrote that she lived in the Alpes Maritimes, as well as in Budapest, Vienna, and Holland, and travelled extensively in Europe. She often climbed with experienced climbers in the Alpes Maritimes, Italy and Austria – no doubt also with John. She skied in the Alpes Maritimes and the Austrian Tyrol. She also wrote that she became a voluntary librarian for the Anglo-American Library in Nice. She and John shared many interests. They both loved to be sociable and fashionably dressed. The south of France was also a wonderful place to enjoy the beautiful scenery and the 'good life' – good food and wine.

It was during this time that Phyllis would have had ample opportunity to practice the language skills she had learnt at the Convent in Verviers in the early 1920s – French, German and Italian, and of course, she could always practice her Dutch with John.

Breeding Dalmatians and the origins of her dogs' Affix: Bellet

Howard mentioned that he never knew how John Kleyn lived, because he did not know how he earned an income. This may be so in relation to John, but we do know that Phyllis continued to breed

Dalmatians and that she took her dogs to the south of France and bred them there. The British Dalmatian Club records show that she exhibited one of her dogs in 1938. Clearly, she felt that showing her dogs and becoming known as a dog breeder would help her sell her pedigree puppies. I believe that it was while she was living in the south of France that she thought through her marketing strategy.

In other domains of her life, Phyllis was very particular in her choice of names, and so I was curious why she chose the affix Bellet. An affix is similar to a surname that is added on to the puppy's name; for example, one of her favourite dogs was called the 'Black Prince of Bellet.' Bellet would identify Phyllis as the dog breeder.

When Howard remarked that Phyllis and John lived at St Roman de Bellet, just north of Nice in the Alpes Maritimes in the south of France, it was possible to deduce that they lived there probably around 1937 soon after they married. I wondered whether this was the clue to her choice of name for the affix.

Rob and I decided to treat ourselves and visited St Roman de Bellet just prior to returning to Australia. It proved to be a fascinating few days. What was so special about St. Roman de Bellet? Why did she give this name to her dogs?

St Roman de Bellet is known for its wonderful scenery, plenty of sun, the beautiful Mediterranean climate, and magnificent wines. It still is a beautiful old village steeped in history with its own chateau, the highly-regarded Chateau de Bellet. The village is made up of many old, stone cottages and 50 hectares of beautiful vineyards clustered around the top of a hill. It is in a most attractive part of France. Walking around the small village imagining how Phyllis must have lived made this a very poignant time.

While there, we hunted around the shops for the wine of the area and only after much searching did we eventually find a few bottles. They were six times the price of other wines and we were told that almost all this wine was sold to the best hotels in Nice. We were about to get on a plane and so I was most frustrated to find the wine so late in our trip, when we could not afford the extra weight.

But it was the descriptions of the wines that triggered my

imagination, and I could not help wondering what memories these wines would evoke for Phyllis.

The white wine from St Roman de Bellet is said to have 'an aroma of pear and white flower'. The rosé wine has a 'delicate bouquet dominated by wild rose'. The intense ruby red wine has a 'potent aroma of wild rose, with notes of pepper and spice and pine when matured in kegs'.

There is nothing as appealing as a rare and beautiful wine enjoyed with good company in the magnificent, historic French Riviera. It was as if Phyllis wanted her dogs to be thought of in the same way – like the wine, as being rare and beautiful, with an exotic French influence and wonderful social qualities. Is this why she chose names like The Black Prince of Bellet, the Black Empress of Bellet, and the Black Knight of Bellet? The names sound so exotic and regal. Cleverly, and by association, she imbued her dogs with elegance, romance, and aristocratic connection – she certainly had a rich imagination and sophisticated marketing skills.

Once again, the advertisement for her stud dog gives a hint of the times she was living through, but it was only after consulting Sally Ann from the Dalmatian Club did the meaning become clear.

In the advertisement, Phyllis wrote 'Shot with five others, one a lovely daughter of Ch. Lucky James, in 1939'. For a long time we puzzled over this, until eventually Sally Ann from France suggested that as war was being declared in 1939, the world was about to change drastically. Travelling from France to England with six dogs through rapidly changing and politically unstable countryside would have made Phyllis and John potentially vulnerable and limited their flexibility. The whole of Europe was rapidly escalating their military preparations and calling for volunteers for their armies, and so they would have started to think about whether they were going to enlist. The market for Dalmatians would have vanished and keeping them fed would also have been very costly.

Irrespective of their reasons, shooting her beloved dogs must have been devastating.

Political turmoil leading up to WWII

The news in the years leading up to the war must have given Phyllis and John a real sense of foreboding. With the German economy depressed, the people of Germany were becoming more and more receptive to the ideological and anti-Semitic policies of Hitler.

In 1938 thousands of Jews were fleeing Germany.[9] Germany had annexed Austria and invaded parts of Czechoslovakia. Anti-Semitism was rife and already, in November 1939, the horrors of Nazi concentration camps (Dachau and Buchenwald) were being documented by British diplomats in Germany.

Huge rallies, and popular discontent across Europe against the extremes of wealth, ideologies and the Great Depression prompted many dictators in Europe to end parliamentary democracy, all imposing fascist or communist governments that tolerated little opposition.

In Spain, not far from where Phyllis and Jim were living in the south of France between 1936 and 1939, more than half a million people died in a devastating civil war.

Was this a factor in their deciding to move away from St Roman de Bellet? We know they also lived in Hungary, Austria, and Holland and it was only in 1939 that Phyllis and John moved back to London.

Peace talks broke down, and Germany and Russia invaded Poland on 1 September 1939. Britain and France declared war on Germany two days later. General mobilisation of troops started in Britain and conscription of men aged 20–22 started on 1 October.

By 1939 Britain and France were left as the only remaining strong democracies in Europe, the others having much smaller populations, such as Belgium, Netherlands, Switzerland, Denmark, and Sweden.

CHAPTER THIRTY-THREE

Phyllis and John Kleyn - back in England – 1939

When Paul visited Phyllis after WWII, she told him that she had been asked by Dutch Intelligence, just prior to the Market Garden Campaign, to travel to Arnhem by submarine and fishing boat to check out the German presence there. Initially, I was sceptical about the credibility of this story. I started taking an avid interest in their lives during WWII, and in particular, Phyllis' and John Kleyn's war-time roles.

This is what I discovered.

On 11 November 1939, Queen Elizabeth issued an appeal to all British women calling them to join the war effort. Phyllis had only recently arrived back in England, and it could be that this appeal strongly influenced her to join the war effort.

Also, in 1939 Britain was making plans to evacuate 2,500,000 children should hostilities begin. However, at that stage this did not apply to Paul, because he was at boarding school and only lived with Jim and his new wife (Caroline) during school holidays.

John would have worried about his parents and brother still living in the Netherlands. Although he could read the papers and listen to the radio for news of the war, much of this was also propaganda. He would have wanted first hand news and it was well known that the Dutch community in exile loved to socialise and catch up on news from the homeland; especially with people travelling from the Netherlands. There were a few pubs where the growing, but still small, Dutch community in exile would congregate – for example, the United Nations Forces Club and the Stage Door Canteen. Those places were havens for people wanting to hear news from Europe and they were known for being less concerned about class than the

British. People from all levels of Dutch society would meet and mix there.

It was around this time that John applied for British citizenship so that he could join the British Army. Phyllis and John may well have talked about this together. Events then moved remarkably quickly.

I found the best way to understand their lives was in the context of what was happening at the time. This involved a fascinating and focused historical journey into those aspects of WWII that they were part of.

Rubber Bridge at Crockfords

I was curious how Phyllis and John managed financially after they arrived back in England, as Phyllis could no longer rely on the income from breeding Dalmatians.

There were two stories that Phyllis told Paul after WWII suggesting that this was the time that Phyllis and John played rubber bridge at Crockfords Club. Rubber Bridge is a form of contract bridge that involves a high level of skill and can be played for serious money.

In 1958, Phyllis asked Paul during one of his visits to see her, how he learnt to play bridge. Paul answered he had read *Bridge is an Easy Game* written by Iain MacLeod (the same book I also used in learning to play bridge). 'Oh, he was one of my partners at Crockfords,' Phyllis had commented. MacLeod was one of Britain's brilliant bridge players who, before the war, lived off his gambling wins. Later, he became a Member of Parliament in both the Eden and MacMillan governments, and on 20 June 1970, was appointed Chancellor of the Exchequer in Edward Heath's Conservative government (1970–74).

Phyllis' association with Iain Macleod, as a bridge-playing partner, helps to explain a rather incredible family story that after the war she was able to raise a considerable sum of money while playing bridge.

Once again, the name that Phyllis mentioned was of someone who was really significant at the time.

Paul and I visited the club at its new location in Curzon Street only to be told politely and firmly that now it is only a gambling club and that no bridge, let alone rubber bridge, was played there any longer. Worse still, they had not kept any of the records and certainly no records dating back to before WWII. How sad. All that social history – lost.

I cannot help but wonder what grandmother and Phyllis' sister, Barbara, thought of her gambling. Was this one of the causes of her estrangement with them?

It was not long before the war took over their lives.

PART THREE
Phyllis's World War II Career

CHAPTER THIRTY-FOUR

Phyllis and John Kleyn – 1940–43

In January 1940, in the UK, more than two million men were called up to join the Army, Navy, or Air forces and casualties were beginning to mount. Captured German documents hinted at a plan to attack Holland and Belgium.

At Easter in 1940, on 23 and 24 March, Paul stayed with Phyllis and John in their tiny flat in Tottenham. One can imagine the tension in their home, because by April Dutch troops were put on full alert along the German border. Denmark and Norway fell.

John, a Dutchman, enlisted as a foreigner and volunteered for the British 'Pioneer Corps' on 29 April 1940. His army record states his 'Trade on Enlistment' as 'Clerk'.[10]

A few days later, on 10 May 1940, Germany invaded the Netherlands; despite the Netherlands declaring its neutrality. They had hoped that, as in WWI, the Germans would again respect their neutrality, but this was not to be. The two countries share a common border; and with so many people in the Netherlands having relatives living in Germany, they were shocked and traumatised.

Another major concern was what would happen to the royal family.

German parachutists landed near the royal palace in The Hague intending to kidnap Queen Wilhelmina. Her bodyguard and Prince Bernhard (Princess Juliana's husband) fought them off. Three days later, Queen Wilhelmina, Princess Juliana, Prince Bernhard, and their children and retinue escaped safely to England[11] and Queen Wilhelmina requested help from her cousin, King George VI.[12] And from then on, the Dutch presence in London became considerably larger. Soon after this, both Belgium and Holland surrendered to the Nazis.

A month after Germany invaded the Netherlands on 11 June 1940, Phyllis' army record shows she enrolled in the British Army; initially with the First Aid Nursing Yeomanry (FANY) and on 22 June 1940 with the Auxiliary Territorial Service (ATS). She enrolled as a driver in the 1st (London) Motor Company. Her army record shows she drove a 27 Humber for about seventeen months,[13] until November 1941. (See the Chronology of Phyllis's life and wartime activities in the Appendices, on pages 289–90.)

What did this mean? And what were FANY and the ATS?

FANY, the First Aid Nursing Yeomanry, was started in 1907 and was called yeomanry because its members (all women) were originally mounted on horseback. In WWI, they transported wounded soldiers from the frontline trenches in Europe in ambulances to field hospitals and set up soup kitchens. They were an elite group of women, often working in highly dangerous situations in Europe and became known for their bravery.

In WWII, FANY recruits were middle-class, educated women who had driver's licences and who could speak foreign languages. When the ATS started in 1939, FANY personnel from their driving sections were transferred into the ATS to create Motor Transport Companies. Few women in the 1930s had driver's licences, so they were a highly-prized, essential part of the War effort. They often were ambulance and staff car drivers, as well as truck drivers in convoys carrying supplies like ammunition, weapons, and food.

Paul showed Ian Bailey, Curator at the Adjutant General's Corps Museum, Phyllis' army record, and in his opinion Phyllis was most probably accepted as a member of FANY *prior* to joining the ATS, and that her role as driver of the 27 Humber would have involved driving high ranking officers to their meetings. Following her commission, she was most probably organising convoys distributing army supplies such as ammunition, weapons, and food. This fit the stories Phyllis told Paul about her wartime activities.

As I began to learn more about her role, I became fascinated by the ATS and the tasks that women performed in WWII.

Initially, Auxiliary Territorial Service officers were drawn from the aristocracy and the upper classes. It officially started in September 1938, before WWII. Perhaps the best-known member of the ATS during the war was Princess Elizabeth, now Queen Elizabeth II, who served as a Second Subaltern and was promoted to Junior Commander.

The authorities conscripted young men into the army from May 1939, that is, into paid service, but there was an initial reluctance to conscript women into the war – it was still felt that the role of women as wives and mothers took precedence. So instead, women were encouraged to volunteer either for the army, navy or air force, or to the Land Army growing food. The ATS was attached to the Army. By April 1941, the ATS was granted full military status and women received a commission the same as their male counterparts. However, they were paid only one-third of what their male counterparts received.

Recruiting sufficient numbers of women was a dilemma, and eventually conscription of women aged between twenty and thirty to the war effort was agreed to, on condition that there would be no compulsion to join for married women, or women with children aged fourteen and under living with them. Additionally, women, like men, could qualify as conscientious objectors and only volunteers would be asked to go into operative roles.[14]

It is interesting (but not surprising) to note the lack of equality in women's army commissions, despite the fact that women had been able to vote and be elected to parliament on the same terms as men since 1928.

Initially, women were in 'non-operational' support duties, such as clerks, cooks (4000 of them), store women, and orderlies. Then, this was expanded to include radar operators, ground gun crews, and military police. Eventually, nearly a third of the 210,000 recruits had qualified in a skilled trade, freeing up large numbers of male recruits to go to the front lines. There were 15,000 drivers, who besides driving vehicles for transport units, delivered vehicles such as tanks and supplies to units and ports all over Great Britain.[15]

A detail in the ATS uniform is mentioned here because it became

Boy, Ethel Hogg (Big Granny) and Phyllis Margaret, 1941

instrumental in dating the only photograph I have of Mother as a British soldier. The ATS uniform was a source of concern for the women, because it was regarded as 'stupid and inelegant.' One of the issues was the fact that the buttons fastened to the left in the male fashion. In 1942 the uniform was redesigned to button to the left and became more acceptable.

A month or so after we first met, my first cousin Jeremy gave me a photograph of Big Granny, Boy, and Phyllis. It was taken in 1941 because the jacket part of Phyllis' ATS uniform buttoned to the right in a male fashion. This provided confirmation of her membership of ATS and FANY. There is a FANY badge worn on the left sleeve of her uniform. It is interesting to note she positioned herself so that her left arm badge, with her helmet and gas mask, could be clearly seen. It was lovely to notice how she was standing – so upright and proud. I was also delighted to be able to recognise at least some of the subtle symbols of her time.

British and Dutch intelligence: an unfortunate legacy – 1940 onwards

At the start of WWII, the Dutch Queen Wilhelmina appointed her treasurer, van't Sant, as head of her intelligence services.[16] The British appointed RV Laming, a much respected, intelligent, Dutch-born and Dutch-speaking, English diplomat as the head of their intelligence organisation responsible for Holland, as in the N Section of the Special Operations Executive (SOE). Unfortunately, in 1916 in WWI, these men had taken opposite sides in an espionage case and from that time on were never able to forgive or trust each other. This was most unfortunate for both sides.

Most of the well-respected and high ranking Dutch citizens who escaped to England were monarchists and were immediately taken to Queen Wilhelmina and Prince Bernhard for de-briefing. They provided immensely valuable information about the German forces in Holland. They were called Engelandvaarders. MRD Foot, the leading expert on the SOE, wrote that Queen Wilhelmina referred these Engelandvaarders to van't Sant, who hating Laming, did not release to the SOE much of what he knew about the conditions in Holland.[17]

This unfortunate relationship between van't Sant and Laming had serious implications for the British in attempting to recruit quality Dutch agents to work for them.[18] For the next two years, British SOE's (Dutch) N section attempted to create a vigorous underground resistance in Holland, but found their attempts to recruit and train agents, send and receive intelligence, and dispatch supplies by aircraft to Holland often sabotaged.

So important were the Engelandvaarders to Queen Wilhelmina and Prince Bernhard that they turned their house in Eaton Square over to the Engelandvaarders, and set up their London Office at 77 Chester Square[19] in Belgravia, central London, very close to Buckingham Palace. Prince Bernhard took an active interest in the Dutch Intelligence Service and when he took on reorganising the service, he transferred it from 77 Chester Square to a house of their own, also on Eaton Square.[20]

This is significant because from at least 16 June 1944[21] Phyllis lived at 5 Little Chester Street, a five minute walk from Chester Square and Eaton Square. And so, Phyllis' proximity to the Dutch Intelligence Service headquarters would have been very convenient, if the story (told in a subsequent chapter) that she had been asked by Dutch Intelligence to go to Arnhem is to be believed.

Special Operations Executive (SOE) – July 1940

Soon after we started trying to retrace Phyllis' wartime career it was suggested that she was gathering information and could have been an SOE agent. So I started exploring the relevance of the history and purpose of the SOE to her story.

Paul and I visited the former training centre, now an SOE Museum at Beaulieu, in the New Forest, Hampshire in the UK. Many books have been written on the subject, particularly by SOE's historian and much respected author, Michael RD Foot, who recently died, but from whom I received some incredibly informative letters.

The Special Operations Executive was set up in July 1940 by Winston Churchill to support resistance groups in Europe to commit acts of sabotage against German occupation, and gathering information useful for war purposes.

The SOE was sometimes called the 'Baker Street Irregulars' (after their headquarters at 64 Baker Street) and operated with as many as 3000 agents across the world. The Nazis caught about 40 per cent of these and many met terrible ends.[22] It was separate from the armed forces and in direct competition with MI5 (British Security Service) and the Secret Intelligence Service.

Recruiting for the SOE was mainly through word of mouth and through pre-war friends or acquaintances, there being no other safe way to recruit. They in turn either brought in other friends or searched Military Intelligence for anyone who might speak the right languages.[23] At the commissioning of a female member into the Army, the commissioning board would have had a member from the intelligence community there to pick out those who had special skills, including any FANY member. (It is also well known that female members of SOE were given commissions in the FANY, but this was to enable them to hold a military rank and receive pay.)

Any prospective candidate would be invited to an interview at 64 Baker Street in London.

Training

Their role could include the use of weapons and explosives or coding and decoding of messages, signalling, and wireless telegraphy, and/or parachute training. It might involve a course at one of the training centres like Beaulieu in sabotage, lock picking, safe breaking, burglary, unarmed combat, silent killing, and living off the land while 'on the run'! According to posters in the Beaulieu Museum, agents were dispatched into enemy-occupied Europe by a variety of methods, often in fishing boats and submarines to nearby countries such as France, and by parachute drops to countries further away. Sometimes the RAF would help with transporting agents, and on those occasions agents would be driven by a FANY driver to Tempsford airport.

This was an intriguing piece of information, as John Leonard Kleyn's war role involved frequent visits to Tempsford airport. Phyllis was a driver from December 1941 to June 1942. Her letter requesting a compassionate posting was written from Castle Ashby, quite close to Tempsford airport.

The role of women in the SOE

The Geneva Convention stated that women could not bear arms in war. As WWII progressed, men who were captured in German-occupied countries were forced to work in the factories in Germany. This released German men so they could take part in their War effort. Consequently, women made up the majority of people in the streets. If men were seen walking anywhere, the Germans became suspicious.

As a result, the SOE considered women better suited than men for carrying messages and information. Once women had been vetted and selected, most female agents were transferred to FANY, because this was considered the best way round the Geneva Convention. The SOE used the ATS and FANY records to find women who spoke foreign languages and who had driver's licences. The SOE particularly selected women who could act independently and would be able to solve problems when they were on their own, for example, in a foreign country.

Phyllis' War Record – 1941

Phyllis and John's army records showed they took leave at the same time on two occasions: once as 'Compassionate Leave' in February and another 'Privilege Leave' in June 1941. Why did she take Compassionate Leave? Was this when John's brother died or when his parents went missing? Or could it have been when her brother, Boy, died?

In November 1941 she was posted to the ATS Officer Cadet Training Unit based in Egham, in Surrey. It had just opened in October 1941, so Phyllis must have been one of the first cadets to pass through. (This was accepted as one of the routes to becoming an intelligence officer, for example, to MI5.)[24]

Paul said that he believed most of the training program would have been at the Duke of York barracks in Central London. The whole process would have consisted of 28 days of basic training, including being kitted out with ATS uniform (which were still in short supply) and being taught skills necessary in the Army; such as use of gas-masks, first aid, basic drill and marching.

Being a member of FANY would have helped identify Phyllis for promotion or commissioning. The commissioning board would have had a representative from the intelligence community to identify those who may have special talents for their work.

At the end of the month Phyllis, recorded as Mrs Phyllis KLEYN (221999), became a commissioned (paid) officer of the ATS as a Second Subaltern – just like Princess Elizabeth. She could now hold a military rank and receive pay.

A notice was put into *The London Gazette* to this effect on 17 April 1942.

As part of becoming a commissioned officer Phyllis completed a second Form 199A. This was a resume of her life's experiences and became the single most important source of written information I have about her. This time her writing was clear and considered. It gives a wonderful insight into her childhood, her life growing up, and her life on the continent before WWII.

She recorded the finishing school she attended – *Le Couvent des Ursulines*, in Verviers in Belgium – and that she worked for the Bank of England for two years. She lived in France for a few years, had a French driver's licence, and lived in Budapest, Vienna and Holland, and travelled throughout Europe. She records she was good at games and climbed and skied in the Alpes Maritimes, Italy and Austria. She acted often with amateur societies, including the Bank of England Dramatic Society, taking the lead. She spoke French, German, Italian, and some Dutch. She was an excellent cook. It was not long before she obtained an army qualification to cook for 100 people, but according to her army record she only did this once. She got paid 2/6d extra, but perhaps she did not like it or it was incompatible with her being a driver.

It is interesting that she omitted that she played bridge and bred Dalmatians. I noticed some other small details. She weighed 124 lbs., which was about 8 lbs. less than when she completed the previous Form 144A eighteen months earlier. She also records her birthday in beautiful, clear writing – 18 July 1906.

John Kleyn's promotion to the Intelligence Corps

An entry in *The London Gazette* confirmed John Kleyn's wartime role in Intelligence: John Kleyn had been moved from P. Corps to become a Sergeant in the Royal Corps of Signals on 3 March 1942, and then on 28 November 1942, Lt JL Kleyn (227554) moved from R Signals to the Intelligence Corps.

The British SOE (Dutch) N Section – the start of *Englandspiel* and the capture of Huub Lauwers

The mistrust between RV Laming and van't Sant, and the consternation and despair in the Dutch and British intelligence agencies, was exacerbated by the enormous counter-intelligence operation launched by the German intelligence agency, the Abwehr, near the start of World War II.

Between August 1940 and October 1944 many British SOE (N) Section agents were parachuted into the Netherlands with the task of building a resistance movement.

On 6 March 1942, one of the secret agents, Huub Lauwers, was captured and over the few days following his capture, he was forced to send radio messages back to the British SOE (N) Section in London. Britain was not initially aware of this, but, from this date on, the wireless radio signals from the Netherlands could no longer be trusted. This became known in Germany as *Das Englandspiel* (The England Game), or *Unternehmen Nordpol* (Operation North Pole), a deadly game of cat-and-mouse by the Nazis. More than 50 of 59 British agents were captured. Almost all of the agents were subsequently executed at the concentration camp of Mauthausen. Although Huub Lauwers tried to warn the British that he had been caught by omitting his personal security code, secret agents and ammunition continued to be dropped into Holland. Within a month, by April 1942, the Germans controlled eighteen radio channels back to London, and wove a web of German deception that caused untold damage to the trust between British and the Dutch intelligence services.

Phyllis and John would have gradually become aware of agents not returning: and as time passed, the suspicions and tension between agents and the secret services would have built up significantly.

Phyllis' letter

And then, out of the blue on 1 April 1942, Phyllis wrote this sad, poignant letter, which was part of her War Record.

'J' Coy. M.J., A.T.S.
Castle Ashby
1st April 1942

Madam
I have the honour to request that my application for a posting to London be considered.

My husband is at War Office, Wing House, Piccadilly. We have been apart except for two months and leave, for two years. My husband has had no leave since last June and will have none for some time, as his work is difficult to leave.

I should greatly appreciate an office job, to enable us to live together.

My husband's parents were killed in Holland, one brother is missing from Singapore and his other brother is a surgeon in the Dutch Army in Java.

I am very interested in Transport, Recruiting, Advertising or Messing. Before going to the OCTU last November, I was driving a 27 Humber, on War Office Pool, for a year and a half. I was in the Bank of England before my marriage.

Thanking you, Madam, for the trouble I know you will take whatever the result may be.

I have the honour to remain Madam, your obedient Servant.

P. Margaret Kleyn

What a revealing and beautifully crafted letter. She would not have written it without a good reason for doing so and I could not help wondering why. Although she and John spent some leave together Phyllis writes that they had been apart for two years. That is a long period of time for any married couple to live apart.

Curiously, the letter was written on April Fools Day! Did this signify anything at the time? I have no basis to think so and consequently will take the letter at face value. My mother! She will always be an enigma! (A photograph of her handwritten letter can be seen on www.janeeales.com)

Another little detail is especially interesting: the address she gave for her letter was Castle Ashby.

Castle Ashby is still today one of the grandest castles in England, set in the heart of a 10,000-acre estate with a serpentine park designed by 'Capability' Brown, with 25 acres of extensive gardens combining several styles, including the romantic Italian Gardens, the unique orangery, and impressive arboretum. The garden is open for visitors and the castle is a much sought after venue for very exclusive weddings. The Castle Ashby wedding website is wonderful and well worth a visit.

Originally built as a Manor House in 1306, it was rebuilt by the Earl of Northampton into an E-shaped floor plan towards the end of the 14th century to celebrate the coronation of Queen Elizabeth 1st, who visited in 1600.

It is rather strange thinking of my mother staying there in April 1942 – it was such a beautiful place. After discovering that during WWII Castle Ashby was the centre of operations for the American Secret Service, serving as a training centre, it seemed natural to explore its proximity to the other well known centres where there were British secret agents. Then, the process of putting Phyllis's story together with John's story took a very exciting turn.

Castle Ashby is only sixteen miles from Bletchley Park, in Milton Keynes, Buckinghamshire, where, during WWII, the German secret military codes, Enigma and Lorenz, were deciphered and where Ultra intelligence was produced. Ultra intelligence, that is, ultra-secret intelligence and its role in Phyllis' life will come later. Castle Ashby and Bletchley Park are also within a reasonable driving distance of Tempsford airport, where secret agents left England to be dropped by parachute into Europe. I presume that Phyllis continued to be a driver and it is eminently reasonable to assume she would have driven and met many high ranking army personnel, secret agents, and pilots driving to and from the airfield and Bletchley Park.

Two months later, on 6 June 1942, her request was granted and she was posted back to No. 1 London District Group. But soon after that, she was posted to B Company LD (Long Distance) Group.

Ian Bailey, Curator of the Adjutant General's Corps Museum, said that at this time she would be no longer driving, but rather would be organising and managing convoys. She may have been based in London and able to live with John. Soon after this she worked for a Postal Services Section Platoon, involving the collection, distribution, and transportation of documents. Then, she went to Norfolk for three weeks to the Postal Services Section Platoon, spreading knowledge and information to country administrations. (She obviously liked Norfolk, as she returned there after WWII.) She moved around various sections within No. 1 London District for the next few months.

A curious tale – John Leonard Kleyn, the Army's pigeon expert

Frequently, while in libraries, and searching through history books, I would often look for Kleyn in the index at the back of the book just in case there was a reference to Phyllis or John. On one occasion, in a book by MRD Foot (Michael Foot) called 'The SOE in the Low Countries', I was absolutely amazed and delighted to discover a reference to a Capt. Kleyn, that is, Captain John Leonard Kleyn.

Foot describes the 'pigeon politics' associated with the rival army and RAF's pigeon services. Capt. Kleyn was the army's pigeon expert and he used to 'go to Stradishall or Tempsford (airports) to deliver pigeons just before agents left.'[25]

This was confirmed in *The London Gazette*, which records that John Kleyn was posted to the Special Section (Carrier Pigeon) on 5 May 1942.

Intriguingly, what did Foot mean when he referred to 'pigeon politics'?

This required a special visit to The National Archives at Kew, in London and as I retrieved the file and undid the ribbon, I could not have anticipated the treasure trove of information it would contain.

Amazingly, there was a manual with instructions on how to use pigeons for communications purposes and a string of recently released letters stamped 'Secret and Personal' about John Kleyn. The letters described his role in some detail. When secret agents planned to carry a pigeon with them, he would deliver the pigeons to the agents just before they left. He had to be present when the pigeons were attached to the agents. After landing safely, an agent would release the pigeon and it would fly back to their loft in England, carrying a message indicating his safe arrival. Pigeon post was considered much less dangerous than the use of wireless radio signals and was a crucial part of communications during WWII.

Soon after this, in August 1942, John's conduct was referred to as 'Very Good' and he was promoted to Acting Captain. In November 1942 he transferred from R. Signals to Intelligence Corp with the rank of T. Captain (Temporary Captain?).

This was the last entry in John's army record until January 1945, further supporting the family stories that from the Intelligence Corps he went on to serve in MI5 and MI6.

However, although there were no further activities listed in John's army record, higher up in the hierarchy, across a whole range of secret services, he was the centre of attention. And he was completely unaware of it.

Pigeon politics and confidential letters in
The National Archives at Kew, Richmond, Surrey.

There were a number of letters and notes from various secret military intelligence agencies referring to John Kleyn dating from 31 December 1942 to 29 January 1943.

The correspondence started because the new head of the Army Pigeon Service wanted Captain Kleyn's position and there were doubts about the discretion and efficiency of this new person. Several letters were exchanged, and then Major MA Frost from MI5 asked for a meeting. Subsequent to this, several letters were written in strong support of Kleyn continuing in this role.[26]

The letters describe how John was used by many secret services, i.e. MI5, SOE, MI14, and PID and SOE's (Belgian) T Section, and how the individual secret services did not know which other services were also using him. They also noted that while Kleyn was never told about the work of the secret agents, he nevertheless had 'a substantial knowledge not merely of the nature of our business but of the details and timings of coming operations...' and that they had 'been very satisfied with the discretion and services rendered by Captain Kleyn.' One letter of 6 January 1943 noted: 'No one could have been more helpful than he has been....'

Director of Counter-Espionage 2 (D/CE.2) wrote on 22 January 1943 that pigeons were used 'when they drop agents in parts of northern France that are within pigeon range of England. The pigeons are dropped either in small containers to a reception committee or in small containers attached to the chest of the agent. When agents are to be dropped with pigeons, they are previously taken to Wing House, Piccadilly, where Kleyn works, and are there given instructions in the art of using and feeding pigeons. Kleyn always goes to the airfield when pigeons are used in operations, as his expert knowledge is required up to the last moment.'[27]

These letters were written at a time when many agents were leaving for Europe and few were returning. Suspicions were building about what might be happening to them and this was clearly reflected in the tone of the letters.

One letter to D/CE (SOE's director of counter-espionage) from 'A/L' reads, 'Although he knows nothing of our organisation, officially his frequent visits to Tempsford make it obvious that he has deduced a good many of our secrets.' This writer was extremely concerned saying, 'It is most undesirable that any change should be made unless essential.... Our only argument for Kleyn's retention in his present job is that our security would be endangered by his removal.' There are some handwritten notes at the bottom of the letter: 'we must be careful' showing their concern.

In another letter to Major Frost from, concern is expressed that the officer employed by the Army Pigeon Service 'should be a man of the highest discretion, and if he hears anything that leads him to suppose that there are leakages, we should be very glad if he would let us know so that we may come and discuss it.'[28]

Phyllis' army record showed that she returned to London in June 1942.

It was at a time when John was meeting many secret agents and he was privy to the workings of various secret services and upcoming operations. He would have been aware of the build-up of tensions and suspicions between the various sections of the secret services. It is not unreasonable to assume that John would have noticed that a significant number of secret agents were not returning. It is also worth noting that John would have had at least two meetings with each of the secret agents who carried a pigeon. How did he feel when he never saw them again?

Phyllis spent eighteen months transporting high ranking officers between Castle Ashby, Tempsford airport and Bletchley Park. At around the same time, John was meeting secret agents from a number of intelligence agencies and assisting them with their pigeons. When Phyllis and John met they might well have talked in general terms about their work, and John certainly would have heard rumours about more than a few secret agents not returning after their missions to the Netherlands, often people he had known or worked with.

This must have been a nail-biting time for everyone involved in espionage. The outcome of WWII was not at all certain at this time.

In July 1942, Phyllis attended an ABCA (Army Bureau of Current Affairs) course. Ian Bailey commented that the ABCA course would have probably been to train Phyllis to lead discussion groups on Citizenship, the scheme being introduced in August 1941. I found this information fascinating.

By the time Phyllis could lead discussion groups, more than half of the army units were participating in ABCA education. These were compulsory, one-hour weekly discussions based on the idea that a citizen soldier must 'know what he is fighting for, and love what he knows'. If the soldiers knew what they were fighting for and something of the facts that underlay the crude news from the battle-fronts it was believed that this would sustain morale through such a lengthy war. Factual briefs were given to the leaders and grew to involve exhibitions, wall newspapers, educational films, special plays about current affairs, and 'Information Rooms' in many of the largest units.

The expectations of the platoon commanders were not only to educate, but also to get to know their soldiers. Often this resulted in political discussions in the most surprising places. There is an amazing story of one British officer in Germany who found himself sheltering in a barn from a mortar attack, only to find a corporal and 12 men earnestly discussing what should be done with the Germans after WWII.

I think it must have been in 1942 or early 1943 that John, while still married to Phyllis, met Diana, the young officer who would become his next wife. Diana's son, Peter tells the story that during the latter half of the war, after completing a mission in France, John flew back to London. He went into the office to write his report. He wrote his report in Dutch, and as he was short of time, he postponed translating it into English. When he returned, he asked for his Dutch report and it was given to him already translated into English. He was surprised; as few English people then spoke Dutch. He chatted with Diana, who had translated his report, and asked her out to dinner. That was the beginning of his relationship with her.

John clearly had quite a lot of contact with secret agents and knew officials in various secret agencies. So it was not surprising to learn that he became a MI5 agent. In fact, there was a precedent for this. Michael Foot referred to another pigeon expert becoming a MI5 agent. This was also substantiated by his son, Peter, who confirmed that his father later joined MI5, and then MI6, and quite frequently went to France and perhaps the Netherlands. Peter said when it was discovered that John could speak French, German, Dutch, and English he was asked to join MI6, which collects intelligence external to the UK. His role then was to fly there to recruit and encourage resistance workers in France.

He had one exceptionally memorable experience when his monoplane landed on pylons. Later, he used this experience as the basis of an episode he was asked to write for a popular BBC TV serial called 'Moonstrike', about the escapades of MI6 agents during WWII. It was filmed in the 1963.

John's engagement announced in The Times – 11 November 1943

Quite by chance, while searching The Times for entries headed 'Kleyn', I came across John's engagement announcement to Diana. I had not expected to find this, although I knew of his next marriage; and I felt terribly sad for Phyllis. I wonder how she discovered the news of his engagement. Did she see the announcement in *The Times* or did someone else tell her?

Phyllis is admitted to the ATS Reception Centre – 11 November 1943

Occasionally, information makes sense when one least expects it. The next time I looked at her army record, I noticed the entry about Phyllis being admitted to the ATS Reception Centre on 11 November 1943. Ian Bailey suggested the ATS Reception Centre was a sickbay attached to the ATS. This was the very same day of John's engagement announcement in *The Times*. This must be significant. My poor Mother.

Curiously, from 13 November nothing more was recorded in her 'Particulars of Service' until 2 July 1945, just before the end of the war when it was recorded that she was sick at home. Why is there a gap in her record?

There was one more significant entry, but this time, in John's army record.

16 December 1943

Five weeks after his engagement in November to his future wife, John's army record has the entry 'Granted Divorce – decree Nisi.' John married Diana a year later, on 27 November 1944.

Phyllis was single again!

CHAPTER THIRTY-FIVE

Phyllis' army record goes blank - 13 November 1943

November 1943 must have been one of the really low points in Phyllis' life. When her second husband, John, announced his engagement to his fiancée her relationship with him must have been well and truly over for some months, if not longer. He married his much younger fiancé a year later. Had she suspected in April 1942 that this might happen, when she wrote her letter asking to be posted back to London?

And then, soon after his engagement, she volunteered for a new role – possibly a very dangerous one. She could not have gone into an operational role without first volunteering for it. It may be true that her own personal events influenced her decision, but could it be that she was also persuaded by circumstances unfolding within the war and intelligence services themselves?

Phyllis was a commissioned officer in the ATS and earning a third of a male salary. There was no market for Dalmatians. Around this time her younger brother, Boy, while in the R.A.F. had been shot down and killed. That must have been an awful loss; Paul said she loved him dearly and that it was Boy who most probably helped her soon after she abandoned Paul. Unfortunately, her relationship with her mother and her sister, Barbara, was not good. Her mother had been diagnosed with cancer of the gall bladder and liver and was living with Barbara. She would die within two weeks of 13 November 1943. It would have been interesting to know whether Phyllis was able to visit her mother and make peace with her before she died. Barbara and her family were in no position to support Phyllis – and then there was eleven year old Paul! He needed her, but she was in no position to support him, let alone herself.

So, her personal life had fallen apart and WWII was going badly. She must have felt terribly alone – perhaps she felt that she had nothing to lose by choosing to volunteer for a dangerous role!

Phyllis' visit to Paul

Working out the time sequences of Phyllis' actions provided clues to her motivation. Paul's story about Phyllis' only visit to see him in the children's home had no specific time attached to it. Life for Paul in the children's home was bleak; he rarely saw his father and knew that his father felt Phyllis' visits unsettled him, so were discouraged. For that reason, Phyllis' visit to his children's home really stood out in his memory.

She arrived in a taxi, smartly dressed in uniform, one Friday evening and whisked him away to stay with her at a Taunton pub. The next day they picked mushrooms and berries together. This visit was extraordinarily significant for Paul and he remembers being extremely sad when she took him back to the children's home on Sunday morning, for that was when she needed to return to London.

Later, in 1958, Paul asked her why she had visited him at that particular time. She explained that she was planning to go on a dangerous mission, and as many people died doing such work, she decided to spend some time with him before leaving. She would have had to convince Jim and get his permission to visit Paul, and no doubt that would have been the argument to use.

The fact that many of the secret agents died was true. In fact, the SOE expected a 50 per cent loss of agents, and even more Dutch agents were killed.[29] It was clear she was well aware of the risks she was taking on.

I longed to identify which weekend Phyllis visited Paul, and wondered if the mushroom picking season could provide a clue. Apparently, autumn is the perfect time for mushroom picking, and I learnt that in 2013 fungi specialists offered expert mushroom picking walks through the beautiful woodlands around Taunton from the 3rd to the 17th November. These dates fit perfectly with Phyllis's release from the ATS Reception Centre on Saturday, 13 November. She might have visited Paul the very next weekend, and still have been just within the mushroom picking time.

What a find! I was elated for days.

Another important piece of information came about during a wonderful visit in 2005 to another new first cousin, Brian, the eldest son of my Aunt Barbara. He and his wife made us very welcome. They showed us their family tree, tracing their family roots to French noblemen who came with William the Conqueror! Crucially, he said he knew of my existence from his mother, my Aunt Barbara, who mentioned to him that Phyllis had given birth to a baby girl. I found this intriguing. He also said that he knew Phyllis was involved in intelligence for *some time* in WWII. But he was not able to be any more specific. He said that everyone knew she could not tell anyone about her work.

These statements provided further substantiation of Paul's stories about Phyllis' spying. I began to accept that perhaps these stories did have substance and should be explored more thoroughly. It showed that her visit to Arnhem as a secret agent was not a once-off, short-term event, but rather that her role was an ongoing one.

I wanted to understand more about the wider context in which she worked, about what the British and the Allies wanted to achieve, and how they wished to do it. And of course, I wanted to explore the connections that led to her work.

Plan Bodyguard

A Bodyguard of Lies by Anthony Cave Brown provided the best insight into Churchill's plan for the purpose and function of the British military intelligence.[30]

When he was young, Winston Churchill was very envious of others who had been to university, so at the age of 22, while in Bangalore in India, he began a process of self-education concentrating on history, philosophy, and economics. He writes: 'From November to May I read for four or five hours every day'[31] and this continued for at least the next two years. What is not so well known is that it was the tragedy of Gallipoli in 1915, for which he was the principal architect, that drove Churchill to further increase his understanding of battles and warfare. Churchill came to the conclusion that critical to winning battles was an unexpected event or strategy, whether it is 'in time, in diplomacy, in mechanics, in psychology'.[32]

As Hitler swept through Europe with his seemingly invincible Nazi army, Churchill knew that Hitler would be expecting the Allies to return to Europe. Churchill initiated a plan to convince Hitler that the Allied invasion into Europe would strike at a different time and a different place to what Hitler expected.[33] Churchill was convinced that there was one factor that could spell the difference between victory and defeat: surprise. Although the planning for D-Day began much earlier, it was in November 1943 (around the same time as Phyllis was planning to volunteer and when her war record went blank) that Churchill in Teheran famously remarked, 'In war-time, truth is so precious that she should always be attended by a bodyguard of lies.'[34]

With that in mind, 'Plan Bodyguard' was launched in December 1943 from the London Controlling Section (LCS), a secret bureau established by Churchill. Plan Bodyguard was an 'overall deception policy' of the high commands of America, Britain, and Russia to mislead Hitler about Allied strategy and tactics. It was within this context the various Allied secret services worked.

The weapons for this plan were called 'special means' – highly devious activities designed to keep the actual military operations secret and to mystify Hitler about the real intentions of the Allies. This applied particularly to the preparations and planning of what later became D-Day in the spring of 1944.[35]

Churchill planned for five main areas of activity, all of which were clandestine and secret.

MI6 and the Office of Strategic Services (OSS), MI6's American counterpart in Europe, were given the task of using both conventional and unconventional ways to discover the enemy's secrets and plans, the strength and disposition of the German forces, and most importantly, foreknowledge of Hitler's intentions. This involved gathering intelligence through conventional means, including reports from spies and informants, the censorship of foreign mail, interrogation of prisoners of war; as well as through two important unconventional means: Ultra, which will be described later, and *Schwarze Kapelle (black orchestra)* – secret information provided clandestinely by high ranking German officers.

MI6 and the OSS were also responsible for the second major area of secret activity: foreign intelligence, counter-intelligence and security. Activities designed to prevent and deny Hitler knowledge about Neptune, the forthcoming invasion at Normandy. This would necessitate destroying the German secret intelligence service outside Britain by MI6 and OSS, and MI5 inside Britain.

One gaffe, one mistake or act of carelessness could destroy the security of the closely held plans to launch D-Day. The safety of the whole plan seemed to be precariously balanced on a knife's edge. The main weapons were secrecy, intellect, stealth, menace, and deception, with only an occasional act of thuggery.[36]

It was in the third area of secret activity of special operations that violence occurred and the agencies involved here were the Special Operations Executive (SOE) and the American Special Operations branch of the OSS (SO). They were part of the planning of Plan Bodyguard in December 1943. Their task was to organise, equip, and guide the French resistance in their acts of sabotage against German lines of communication and transportation in an attempt to delay or disrupt their response to Neptune.

The fourth area of secret activity was political warfare in the specially-created British Political Warfare Executive (PWE), which, with the LCS (London Controlling Section), was instructed to launch a war of words against the Third Reich, driving a wedge between the Nazis and the people, by using elaborately sustained fictions designed to appeal to the selfish, disloyal, individualistic motives in the German soldier and citizen.

The fifth arena of covert activity was deception, the most secret of all the secret operations, in which the London Controlling Section was instructed to plant an unusually large number of bits of information, like puzzle pieces; which, when put together by the enemy, amounted to a plausible but false picture of the Allies' military intentions. This would involve double agents, whispers and rumours, sacrificial military operations, the creation of fictitious armies – in short, nothing would be overlooked to create a false impression of the location and timing of the Allied invasion.

Could *Englandspiel* have been part of this deception? And would John and Phyllis Kleyn have been caught up in this?

Anthony Cave Brown makes another interesting comment: 'Deception, like intelligence, was the pursuit of gentlemen.'[36] The men (and women) involved in this deception were united by one thing – class! It is interesting to speculate why this might have been so.

Clearly, Plan Bodyguard could help to explain some of the enigmas that occurred throughout WWII in relation to intelligence and some of the campaigns. Could there be, at that time, other big-picture aspects of the war that were impinging on British intelligence and possibly Phyllis' life?

Englandspiel

The story about *Englandspiel*, starting in late 1940, was briefly described in the previous chapter. How it was eventually unmasked is an extremely gripping story in itself. Two Dutch agents, Ubbink and Dourlein, captured in August 1943, escaped to Switzerland and eventually warned the British that the whole Dutch Resistance Radio Program had fallen into German control and that SOE Agents were being 'received' by Germans in Holland.[37]

When they returned to England two months later, Prince Bernhard learned that they were detained by the British on suspicion that they were German agents. The Prince said, 'I personally had shaken hands with those boys and said goodbye to them when they started for Holland.'[38] Only on the Prince's personal representation were the men released and could tell how their radio service had been infiltrated.

So it was that in November 1943, SOE reported to the Allied chiefs of staff that the organisation 'had been penetrated several months ago and wiped out'.[39]

But communication to Holland from Britain did not stop until Aprils Fools Day 1944, when a cheery, heavily ironic message came from the Germans acknowledging their part in the deception and saying 'so long.'

Despite this being tragic for the Allies, *Englandspiel*/Operation North Pole did *not* provide the Nazis with the information they most desired: the location and date of the planned D-Day invasion of France in Normandy.

New evidence came from recently-released British Foreign Office files from 1949 in The National Archives in Kew suggests that there was an official cover up of the full story. In fact, Pieter Hans Hoets, in his Dutch book, *Englandspiel ontmaskerd*[40] published in 1990, advocates that Dutch secret agents were pawns of D-Day and were deliberately sacrificed in Nazi-occupied Holland. He is a much revered Dutch war hero, knighted at twenty-six for his role in military intelligence.

The distrust that existed already with van't Sant and Laming was not helped by *Englandspiel*, making it much harder for the secret departments to cooperate.[41] This background of tension, anxiety and suspicion was clearly evident in the letters between the secret services such as MI5 and SOE, concerning John Kleyn's pigeon 'post' and his contact with secret agents.

It is still interesting to note that what the Germans had done for eighteen months to the SOE agents coming from Britain, the British did to the Germans. Every single German agent sent to England during WWII, bar one, was captured and asked to change sides. Those that did not change sides were tried and hanged.[42]

It was clear that Churchill's Plan Bodyguard and the secret services had a crucial role in WWII.

SOE's new recruitment drive

When it became known that the Dutch section of the SOE had been penetrated and 'wiped out' (November 1943), the SOE started a new recruitment campaign. This was just at the time Phyllis volunteered for a new role and it was from this date that there was nothing more recorded about her activities.

Cooperation between the British and Dutch secret services involved in the Netherlands

After the discovery of *Englandspiel*, cooperation between the secret services improved significantly. For example, when Ubbink and Dourlein were released, they told how their radio service had been infiltrated. Prince Bernhard said, 'Then, the balloon went up.' Hatch goes on to write, 'He (Prince Bernhard) and Colonel Somer force-fully fused the split between intelligence and sabotage.' According to Hatch, the Dutch Intelligence became the most efficient operation in any of the occupied nations.[43] This is supported by Foot, who said that after April Fools Day, when the Germans publically admitted to *Englandspiel*, a significant effort was made by both the British and Dutch secret services to cooperate – with a lot of success.[44] The Dutch were able to carry out their own security checks and Dutch officers were allowed to monitor British training courses and were informed of the precise orders given to agents. Also, all messages received from the Netherlands were shared between the secret services in their entirety.[45]

Distrust continues: Charles Lindeman's 'King Kong' Nazi double agent

However, things did not get better for long. Just as the intelligence services for the Netherlands began to work more efficiently, more secret agents began to go missing – 176 in total – and reports gradually filtered through that the Nazis were arresting them. Charles Lindemans, a member of Dutch Resistance, became a Nazi double agent in the summer of 1944 and was responsible for this tragic scandal.

It was while this was happening that Phyllis was asked to go to Arnhem.

CHAPTER THIRTY-SIX

Phyllis is sent to Arnhem

8–15 September 1944

In 1958 Paul visited Phyllis in East Anglia. He was twenty-six and this was the first time he had seen Phyllis since 1947. They talked constantly and after she told him why she visited him at the children's home in Devon in 1943, she told Paul another wartime story. When Paul told me her spying story, on the first day we met, I listened to him spellbound. I shivered. Goosebumps rose on my arms. I could not believe what I was hearing.

Phyllis related to Paul that early in September 1944, she was asked by the Dutch Intelligence Service to travel to Arnhem to assess and report on the German military presence there. She explained that she was chosen to go because of the distrust that existed between the Dutch and British intelligence.

She travelled to the Netherlands by submarine and was transferred to a fishing boat. On the fishing boat, she assumed the identity of a woman who was a cook. She explained that this had to be done carefully, so the Germans would not find her out. She changed all her clothes, including her underwear, and exchanged identity documents with the woman.

She told Paul that she stayed at the cook's apartment at a fishing port in the Netherlands and the cook stayed at her apartment in London. She gave the cook her keys to her home in Little Chester Street. She was given Dutch money and travelled around by train. She was to assess the German military presence near Arnhem, particularly around the bridges. Paul also said she took a letter, but was unsure who this letter was for.

She returned to England and visited her friend Daphne. She was invited to lunch with her friend Daphne and Daphne's husband, Lieutenant General 'Boy' Browning. He was the commander of the British First Airborne Division. Phyllis reported back about her trip to Arnhem and said that she found the 9th and 10th SS German Panzer Divisions at Arnhem near the bridge, but little German presence around the Nijmegen and Eindhoven bridges. She said that there were large numbers of tanks at Arnhem; the German soldiers there were resting and refitting.

Lieutenant General 'Boy' Browning listened very carefully to what she had to say. Then he told her that many thousands of men were ready for battle and that many previous campaigns had been cancelled. He explained that the Market Garden Campaign was to be launched in two days' time, and that it was too late to stop it.

Paul then told me a little about the Market Garden Campaign and advised me to read the book, *A Bridge Too Far*. It became clear after extensive reading that Phyllis' intelligence about the recently arrived Panzer Divisions in Arnhem was significant, and perhaps a *new* part of the same story, but one that had not been reported anywhere in the literature about the Market Garden Campaign.

Understanding the context of the Market Garden Campaign

In the six weeks that followed the success at the D-Day landings in Normandy on 6 June 1944, the Germans retreated so quickly that sixteen Allied campaigns designed to halt the Germans in their tracks had to be cancelled at the last minute.

Then, on 10 September, the plan to launch the Market Garden Campaign (all the others were called by different names) was announced and the launch date was to be 17 September 1944. A large number of airborne forces were to land by parachute and capture the series of bridges over the main rivers of German-occupied Netherlands. It was hoped that this would allow the Allies to cross the Rhine and advance rapidly into Germany by Christmas.

The book and film *A Bridge Too Far* told the story of how the strength of the German defences prevented the British 1st Airborne Division, headed by General 'Boy' Browning, from holding Arnhem bridge, and the British XXX Corps, travelling along the road on a one-tank-wide dyke, were unable to relieve them.

After hearing this story from Paul in 2005, one of the first pieces of research we did was to phone the Imperial War Museum to ask for advice. We were immediately asked whether we knew who Daphne was. We did not know.

'Oh,' said the representative from the Imperial War Museum. 'Daphne, who was the wife of General 'Boy' Browning, was Daphne du Maurier, the well-known British author.'

I was astonished. I knew that Daphne du Maurier was a famous author. How did Phyllis come to know her? Through her ballet lessons or perhaps her love of performance and theatre? Would Daphne have been to Crockfords? Was she truly a friend? I'll never know.

I asked Paul to describe Phyllis' mood after telling her story. Paul said that she seemed very sad that her intelligence did not change anything. She was especially sad because so many – some 17,000 – people were killed during the campaign.

I admire her courage and her willingness to risk her life.

However, I was still sceptical and very curious. I wanted to know more and to substantiate as much of this extraordinary story as I could. To do this, it would be necessary to dissect and attempt to understand the story in light of the wartime events that were happening at the time. Perhaps with that knowledge I would be able to establish whether it was plausible and possible.

CHAPTER THIRTY-SEVEN

Checking Phyllis's spying story

Paul was very patient with me. I often asked him to repeat a story just to check my understanding. I really appreciated his excellent memory and the steadfastness in his storytelling. When I badgered him with questions he did not elaborate on the story, but rather kept to what he knew and remembered, and trusted his memory. Time after time aspects of the stories I thought were just coincidental were found to be plausible and were often substantiated. That was most reassuring!

One of the real pleasures of my journey was discovering how kind and good natured Paul was and how generous the people we consulted with were with their time and in their efforts to assist us.

Phyllis' intriguing wartime career

One aspect of Phyllis' army record puzzled me for a long time. There were no more entries after 13 November 1943 about what she was doing, where she was, or which platoon or company she was part of, yet she continued to be promoted. Why? Her first promotion was on 11 July 1944 when she became Acting Junior Commander. Her second promotion was dated 11 October 1944[46] when she was promoted to Temporary Junior Commander, this being the male equivalent rank of Captain. Why was she promoted in both July and October?[47]

Both Sue Tomkins, Archivist to Lord Montagu of Beaulieu, and Ian Bailey, Curator of the Adjutant General's Corps Museum, independently suggested that the anomalies most probably meant that she was transferred to the Special Operations Executive or MI5.

They said that her skills and background matched the profile typical of the secret agents that were recruited to the SOE or MI5.

In 2009 I wrote to Howard Davies, who at the time was Head of Supervision and Selection at The National Archives, attaching copies of relevant pages from her army record and briefly relating what Sue Tomkins and Ian Bailey had suggested. His reply was: 'I think your analysis of your mother's service record is pretty strong – the gap from 1943 to 1945 is bound to be significant when coupled with the continuing promotions. We know that SOE, for instance, as a matter of routine gave promotions to personnel about to go behind enemy lines just before they went, because, if captured, it was felt that officers would receive better treatment than the rank and file. This may be what has gone on here, though whether SOE or another service, we cannot tell.'

I was genuinely pleased to receive this advice in writing from Mr Davies.[48] I felt much more confident that it was a reasonable assumption that she was involved with the secret service, possibly MI5 or the SOE.

Sue, Ian, and Howard all suggested that it might be difficult to find any further confirmation. For example, Howard Davies wrote: 'Thank you for this enquiry. I am afraid I have not had much success with it for you. I can confirm what you have found, that there is no SOE personnel record for your mother, Mrs Kleyn, held here – and that means that none will have survived. We now hold all the surviving SOE personnel records. It does not mean that she was not attached to SOE – we know for instance that a number of personnel records, including those of many female personnel, were lost in the fire at SOE's Baker Street headquarters at the end of WWII. But I have not been able to find any concrete evidence that she served with SOE.'

Only 13 per cent of the SOE personnel records survived. Phyllis' records were missing. This was disappointing and I was sad for days, until I remembered Sue Tomkins' reassurance that although proof may be hard to find, this did not mean she did not join MI5 or SOE.

Which organisation did she work for?

Phyllis told Paul she was asked to go to Arnhem by the *Dutch Intelligence Service*. We knew she spoke some Dutch, that she knew Europe well, that she was Dutch by marriage, and that her ex-husband was himself in close contact with Dutch secret agents.

But, in spite of this, I wanted to be able to reconcile the request coming from the Dutch Intelligence Service when she was a British soldier, a member of FANY and the ATS, and possibly a secret agent working for either SOE or MI5. Could it really be true?

Eventually, Michael Foot, an expert on the Special Operations Executive in the Netherlands, provided a possible explanation. After the deception of *Englandspiel* was discovered, the Dutch Intelligence Service (SIS) and the British (N Section of the SOE) actively worked closer together and were so successful that as early as May 1944 they cooperated 'so closely that they were almost two halves of the same organisation'.[49] This was also supported by Hatch, Prince Bernhard's official biographer.

Further evidence that the Dutch Intelligence Service, headed up by Prince Bernhard, was involved in the planning of the Market Garden Campaign with General 'Boy' Browning is contained in a transcript of a conversation on 19 March 1996 between Sir Brian Urquhart and Harry Kreisler at the Institute of International Studies, UC Berkeley; as a result of the publication of Sir Brian's autobiography, *A Life in Peace and War*.

He said, 'Our general, who was a very dashing figure called 'Boy' Browning, said to Prince Bernhard of the Netherlands that the Allied forces were going to advance into Germany over a carpet of airborne troops. And I (Sir Brian Urquhart) said to our chief of staff, "I wonder if they're going to be alive or dead airborne troops?"'[50]

Sir Brian Urquhart said his comments didn't go down well at all and he was sent away. Urquhart was the chief intelligence officer for the First Airborne Division and his role was to evaluate what the enemy reactions were going to be. He had reported to General Browning that there were two Panzer Divisions right next to where the British troops were to be dropped in Arnhem.

Now it seemed very plausible that Phyllis could have been asked by the Dutch Intelligence Service to go to Arnhem. Were there any more clues supporting this?

5 Little Chester Street – June 1944

We knew Phyllis lived at 5 Little Chester Street because Paul stayed with her there in 1946, when he met the Dutch General. But I still wanted to substantiate his story.

The earliest record of her address was found in an entry in John's army record: '5 Little Chester Street, SW 1: 16 June 1944 Phyllis Kleyn.' This same address is mentioned at her discharge from the army in 1945 and in the 1948 London Telephone Directory. So, it is reasonable to deduce that she lived there from at least June 1944 (before she went to Arnhem) to 1948 or 1949 (after I was conceived and born).

Phyllis told Paul she always wanted to live 'north of the river and south of the park' and Little Chester Street fitted the bill. It is a small Georgian terrace house in the fashionable suburb of Belgravia. She was able to keep her three dogs there and was pleased to live so close to Buckingham Palace and within easy walking distance to Crockfords Club, where she played bridge.

But imagine my surprise when I looked up the address of the Dutch Intelligence Service and found her home was, very conveniently, only a short walk from Chester Square and Eaton Square, where the Dutch Intelligence Service offices were located. Surely, this was more than a coincidence!

The statement that she was asked to go to Arnhem by the Dutch Intelligence Service now seemed even more plausible. Could there be any further links with the Dutch Intelligence Service?

*The author and her husband outside Phyllis's wartime home
5 Little Chester Street, Belgravia. SW1, 2005*

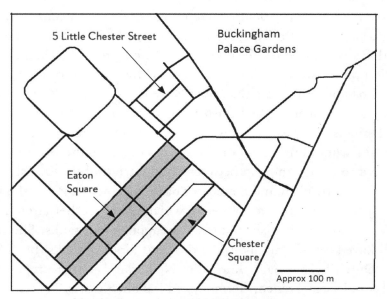

*Map showing proximity of 5 Little Chester Street, to
Eaton Square and Chester Square, London*

General Pieters

Paul's story about meeting General Pieters, while he was staying with Phyllis in 1946, now takes on much more significance.

We were astonished to discover General Pieters (not his real name) was very senior in the Dutch establishment, and that he was a military attaché at the Dutch embassy in London, continuing in this role until the end of WWII. He regularly visited the British War Office and, as such, he had a working relationship with General Eisenhower. I mention this here because I think Phyllis' association with this General adds to the assertion that Phyllis had a wartime connection with the Dutch. It also significantly strengthens the possibility of a connection with the Dutch Intelligence Service, and makes her story that she went to Arnhem much more plausible.

But why was Phyllis selected to do this piece of surveillance?

Why Phyllis?

I read that agents were almost always selected for the SOE through pre-war friends or personal acquaintances.[51] Did John Leonard Kleyn, while he was the British army's pigeon expert or when he started to work for MI5, bring Phyllis into contact with secret agents in the SOE N Section or during their social activities? Did they recruit her later? It's also known that from the end of November to early 1944 there was active recruitment for the British SOE to work in Holland.

Perhaps they asked Phyllis to go to Arnhem because the information she would bring might be more acceptable to the British – she seemed to bridge the gap between the Dutch and the British. She was British by birth and a member of FANY and the ATS; she had just spent six months at Chilwell, which, among other attractions, was a centre for British motorised weaponry and tanks. She may well have been taught about the different kinds of tanks there. She was Dutch by marriage, knew the Netherlands and Europe well, and could speak French, German, and Italian. She was an accredited cook, so when she assumed the cook's identity, she was credible. She was known among some of the high-ranking British people. Some could have been long-standing friends, some she might have met at Crockfords playing bridge, and others she may have known when she was a driver with the 1st (London) Motor Company ATS driving high ranking officials around.

How plausible was Phyllis' story?

When Paul first told me that Phyllis travelled by submarine and transferred to a fishing boat on her way to Arnhem, I was astonished and very sceptical.

My doubt increased very early on in my research when a staff member from the Imperial War Museum, during a telephone conversation, doubted this could be a credible way to reach the Netherlands. I was worried. If one aspect of the story was not plausible, how could I be certain the rest of the story was valid?

But I need not have worried. A few weeks later, Paul and I spent a lovely day at Beaulieu visiting the SOE Museum. Beaulieu became known as 'The Finishing School for Secret Agents' and their poster exhibition with photographs confirmed without doubt that travelling by submarine and connecting with a fishing boat was one of the methods used by the SOE to land secret agents in Europe. We checked this again with Sue Tomkins, who also confirmed this.

The practical aspects of assuming the cook's identity fascinated me. Did she look like her? Did she have a false passport? Did she get seasick? Paul said she exchanged even her underwear. They must have been of a similar size; otherwise, their clothes might not have been able to be exchanged. In the film, *Black Book*, the Gestapo inspected the underwear of the secret agents they caught. If Phyllis had been wearing British-made underwear, she would have been revealed to be a spy.

Another question that puzzled us for a long time was how she returned to London after her trip to Arnhem.

Secrets, Spies and Spotted Dogs

How did Phyllis return from Arnhem?

On one of my trips to The National Archives at Kew, Richmond, Surrey, I discovered a tiny piece of information, but a real gem. In the substantial British Foreign Office Records Index, there was a single entry with a file reference to correspondence in 1944, which, according to the Archives librarian, has since been lost. I checked this on three separate occasions with no luck, but the file reference is there, as large as life.

The entry was: 'M Kleyn. Priority air passage from Stockholm to the UK'.

At first I was not certain this referred to Phyllis Margaret Kleyn. Perhaps there was another person who could be called 'M Kleyn'. But, after checking through *The London Gazette*, where everyone who signed up to serve is listed, plus telephone books and *The Times*, there did not appear to be any other person with the same name. Eventually, I concluded that she was the only M Kleyn in the British Army at the time.

Hers would not have been the only request for a flight from Sweden to the UK. There is another file reference, this time to Prince Bernhard, who was very involved in the Dutch Intelligence Services. This referred to 'Prince Bernhard's arrangement for transport of Dutch flyers from Sweden' in 1944.[52] Could he have written a similar letter asking for permission for Phyllis to have a seat on a flight from Stockholm as a matter of priority? She did go to the Netherlands, so it is conceivable that it was written by a Dutch official. As the entry was in the British Foreign Office Records, it seems logical to deduce that this was a request to the British Foreign Office by a foreign government (that is, the Dutch government).

This is an independently documented piece of evidence of her involvement during WWII, separate from her army record and unrelated to Paul or any other family stories. It also suggests that her activities were being directed by a foreign government. It also would be reasonable to assume that obtaining permission for her to fly from Stockholm to England would have taken at least a few days to plan, organise, and receive approval. This raises the question whether this was done specifically for the trip from Arnhem or whether she was involved in this role over a longer period. Either way, it is a good bit of evidence and I was absolutely delighted to find it.

However, I wanted further substantiation that there was indeed an escape route from Arnhem.

Evidence of this came through a wonderful Dutch friend, who on my behalf read and translated some Dutch books, and started an amazing interchange of correspondence in Dutch with Pieter Hans Hoets, an eminent Dutch war veteran.

Pieter Hans Hoets was knighted by Queen Wilhelmina at twenty-six just after WWII. He qualified in law at Yale University and became a distinguished attorney in America and a respected author. (It was through his efforts that more than $630 million of the assets were returned to the Philippines in what the *Guinness Book of Records* has called 'one of the greatest thefts of history' by the Marcos family.)

In his book, *Vrijgevaren!* he describes how in 1944 hundreds of American Air Force crews waited in a camp called Falun in the Netherlands, before taking refuge in Sweden after their bombers had been damaged. The Americans put pressure on the Swedes, and in an amazingly short time, enormous bombers, Consolidated B-24 Liberators, called 'Black Birds' started transporting thirty stranded Americans at a time to Scotland. This was on a completely different scale to the single passenger that a RAF Mosquito would carry once in a while.[53]

Pieter Hans Hoets goes on to write that Prince Bernhard had a meeting with General Hap Arnold, Commander of the American Air Force, and managed to arrange, on a short-term basis, for all Dutch volunteers in Sweden to fly with the Americans to Scotland.[54]

Finally, on 13 October 1944, Pieter Hans Hoets himself was allowed to fly to Scotland in one of these Black Birds with twenty-nine other so-called Dutch volunteers.

During the war, Pieter Hans Hoets worked with MI5, MI6, and the SOE, and is the first person I have had direct contact with who actually lived and worked in WWII at the time and in the areas that are connected with Phyllis' story. It was he who suggested I read *Bodyguard of Lies* by Anthony Cave Brown, which gives real insight into Churchill's purpose for the British intelligence services.

Pieter Hans Hoets was extremely helpful, especially in relation to Phyllis' possible return from Stockholm. In an email to me, he wrote saying that in 1944 he 'was [serving] in Stockholm with the staff of the Bureau of Information. There was indeed an air bridge to Scotland via the RAF and the United States Air Force with whom we worked closely.'[55]

He went on to write: 'Of Margaret Kleyn's eventual passage I, however, know nothing.'

I was very pleased to know for certain that an air bridge did exist from Sweden and it was being used for Dutch volunteers to fly to the UK.

Phyllis' War Medals

I wrote to the War Medal Office asking if Phyllis had been awarded any medals and whether any had been claimed. I was delighted one day when a small rectangular box wrapped in brown paper came containing her two war medals. The medals remained unclaimed for more than 50 years! Why did she not collect them? I did not mind – it felt like a gift from her and I was thrilled!

She was awarded the usual War Medal given to everyone who served full-time in operational or non-operational service from 1939 to 1945 as well as The Defence Medal given to members serving for six months in specified non-operational areas subjected to *enemy air attack or closely threatened*. Did she become eligible for this as a result of her trip to Arnhem or could she have been subjected to enemy attack or closely threatened in other intelligence missions?

In the letter that came with her war medals she was referred to as Junior Commander, so she would have been promoted from being Temporary Junior Commander, as indicated in her army record.

This was the female equivalent of Captain in the men's army rank structure as organised from July 1941. Junior Commander in the ATS was the rank given to Princess Elizabeth in WWII.

Piecing together the story of her life out of these few fragments of information makes me realise how much she could have told me and the wealth of information that would not have ever been recorded in her army record.

I feel a profound sense of loss.

221999 JNR CMDR PM KLEYN ATS, War Medal and Defence Medal, 1939-1945

CHAPTER THIRTY-EIGHT

Solving the logistical issues

The timing of Phyllis' story about her visit to Arnhem troubled me. If the Market Garden Campaign was only announced on 10 September, how could it have been possible to organise Phyllis' trip to Arnhem and back at such short notice?

After the Dutch made the decision to send someone to Arnhem, Phyllis would have had to be asked, and then she would have needed a few hours to be briefed and to prepare herself for the mission and her home for her absence.

Her place on the submarine would have had to have been booked, the owner of the fishing boat contacted, and arrangements made about where to meet on the ocean. I imagine (but do not know) that the submarine and fishing boat would most likely have met under cover of darkness.

And how did they find the Dutch cook? The underground resistance movement or a trusted person in Holland would have had to be asked to find a cook – and then the cook would have had to be asked, and then briefed in Holland. She would have to be someone who looked like Phyllis and who wore the same size clothes. There would have had to be discussion about passports – and a copy of the cook's passport would have had to be forged with Phyllis' photo in it and given to her before she landed in The Netherlands. Paul mentioned that she was given money so that she could travel by train. I wonder where the fishing boat left her and how she travelled on from that point. Could she have been met by a member of the Dutch resistance?

Her return trip would have had to be organised ahead of time. A letter would have to have been written seeking permission from the British Government for the agent (Phyllis) to fly from Stockholm to the UK. Obtaining a written reply would have taken some time, at the very least, a few days.

The latest she could have left for Holland would have been on Sunday, 10 September, on the day the Campaign was announced. But I do not think there would have been enough time to arrange her trip, if the decision for her to go was made on the day it was announced.

The decision must have been made earlier, but how would this have been possible?

A look at what was happening behind the scenes at the warfront might give some explanation.

There was no doubting the willingness of the Dutch to contribute to British Intelligence. There was great suffering in The Netherlands and the Dutch community in London was extremely anxious that the Allies defeat the Nazis and free their people as soon as possible. But as days passed, they were totally perplexed by the Allies who instead of advancing quickly, slowed down, and eventually stopped. The Allied supply lines were overstretched and petrol, food, and other supplies dwindled and ran out.

This could not have happened at a worse time. The Germans, after the successful D-Day landing, were in such a rapid retreat that at least sixteen Allied plans to land behind German lines to cut off their retreat were cancelled at the last moment.

The Allies were euphoric, believing the Germans were close to defeat. The Dutch understood that intelligence had to be constantly updated and they tried to provide the Allies with advice and guide the Allied plans, but found it difficult to be heard.

An example of this was when Prince Bernhard and his retinue travelled to Brussels to meet with Montgomery on the morning of 7 September 1944.

Prince Bernhard's visit to Field Marshall Montgomery

Cornelius Ryan's well-known book, *A Bridge Too Far*, describes the meeting between Montgomery and Prince Bernhard in detail which is confirmed in Prince Bernhard's official biography written by Alden Hatch. It provides intriguing background to what was happening at the time.

Immediately after collecting valuable intelligence about Dutch resistance to the Germans in Holland, Prince Bernhard, with some close advisers, decided to fly to Amiens in France on the evening of 6 September, in preparation for meeting with Field Marshal Montgomery the next morning in Brussels. Bernhard recalled that 'He (Montgomery) had a lot on his mind' and obviously 'was not happy to see me'.[56]

Bernhard fully appreciated Montgomery's renown as the greatest British soldier of WWII and how this had made him the 'idol of millions of Britishers'. Once there, Bernhard reviewed the situation in Holland as reflected in the underground reports and advised that 'The Germans are running out of Holland like madmen'.[57]

Montgomery retorted, 'I don't think your resistance people can be of much use to us.' Then went on to say, 'Just because the Dutch resistance claim the Germans have been retreating from 2 September doesn't necessarily mean they are still retreating'.[58]

I thought this was a particularly strange comment. Did General Montgomery know something Prince Bernhard did not know? Bernhard had to admit the retreat was 'slowing down' and there were signs of re-grouping. He knew the situation changed daily. Still, in his opinion, there was a valid reason for an immediate attack.[59]

Prince Bernhard was startled by Montgomery's response and realised that he apparently 'did not believe any of the reports that came to me from our agents in Holland.'[60] 'But,' as he told Cornelius Ryan, 'in this instance, I knew the Dutch groups involved, the people who were running them, and I knew the information was indeed, correct.'[61]

Eventually, Bernhard asked Montgomery why he couldn't attack right away and Montgomery admitted that his forces had outrun their supplies. His tanks had no petrol and were running out of ammunition. This astonished Bernhard. He was anticipating the liberation of Holland within a matter of days.[62]

Bernhard said later, 'We had absolutely every detail on the Germans – troop strength, the number of tanks and armoured vehicles, the position of anti-aircraft guns – and I knew – apart from immediate front line opposition, that there was little strength behind it. I was sick at heart, because I knew that German strength would grow with each passing day...Nothing I said seemed to matter.'[63]

Montgomery said, 'I am just as eager to liberate The Netherlands as you are, but we intend to do it in another, even better way.' He paused, and then admitted that he was planning an airborne operation to land near the bridges ahead of his troops.

All this is based on information that is publically available – and no doubt there will be more in private, personal archives. Nevertheless, one cannot help but wonder whether Prince Bernhard and his generals came away from this meeting seriously concerned. It appeared that Dutch intelligence was being ignored, as well as the advice of Dutch military experts about the terrain.[64]

Perhaps it was the outcome of this meeting with Field Marshall Montgomery that spurred the Dutch to do whatever it took to continue to keep providing up-to-date intelligence – information that would be acceptable to Montgomery and would hopefully persuade him to rethink this strategy.

If Phyllis' trip was planned after the meeting between Prince Bernhard and Field Marshall Montgomery on 7 September 1944, they would have had three extra days to plan. The timing of her trip would then become entirely plausible.

But there was one other question: Did General Montgomery know something Prince Bernhard did not know? He would have been aware of information supplied by Ultra that he might not have wanted to disclose to the Prince. Could it be that Prince Bernhard was not aware of Ultra? Ultra was ultra-secret – and an indispensable part of Plan Bodyguard.

CHAPTER THIRTY-NINE

The dissemination of military intelligence

Role of Ultra Signals Intelligence

Ultra was a well-kept secret until 1974, when F.W. Winterbotham published *The Ultra Secret*. It was the British code name for the information received through the interception and decoding of German signals and instructions to the German army. It was so important to WWII that Churchill famously said after the war: 'It was thanks to Ultra that we won the war.' This intelligence centre was located at Bletchley Park, in the town of Bletchley, in Milton Keynes, Buckinghamshire, England.

Ultra was one of Churchill's unconventional 'special means' referred to earlier that was employed by MI6 to obtain knowledge about the enemy. It was the most significant source of intelligence for much of WWII and in order not to warn the Germans that their code had been broken, a decision had been made not to make the information available to ranks below army headquarters. Therefore, only a select few top personnel (for example, General Eisenhower, General Patton, and Field Marshall Montgomery) knew about Ultra and received reports. So valuable was the information received that it was resolved not to act upon it until the same information had been received from another credible source. Thus, a secondary source of information about any wartime event was essential before a decision could be made to act!

This meant that the role of intelligence confirming Ultra information became a crucial pre-condition to being able to act on intelligence Ultra provided.

On 5 September 1944 the Allies' high command would have been aware, through Ultra, of the Nazi instructions to the 9th and 10th

Panzer Division to rest and refit in Venlo-Arnhem-s' Hertogenbosch.[65]

This was two days before Prince Bernhard's meeting with Montgomery and five days before the announcement of the Market Garden Campaign.

This might explain Montgomery paying scant attention to Prince Bernhard's intelligence, and his saying, 'Just because the Dutch resistance claim the Germans have been retreating from 2 September doesn't necessarily mean they are still retreating.'[66]

Hatch, Prince Bernhard's biographer, does not mention Ultra or that Prince Bernhard was aware of Ultra. Indeed, his astonishment that his up-to-date and reliable intelligence was not being listened to might imply that he was not aware of it. Clearly, he was alert to the dissonance in the information that he and Montgomery were privy to.

Paul thought that General Pieters, who he met at Phyllis' home in 1946, might have been a very senior military man in the Dutch Forces. We subsequently confirmed this – he represented the Dutch Forces at very senior levels and attended meetings with General Eisenhower, so he would have understood how intelligence was circulated through the ranks. Perhaps as a result of Prince Bernhard's meeting with Montgomery, plans were made to disseminate the intelligence to as many levels of the military hierarchy as possible, particularly to decision-making leaders.

Is there any evidence of this in relation to the intelligence gathered by Phyllis?

Tracking the information discovered by Phyllis and how it was used

My next step was to see if I could track down where the information about the 9th and 10th Panzer Divisions resting and refitting near Arnhem came from and where it was received. As I read and re-read the literature, I looked specifically for the sources of the intelligence concerning the Panzer Divisions seen in Arnhem. Gradually, I became aware that Phyllis had direct and indirect links with the way the intelligence about the 9th and 10th Panzer Division was distributed to the different levels of the Allied forces, from SHAEF (Supreme Headquarters, Allied Expeditionary Force) downwards.

This was very curious. What did it mean?

Through Ultra intelligence, it was known that on 5 September 1944 the Nazis had given the instructions for their 9th and 10th Panzer Divisions to rest and refit near Arnhem. Phyllis' intelligence confirmed that this instruction was obeyed; so theoretically, her intelligence was a credible secondary source of information that allowed the Allies to take action without threatening the Ultra source of intelligence.

This intelligence was known at various levels. Examples are given below.

First, Lieutenant General 'Boy' Browning, the husband of Phyllis' friend Daphne (Daphne du Maurier) acknowledged that he had received a report about a Panzer group around Arnhem. Hibbert wrote: 'General Browning, having heard a report that a Panzer battle group, which was driving towards Germany to refit had been halted in Holland, referred the matter to 21st Army Group (headed by Field Marshal Montgomery). Browning was assured that the battle group was 'no longer a threat' on the British front.'[67]

Could this have been Phyllis' intelligence? General Browning did the right thing. After referring the matter to his superiors, General Browning could legitimately not be held responsible for ignoring the warning.

Second, the intelligence officer, Major Brian Urquhart of British Airborne Corps, which was headed up by General 'Boy' Browning, claimed he had received similar information from the Dutch Resistance via Second Army (headed by Lieutenant-General Dempsey) and the *Dutch Liaison Officer* at the Corp's Headquarters.[68] Could this have been General Pieters?

In any case, on 12 September, Urquhart had requested air reconnaissance of the Arnhem area. When General Browning was shown the photographs of the tanks parked under trees, he was reputed to have said, 'I wouldn't trouble myself about these if I were you.'

Subsequently, Urquhart was ordered to go on leave due to 'nervous exhaustion'.[69] This report was the source material for the film, *A Bridge Too Far*.

Third, yet another report stated, 'Dutch agents confirmed the large concentration of armour in the Arnhem area'.[70] This could have been provided by other Dutch agents. However, it would have been possible for Phyllis, when she reached Stockholm, to telephone or send a telegram to the Dutch Intelligence Service in London; thus allowing the Dutch Liaison Officer at Corps Headquarters to immediately alert those involved with planning the campaign.

Fourth, in Prince Bernhard's authorised autobiography, Hatch wrote that Prince Bernhard spent time with Montgomery for three days before the battle, that is, from 7 September. During that time, Bernhard would have attempted to provide intelligence from Phyllis and perhaps also from other sources from the front line in the Netherlands, as well as give advice about the conditions of the terrain in Holland.

The reaction he received from Montgomery was not reassuring. Hatch wrote that Prince Bernhard said, 'Monty did *not* believe the *absolutely accurate* information I gave him about the number and disposition of all the German troops in the area.' Hatch went on to write: 'Prince Bernhard did not receive any credit for the brilliant intelligence work of his agents at Arnhem.'[71]

Further, Montgomery seemed determined to ignore Prince Bernhard's comments about the terrain. Hatch quotes Prince Bernhard as saying: 'Monty *absolutely* would *not* believe us. He would not believe that the tanks could not go alongside the road through the soft, swampy fields and over the dykes of Holland as they could go through the firm fields of France and Belgium.'[72] Bernhard knew that this would be a one-tank-wide Allied front.

Fifth, news of the 9th and 10th SS Panzer Divisions near Arnhem reached SHAEF, which caused SHAEF's Intelligence Chief, British Major-General Kenneth W Strong to bring it to the attention of American-born Lieutenant-General Walter Bedell Smith, Eisenhower's Chief of Staff.[73]

General Walter Bedell Smith was 'destined to become one of Prince Bernhard's closest friends'[74] and may have heard the intelligence from the Dutch Liaison Officer at SHAEF (General Pieters, perhaps?) or from Prince Bernhard himself.

Bedell Smith was reported to be 'alarmed' and thought that the First British Airborne Division due to land at Arnhem 'could not hold out against two armoured divisions'. He recommended to Eisenhower that another airborne division be added to reinforce the current plan. Not wanting to challenge Field Marshall Montgomery's authority and not wanting to cancel yet another campaign at the last moment, Eisenhower suggested Bedell Smith fly to Brussels and talk with Montgomery directly. Bedell Smith took up this suggestion, but Montgomery 'ridiculed the idea' of taking another division and waved Bedell Smith's objections 'airily aside'.[75]

Bedell Smith reportedly said, 'At least I tried to stop him, but I got nowhere.'[76] Despite all those with a decision-making role being aware of the Panzer Divisions being at Arnhem, the information was not passed down to the next level of the hierarchy.

For example, Lieutenant General Horrocks, who directly reported to Montgomery, said, 'I had no idea whatever that the 9th and 10th Panzer Divisions were re-fitting just north-east of Arnhem, nor had Dempsey (Lt-General Dempsey of the Second British Army also reporting directly to Field Marshall Montgomery).'[77]

Nothing was allowed to conflict with the prevailing optimism about the retreating and defeated Germans. This campaign was not going to be allowed to be cancelled. All the while the Dutch intelligence community, who knew what was happening, must have been extraordinarily frustrated, fearful, and in despair. The Market Garden Campaign went ahead with devastating consequences.

It would appear the Dutch distributed the information in a deliberate and planned way to the key people at the different levels of the Allied command structure. The key people who could have distributed the intelligence included Prince Bernhard, a Dutch 'Liaison Officer' – perhaps General Pieters, the American General Bedell Smith to General Eisenhower, and Phyllis to General 'Boy' Browning; not to mention Browning's intelligence officer, Major Brian Urquhart.

There is no doubt that Phyllis' intelligence was of strategic importance and that she played an important role in bringing that intelligence to the notice of General 'Boy' Browning. It also provided a credible secondary source, which technically would have made it possible for the Allies to act on if they wanted to. Was this a function of history and the lack of trust between the Allies and the Dutch intelligence services or was this more due to bigger forces at play within the higher echelons of the Allied forces?

The failure of the Market Garden Campaign was an immense disappointment. Allied forces suffered more casualties in the Market Garden operation than in the mammoth invasion of 160,000 Allied troops on D-Day in Normandy; which in the 24 hour period following 6 June 1944 amounted to 12,000. In the nine days of Market Garden, the casualties, including those killed, wounded, and missing, amounted to more than 17,000.[78] No one quite knows how many Dutch civilians died or were injured. The dream of ending WWII by Christmas did not materialise and the horror of the 'Hunger Winter' is still remembered with great sadness. More than 16,000 people died from starvation in one of the most fertile countries on earth.[79]

Many authors have written about why this happened and crucial factors often mentioned are the failure to heed the intelligence about the 9th and 10th SS Panzer Division resting and re-fitting in Arnhem and the failure to make use of sound Dutch information and advice about the best approach to Arnhem.[80]

I was amazed to learn about these events and Phyllis' involvement. I was intensely proud of her – and sad at the outcome. But I cannot resist sharing the statement Major-General RE Urquhart wrote in his book, *Arnhem*:

None of the operations that were planned before Market Garden came to anything: two of them might have been utterly disastrous. They had the effect, however, of sharpening our state of readiness and advancing our planning to a fine art, and also of creating a common attitude of eagerness to be off. By September 1944, my division (the British First Airborne Division) was battle-hungry to a degree which only those who have commanded large forces of trained soldiers can fully comprehend. In fact, there were already signs of that dangerous mixture of boredom and cynicism creeping into our daily lives. We were ready for anything. If there was a tendency to take light-heartedly the less encouraging factors, and even the unknown ones, it was understandable. Certainly it is impossible to over-emphasise the ultimate significance of this processing of operations that never were. In the cold after light the historian and military critic has his licence to juggle the arithmetic equations of battle. Only the participant can adequately apportion the invisible factors, such as the effects of the sixteen cancelled operations in a row.[81]

This gives some sense of the tragic dilemma the military leaders faced at that time.

I wonder how Phyllis reacted, as the Market Garden Campaign was launched on 17 September and the reports trickled in of the catastrophic failure it turned out to be; as men in parachutes landed in the fields so close to where the 9th and 10th Panzer divisions were waiting.

If only I could have talked with her.

It is interesting that I could find little or no mention of the role the Dutch played in providing relevant and valuable intelligence in the Market Garden Campaign in any English history books about WWII.

PART FOUR

Phyllis's Life After World War II

General Pieters and
Dick Barton Special Agent 1946

Paul hovered expectantly near the wireless set on the mantelpiece in the sitting room. It was Friday evening, and the first night of his long awaited mid-term break from boarding school.

He was pleased as punch to be staying with Phyllis, his mother; although he saw her rarely and had not visited her in this house before. However, he knew her well enough to know that this small Georgian terrace at 5 Little Chester Street, Belgravia, within a stone's throw of Buckingham Palace, fulfilled a long-held dream of hers. She had always yearned to live 'north of the river and south of the park' – one of her favourite sayings.

It was a wonderful location and she had asked if he would like to take her four Dalmatians for a walk in Hyde Park the next morning.

Phyllis was upstairs preparing to go out for dinner as he eagerly anticipated listening to the next episode of his favourite radio serial – 'Dick Barton Special Agent.' It was the BBC's first ever radio serial and lasted only fifteen minutes, starting at 6.45pm every evening Monday through Friday. At school, he and the other boys had made a habit of listening to it ever since it had started a few weeks earlier on 7 October.

Just as he moved his chair closer to the wireless set, his mother stepped carefully down the stairs and into the sitting room.

Phyllis smiled at Paul. She would have noticed how tall he was for his fourteen years and how his short dark brown hair framed his large brown eyes. He had a typical boy's grin, with the edges of his mouth turning down lightly. She clearly felt good and was wearing a skirt and jacket and high heels. An evening coat and a clutch bag hung over her left arm.

'How do I look, Paul?' she asked.

Paul was flattered at her asking for his opinion. As a young lad, this was a first. Never having been asked to give an opinion before about the way his mother dressed, he wanted to make an impression.

Paul replied, as confidently as he could, 'Mother, you look lovely, but I do think you should wear red lipstick.'

Looking directly at Paul and standing as straight and tall as her small frame would allow, Phyllis' radiated assured self-composure. She spoke slowly and confidently, saying, 'If I were a flower girl going out with an author, perhaps then I would wear red lipstick. But, as I am a lady going out with a general, I need to be more discreet.'

That left Paul speechless. She put her coat and bag down on the couch and disappeared up the stairs again. At that moment, the radio serial started and Paul became engrossed.

Suddenly, a loud rat-a-tat tat on the front door interrupted his concentration.

Phyllis rushed down the stairs and opened the door, and as he feared, she asked him to turn the wireless set off. It was his intense frustration, as he switched off his favourite radio program that would burn this incident into his memory. He turned toward his mother and watched as she invited a tall, fair-haired man of about fifty inside.

'Paul, I would like to introduce you to General Pieters,' she said. Paul noticed she pronounced his name in a very strange way. He was slim and elegantly dressed in a uniform with red epaulets on the shoulders. The General looked relaxed and had his left arm around Phyllis' waist while he shook Paul's hand with his right hand. They clearly knew each other well and were good friends.

For Paul, after living at the children's home and then at boarding school, the opportunity to observe body language of this kind was most unusual. This was clearly a significant relationship and Phyllis appeared to be exuberant.

She said goodnight to Paul, gave him a kiss on his cheek, and she and the General left to go out to dinner.

Paul raced to the wireless and switched it on, only to discover that that evening's episode of the radio serial Dick Barton Special Agent had already ended. He was bitterly disappointed.

He would never forget the feelings he experienced that day when Phyllis introduced him to the General. But it would be nearly sixty years before he would understand the real significance of that meeting.

For, unbeknown to Paul, Phyllis, now *our* mother was four month's pregnant with me – a secret we were never meant to know.

Later, when Paul and I met again, I asked him to retell that story, and then we searched for General Pieters' name on the internet and found him straight away.

'Good heavens!' I said. 'There he is!'

Paul was thrilled. His memory of events sixty years before had not failed him and he was convinced this was the right person.

We were curious about the context in which she came to meet and know him. Could he have been working with her during the war in Dutch Intelligence when she went to Holland in 1944? Was this the relationship, according to the family stories, she had had for some years, and with whom she was going to make a 'brilliant marriage'? Could she have met him while still married to John or was it later?

At this stage, all we knew was that they were close friends and might have been friends from 1944–46. Clearly, this was not enough information to draw any conclusions.

We were absolutely delighted when we were able to confirm on the internet General Pieters was very senior in the Dutch establishment. He arrived in Great Britain in May 1940 and in 1943 was inspector of the Dutch forces in Great Britain. After that, he was military attaché at the Dutch Embassy in London until the end of the war. He also had a senior role in the Dutch military mission and regularly visited the British War Office. This was also confirmed in an article in *The Times* indicating he had a working relationship with General Eisenhower.

It seemed reasonable then to assume that Phyllis met him during the course of her wartime activities. If this was the case, they would have known each other for at least two years, and possibly more.

Rob, Paul, and I visited the national archives in The Hague in 2005 and discovered that during WWII he had had to leave his wife and two children behind in Holland. So, he was married! That certainly made it less likely that he was my father. Nevertheless, while in London he lived in W1 within easy walking distance of Phyllis at 5 Little Chester Street, and where the Dutch war and intelligence offices were at Chester and Eaton Squares.

Given that Paul met him while Phyllis was pregnant with me, it was an obvious avenue to explore further. What did he know about Phyllis and her pregnancy, if anything?

We were living in Sydney, but were about to leave for a holiday in Europe and were looking forward to seeing Paul and his family and our other UK friends. Could we possibly make contact with General Pieters' family and arrange to go and see them in Holland?

I hesitated for a long time; I really loathed the idea of imposing myself and my story on them. But there were four questions I did so want answered – did he tell his family anything about his friendship with Phyllis? Did they know anything about me? Could they confirm her spying activities? And – could he be my father?

I turned to my dear friend Mary, who acted as my intermediary with Paul. I have enormous respect for Mary and her wisdom gained from many long years in the medical arena. She is a linguist, speaking seven languages, understands a wide range of cultures, knows Europe well, and has a very warm personality. I trust her judgement and wanted an independent sounding board, so I wrote asking her whether it would be unreasonable for me to contact General Pieters' family. What did she think of the appropriateness of me approaching the children of this general?

This is her very hastily written reply.

'None of it [Phyllis's spying story and her story about meeting the Dutch General] seems to me unlikely, in fact, it hangs together well and it has become essential to you to find out [who your family are] – so you really have to go on now. I think anyone born in 1914 is now either demented

(but then why would they still have a phone number?) or past the age of prissy convention, so there is no reason why you should not make contact and ask. But it needs to be done by letter, by you. Not a phone call, which for someone of that age is impolite and may be too sudden to absorb. You need to write quite a long letter, starting with the obvious and gripping statement that you may be a sister, and there is no time to waste.

'The children of a general would be well educated and will have seen enough of the world to speak English and know that many things happen in wartime.'

I was grateful for Mary's clarity of thought, but I still felt vulnerable. I also felt I had no real choice but to do it – if only for the sake of our eldest son and the future children of our other son and daughter.

At this point, I would have much preferred to be someone else. But I could not stop now. So, thinking of Adam, our son, and with my heart in my boots and three weeks before leaving home, I wrote a letter to each of the two children in Holland asking whether it would be possible to meet.

I could never have anticipated the warmth and kindness we received. They offered to meet, which we did in the Netherlands, and soon after this, they suggested doing a DNA test with a close family member of the general. We were hopeful, and within a few months after our meeting in Holland, it was done.

We knew the results would take some time, but even so, the days passed exceedingly slowly.

And when the DNA test result finally came, it was no. Without doubt, General Pieters was *not* my father.

Fortunately, one side of the family had foreshadowed that this might be the outcome of the DNA test. His family said that they were convinced their grandfather was ethical, trustworthy, and very well respected; and that it would have been most unlikely for him to have had any extramarital affairs. And so, the shock was cushioned a bit and since then, we have become firm friends.

After the test was complete, another very intriguing puzzle piece emerged.

In 1947 General Pieters apparently knew about the adoption of a small baby in London and also knew Dr. Davidson, who had arranged it. General Pieters disliked Dr Davidson intensely and expressed this for some years to his family. I was amazed at the strength of his feelings as related by his family. It was not something one could ignore. General Pieters was upset that a German doctor had been chosen to arrange an adoption, which he thought was most inappropriate seeing that both the UK and the Netherlands had been at war with Germany. He knew the family chosen to adopt the baby were planning to emigrate from England. Why he knew this, and in what capacity, remains unclear. This small fragment of information has all sorts of implications.

We were told that General Pieters talked about his frustration about the adoption for years and years. I've thought much about this, but can come to no conclusions. Did Phyllis confide in him? What was it about Dr Davidson or the arrangements relating to my adoption that he was so concerned about? The secrets remain.

I include this also because of General Pieters' involvement with the role Phyllis had during the war. There were still so many unanswered questions. Could General Pieters have known about Phyllis being sent to Arnhem? Did he go with Prince Bernhard to General Montgomery's meeting on 7 September? And was he involved in the dissemination of the intelligence about the 9th and 10th Panzer Divisions? Once again, the unanswered questions are particularly significant.

There was one nice story to emerge – from and about his grandson. As a small baby, he was critically ill, and there were no medicines available in post-war Netherlands. On one of his grandfather's visits to the United Kingdom, which had something to do with arrangements about me, he was able to obtain the much-needed medicines and the grandson survived – grateful that he could tell me this story.

CHAPTER FORTY-ONE

My twelve months with Phyllis

Phyllis and I were intimately connected for the best part of a year. I was conceived in July 1946. Phyllis endured an unwanted pregnancy, stayed in a confinement home, and gave birth to me in April 1947. She cared for me for five weeks, and then carried me to Dr Davidson's rooms. She signed the adoption order in July 1947.

Phyllis conceived me within a day or two of her 40th birthday in July 1946, before the pill made contraception so accessible. Love-making would have been hard to refuse while celebrating such a significant birthday.

During WWII, she told her family she hoped to make 'a brilliant marriage'. Was this to my father? It must have been very disillusioning indeed to have this relationship end within days or months of her discovering she was pregnant. How did this come about? There is so much I would love to know.

Being pregnant with me could not have been a good experience for her and I certainly would not have been a 'wanted' baby. She would have been reminded of her own mother not wanting her and of her own experience giving birth to Paul, with her subsequent depression, being out of control, and then abandoning him.

She had two issues to resolve: her emotional, and possibly, financial vulnerability and the need to decide what to do with me. If she was working in any capacity, that would soon not last. She needed to ensure that she took good care of herself emotionally and physically.

Phyllis was already forty, and once it was obvious her partner was not going to marry her, she would have had to think through her options. Did she consider at all whether she could keep me? She would have been a single mother, which in those days and even without her history, would have been an unenviable position to be in. Would she have been able to provide for herself and her baby?

Big Granny was no longer alive and Barbara had her family to care for. Boy, her beloved brother, died in 1943, when his plane crashed. Phyllis could not expect any help from her family and must have felt very alone.

Phyllis' pregnancy appeared to proceed normally. Paul stayed with her again a few months later in January 1947 in their first family home in Matlock Road, Caterham, called 'Bandol'. It was freezing cold that January, and although Phyllis was six months pregnant, Paul never suspected a thing. By this time, her pregnancy would have been noticeable, but because it was so cold, she could hide her swelling belly inside a coat. Her wartime training as a spy would have made her a master of concealment and Paul, as a fifteen-year old teenager in boarding school most of the year, would not have been attuned to those sorts of details.

In January 1947 Phyllis was preparing the family home for sale. Was this part of her plan to become more independent financially? Or was there still a mortgage on the home? Perhaps another part of her plan would have been to ask for help from her partner, my father. Did she do this?

After deciding to place me for adoption, the next step would have been to do whatever she could to ensure I had the best possible chance in life. How could she find a suitable family who wanted a baby to love and who would be financially sound? In those days, the government's social services arranged adoptions; but if one needed more discretion, arranging an adoption through a doctor could be a better strategy. Did she have any say in selecting her doctor? I'll never know. But I do know that within the social circles she mixed, she could have made discreet enquiries about doctors who served the right kind of families. However, I believe it was more likely that her partner selected Dr Davidson, as she would have been unlikely to have chosen a German doctor, and an expensive one at that. The fact that General Pieters knew about and disapproved of Dr Davidson supports the conclusion that Dr Davidson was chosen by my father. General Pieters would have been more circumspect if he had known Phyllis chose the doctor, and perhaps then he wouldn't have been involved.

Dr Davidson's surgery, being located in fashionable Regents Park, clearly administered to the well-to-do members of town. Dr Henry Davidson was a German Jewish refugee, fleeing from Berlin in 1933. In Germany, he qualified as a medical doctor and was known there by the name of Dr Heinrich Davidsohn. In England, he was known as Dr Henry Davidson and obtained his medical qualification to work in the UK in 1934, in Glasgow.

When did my adoptive parents start to consider adopting a baby?

Dr Davidson and Dad (Benjamin, my adoptive father) may well have known each other in Berlin. He would have been a natural confidante for Dad and Mum (Elizabeth, my adoptive mother) told me Dad had insisted that Dr Davidson be their family doctor. Unfortunately, Mum did not share Dad's faith in his doctor; in fact, she had quite strong feelings about this, and more than once in Rhodesia when I was a child, Mum lamented the fact that they had relied on his advice.

Although WWII was over when Jonathan was born, Mum and Dad would still have been shocked and distressed. Many of Dad's family were murdered in concentration camps and he would have found the British anti-German sentiment very uncomfortable. The bombing raids would have been difficult (for everyone no doubt). And the emotional roller coaster of two miscarriages would have been compounded by the subsequent birth of Jonathan with Downs syndrome, with his severe disabilities. Consulting their family doctor would have been perfectly natural in those circumstances.

When it became clear that Mum and Dad were not coping with Jonathan, my brother James was put into a boarding school on a short term basis possibly to give them time to think. Dr Davidson then suggested they put Jonathan in a children's home. Mum said both she and Dad were grief-stricken, but said it was for the whole family's sake that they eventually decided that this was the right thing to do. This was the accepted practice at the time, and Mum had been assured that the people in the institution were skilled in caring for babies like Jonathan. He would need special care which they felt they could not give him. Additionally, they were planning to emigrate and could not be certain that they would find appropriate help for him in Southern Rhodesia.

It was a time of real crisis. Mum was distraught and Dad hated Mum talking about Jonathan and couldn't cope with her tears. He eventually forbade her from talking about Jonathan. 'You only make things worse,' he would say. Then, and even years later, Mum had no one to speak to or to console her – having to keep her grief secret would have made coming to terms with it much harder.

Dr Davidson on the other hand, had experience with families facing similar issues. I discovered that Dr Davidson, whilst practicing in Berlin, wrote some articles for a medical journal which indicated he had an association with a children's home and some experience in arranging adoptions. So, when he suggested adopting a baby, he said this from a position of being familiar with the process.

At about the same time all this was happening with Mum and Dad, my biological mother, Phyllis, was staying at Torwood, Torwood Lane, Whyteleafe, Surrey. This was the address she put on my birth certificate. I suspected Torwood might well have been what they used to call a 'confinement home' where pregnant single mothers wait out their pregnancy.

Paul and I decided to try to find Torwood, in Torwood Lane.

It was a dark grey day, and we drove along a long, heavily wooded lane, with old established trees and fields on one side and large homes on the other. It was a cul-de-sac and right at the end of the road was a large two or perhaps a three storey 19th century mansion, with a single front door, lots of chimneys, many roof turrets, and a large number of small windows. It might have come out of a Hitchcock movie – and may well have been a manor house in the past. As we observed the building from the car it seemed just the sort of place pregnant women might stay in if they wanted to be isolated during the last stages of their pregnancy.

I felt as if I was in a nightmare and was not prepared for the strength of my emotions. All I wanted to do was to escape, so Paul turned the car around and we drove away. As far as I was concerned, we could not leave soon enough. I just *could not* take any photos!

Recently, I tried to find the house on Google Maps, but without any success. It has vanished and so remains a bit of a mystery. But Paul and I saw it together.

My birth certificate also states that I was born at 12 Lancaster Drive, Hampstead. While we enjoyed many happy walks on Hampstead Heath, for a long time I felt too raw emotionally to search for my birthplace.

Rob and I left this to last, just before we were due to return to Australia.

12 Lancaster Drive is a wide, three-storey, free-standing white house with a basement and large, white-painted, bay windows on the second and third floor. As I looked up at the windows, I couldn't help wondering which room I was born in. I liked the location, quite close to the trendy village of Hampstead and the large open expanse of Hampstead Heath.

The 1947 telephone book recorded the location as the Lancaster Nursing Home. Six women were registered as living there on the 1946 electoral roll, and seven women in 1947.[82] One woman, Jean Davidson, was registered as being there both years, and an experienced midwife from Wiltshire, Margaret Doherty, was there in 1947. Having an experienced midwife there adds further weight to the nursing home entry on my birth certificate and lends credence to the idea that this was where I was born.

Jean Davidson was a possible link with Dr Davidson and it is not unreasonable to assume that he may well have had a financial stake in the nursing home.

I was thrilled to have found this information. It provided some sort of closure. At least now I knew where Phyllis lived during her confinement and where I was born, and that it was possible there was an experienced midwife to help her. I might have been an illegitimate baby, but I couldn't complain about being born in Hampstead.

Soon after I was born, Phyllis gave me my name: Jane. I often wondered how my name was chosen. As soon as Paul heard my

12 Lancaster Drive, Hampstead, where the author was born

name, he remembered that Phyllis had a friend also called Jane. Paul said Phyllis always chose names carefully and I was probably named after her 'dear friend Jane'. He said he thought Jane was related to the family who owned Harvey Nichols department store in London, but I haven't yet found any evidence of this.

Also around the time I was born, Dr Davidson might have asked my adoptive parents to come and see him. I don't know when Jonathan was taken to the children's home, whether it was before or after this interview, but it might well have been at this interview that Dr Davidson told Mum and Dad about the baby girl that was available for adoption. He might also have used the opportunity to talk through the process of adoption.

He might have argued that adopting a baby girl would complement their family, providing a sister for their elder son. He might have suggested that in contrast to their recent experiences, this would be a happy experience for their family.

He would also have been able to say he had known the baby's mother for some months, that she was a good 'class of person' (I think I remember Mum telling me this) and a healthy woman. He most probably could also say that the child's father was contributing financially to her care. He would be able to state that the baby's mother had been cared for at a confinement home at Torwood, and had given birth under the careful supervision of an experienced registered midwife in the Lancaster Nursing Home in Hampstead, which he knew well.

Dr Davidson might have also said that they would be helping my mother and her partner enormously by providing a home to a baby, who otherwise, might be homeless.

It sounds so natural and good. And it's true, they might have been very hopeful that caring for a baby girl would help them more easily come to terms with the recent, very traumatic, events in their lives.

But why did Dr Davidson not understand that their unresolved grief would have significant consequences for their ability to bond with me? This was hardly a happy family situation. Wasn't that obvious?

Perhaps it was very difficult after WWII to find appropriate families to adopt children. Did General Pieters and Phyllis know about Jonathan and his disability, and that he had been placed into a children's home? Was this why General Pieters disapproved of Dr Davidson? I hope Phyllis did not know – she would have had more than enough trauma and guilt to work through, and knowing this could have made it doubly difficult.

Another scenario could be that Dr Davidson felt under pressure to do whatever he could to effectively make me 'disappear' and felt that he had to 'strike while the iron was hot'. From that perspective, placing me with my adoptive family, who were planning to emigrate, seemed ideal – what better way could there be to make me vanish?

Judging by what happened to me many years later, I think Dr Davidson insisted my adoptive parents delay disclosing the truth to me about my adoption, for as long as possible. He would have advised them that they would also need to insist their six year old son keep the adoption secret and might have also advised to keep the child out of the public eye. His approach might have been that it would be in the child's best interest, as illegitimate children were not regarded highly and often not well treated. It would be better for the child if she grew up as if she was their own child.

Furthermore, if they allowed the adoption to become known, they could be asked very awkward questions about the adoption. If it was then discovered that they had a disabled child, and had abandoned him in a children's home in England, it could reflect badly on them. Mum and Dad would know that few people would have understood their predicament and that keeping it secret would simplify everything.

The possibility of their secrets being discovered must have haunted them all the years they were in Rhodesia, later renamed Zimbabwe, and especially after they told me I was adopted.

Dr Davidson might have encouraged them to commit to a whole raft of lies that would have to last all their lives. Very neatly, keeping my adoption secret met the needs of both my biological and adoptive parents.

To complete the process, when their son returned home, traumatised by the separation from his Mum and Dad, he was told that his brother, Jonathan, had died. Very soon after this, in May 1947 (just after he had turned seven), he would have accompanied Mum and Dad to collect me, his new baby sister, from Dr Davidson's surgery in Regents Park.

One day in 2007, during a visit to the UK, I went on my own to Park Square East, NW1, Regents Park in London, where Dr Davidson's surgery used to be. I stood on the pavement opposite the very elegant, cream-coloured Nash terrace where his surgery would have been and tried to imagine what it must have been like for Mother to carry me there, knowing she would never see me again. I was five weeks old. I tried also to imagine what it must have been like for Mum and Dad, along with my brother, as they walked toward the surgery. It seems fitting that it was raining that day. Mum said she saw my mother in a black raincoat holding an umbrella. It's not hard to imagine Phyllis, a solitary figure in her raincoat walking down the street, with the regular sound of her high heels on the concrete pavement slowly fading as she turned the corner.

Now, there is only silence and I feel as if I'm in a void.

Having a new baby in a family is usually a happy event. But, inadvertently, I must have become a constant reminder of their recent traumas. Poor Mum. I understand now why Mary, an au pair from Switzerland, was engaged to look after me, and why Mum was sometimes so distant and depressed. It was not something that could be reversed or ever easily talked about.

The nursery rhyme my Dad used to make me repeat,

'Was bist du? Du bist ein dummes kind!
Was bist du? Du bist ein stupide kind!'

echoes through me at times. Had Dad unconsciously turned me into their *dummes kind*?

Keeping these secrets seriously affected our family's relationships for all our lives. In 1947 there were strong personal reasons on the part of both sets of parents to keep my identity a secret. Their need for secrecy took precedence over truth, integrity, and honesty in their relationship with me. Eventually, we were all trapped in a web we could not unravel. Although I gained a well-intentioned 'good' family, and lacked for nothing as far as material things were concerned, because of the secrets I would always be an outsider.

Maybe my adoptive parents saw me as an illegitimate child who could have potentially been orphaned, a child 'in need.' Perhaps they thought that by adopting me they were doing what they could to erase their debt. From their perspective, that would seem reasonable.

Amazingly, one day I was searching the website of The National Archives for Dr Davidson and up popped a reference to a Dr Dav-

Dr Davidson's surgery in Park Square East, N.W.1, Regents Park, 2007

idson, and to a file about a matter in 1938 that was embargoed until 2040 – more than a hundred years after the events happened. Clearly, Dr Davidson was no stranger to secrecy and events that had to be kept out of the public eye. This was much more than the customary seventy years imposed on files at The National Archives – very curious.

As I began to understand more about the circumstances of my adoption, tears were a constant companion, not just for me but for the lost opportunities for all our family.

Would Mum and Dad have made the same decisions now? I doubt it. And the advice they would be given would be very different.

Mum was an intelligent woman who would have observed and understood how attitudes and practices in the care of people with disabilities and adoptions had changed. She also watched us caring for our children, including Adam, our son with a disability. In the garden in her hospice, a few days before she died, she said, 'Jane, if I could have my life over, I would have done things differently.'

The insight I have now into my adoption gives new meaning to Mum's statement. I sensed she was referring to my adoption and Jonathan. But she was already very weak and finding it difficult to talk, so I didn't have the heart to question her more deeply about what she meant. The crushing feeling I experienced when learning of my adoption returned. I was still honouring my promise not to search for my biological family. This meant she could not talk about it either: the barrier had to stay. If she did know anything more, she couldn't yet tell me. What could I say? In the end, saying nothing seemed the kindest thing to do.

We both knew things could have been very different. Given our own family's circumstances with Adam, I would like to think that she would understand and accept our need to know more about the genes I had inherited.

CHAPTER FORTY-TWO

East Anglia– 1949–63

After WWII, and fairly soon after relinquishing me for adoption in 1947, Phyllis moved to Norfolk. This must have been a very welcome change. But, why Norfolk? In her war record there was a reference to being posted to Chilwell in Norfolk. This must have been a positive experience and perhaps she made friends there.

Finding information about her life in Norfolk and subsequently Cambridgeshire was quite a challenge. Apart from Paul, no one else from her family knew about her life in Norfolk. As often happened, an amazing sequence of events helped to provide information that fleshed out her life there.

Phyllis's death certificate recorded Phyllis's last address as The School House, in Rings End, Cambridgeshire; and after the shock of finding it had subsided, it occurred to me that it might be worthwhile to find out whether Phyllis had bought or rented this house, and how long she had lived there. I wrote to a librarian in Cambridgeshire to enquire about this and it was she who found the obituary about Phyllis.

This was a wonderful breakthrough.

Paul knew nothing of this obituary and he, like me, was delighted to read it because it supported and added to the stories he had told me of her life there.

Other information came as a result of the excellent record keeping by the British Dalmatian Club. Every time Phyllis won a prize for her Dalmatian, they recorded her address.

Paul told me that soon after arriving in Norfolk, Phyllis became a Home Help Organiser, arranging care for people in their homes. This was such a revelation. I have been a social worker for almost forty years, and to discover that Phyllis worked in a very similar area was almost surreal. According to Paul, Phyllis was delighted, when as part of her role, she was given a car. This made it possible for her to exercise her dogs by driving around the lanes of Norfolk with her dogs following behind her.

What a change and what a contrast to her previous life. No longer did she need to compete to be part of the elite and the high life or strive to live 'north of the river and south of the park.' Now she was organising home help for people who were confined to their homes due to illness, disability, or perhaps war injuries. The National Health system only started in 1946 and Phyllis would have been working in a pioneer role. Her wartime career and her ability to work independently must surely have helped her in obtaining this position. Being a social worker myself, I can imagine her in this role and find myself feeling closer to her. I hope she found it rewarding.

Marriage to Alan MacRobert, Norfolk – 1949

In 1949, Phyllis married Alan MacRobert in Norfolk. Paul said they met at an army hospital.

Jeremy, my new cousin, tells a wonderful story about Phyllis and, given the choice, this is the way I'd like to think of her. He was a young teenager, and in 1949, he met her for the last time.

> 'She arrived at our little farm. She was triumphant. She had this rivalry with my mother [my Aunt Barbara], and now she had a husband of her own. She was so thrilled; she swept in, and she was just like my mother, full of confidence, full of charm, tremendously energetic, and I thought, where had she been all my life? We had seen so little of her. This was my aunt! This was Phyllis. I was swept off my feet. I was amazed. I was about fourteen or fifteen at this time. That was the last I saw of her.'

I love that description of Phyllis. Thank you, Jeremy.

Captain Alan MacRobert was one of the few survivors from a Japanese prisoner of war camp; he had been on starvation rations in Singapore and had been forced to work on the Burma Railway in WWII. Paul said he thought Alan had been driven insane through these experiences and that this was the reason he had been given a war pension. Paul said he did well to survive WWII. He had fair hair, freckles, and was fearfully thin. Paul often commented on how thin he was. He also thought that Alan, despite his name, probably didn't come from Scotland. He was a quiet man, lacking in self-confidence. He was always cool to Paul. The first home that Phyllis and Alan MacRobert bought in Norfolk was quite a large thatched cottage in Cheney's Lane, Tacolneston.

Phyllis told Paul that Alan had bouts of insanity, and in 1951, he killed some of the livestock with a pitchfork. She told Paul that she survived an attack only because the dogs protected her, barking like mad and keeping Alan from attacking her. After such episodes, he would come back to reality.

Then she told Paul that later (possibly in 1954), her thatched house burnt down! That must have been enormously traumatic. Paul and I were keen to find out more, and so, in 2005, we drove to Cheney's Lane in Norfolk. At first we found nothing. It was a beautiful country lane with farm land on the one side, with lovely homes behind trees, hedges and gardens on the other. Then a 4WD vehicle reversed out of a driveway, so I jumped out of the car and asked the driver if he knew where a house had burnt in the 1950s. He said we had driven past it, so we returned in the direction we had been. Right next to the road was vacant land with a large concrete slab with tall spreading trees on two sides of it. We assumed that this was where Phyllis's home might have been.

But ten years later, I returned hoping for confirmation. The local community were a great help. The editor of the *Tacolneston Times* wrote some fascinating articles about Phyllis and my search for where her house had been. Apparently the vacant property was where sugarbeet was stored before market. Later, I had two wonderful and illuminating conversations with long-time local residents. Apparently in the early 1950s, Phyllis was burning old documents in the garden (war-time documents, perhaps?), and the fire spread,

Cheney's Lane, Tacolneston, Norfolk, 2005
where we assumed Mother's thatched house had been

very rapidly burning down their thatched home. One resident
was a neighbour, a little girl at the time, and was terrified that her
home would also burn. Fortunately, that didn't happen. Eventually
Phyllis's land was sold, and a new home built. I was delighted to
have this mystery resolved.

That was not the end of the story. After the house burnt, Phyllis
was left with a sizable mortgage that still needed to be repaid. She
told Paul she went to live in London for six weeks and played rubber
bridge for money at the Crockfords club. She told him that when she
had earned sufficient money to pay off the mortgage, she returned
to Norfolk.

Initially, I could not believe this. We knew Phyllis said that she
had been one of Iain MacLeod's bridge partners, but I hadn't understood the significance of her mentioning this.

A couple of years later, at my desk in our home in Australia,
I explored Iain Macleod's illustrious career on the internet. There,
to my great surprise, I discovered that Iain MacLeod's lived off his
winnings from playing rubber bridge in the 1930s. In a story to be

told later, Susan, a Dalmatian dog breeder we met in 2005 and the daughter of one of Phyllis' Dalmatian breeder friends, said she knew about Phyllis's house burning. I felt embarrassed for not initially believing the story!

Phyllis's success at Cruft's and breeding Dalmatians

Phyllis's life story would not be complete without describing the hobby that provided her with so much pleasure. It must also have given her a significant identity as one of the first sought-after early breeders of quality Dalmatians in the UK. To understand what this meant to her, I wanted to know more about why she was attracted to breeding Dalmatians and why showing her Dalmatians at the British Dalmatian Club became such a passionate and sustained interest.

Evidence of the prizes her Dalmatians won, her home addresses, and three photographs were given to us when Paul and I visited The Kennel Club in London. We were shown entries in their catalogues confirming the occasions when Phyllis showed her dogs; for example, in 1938, and also in 1955, 1956, and 1961, each time providing her address. That was such a happy and poignant day. Had Phyllis not bred Dalmatians and had The Kennel Club not kept such meticulous records, I would not have been able to discover so much about her.

Paul, Rob, and I added to this information by driving around the country lanes visiting all her recorded homes in Norfolk and Ely, and speaking to a few elderly Dalmatian breeders around the country who remembered Phyllis during that time. This proved to be quite an adventure. Howard and Margaret Kleyn very kindly invited us to stay and enthusiastically supported our quest.

There is no doubt that Phyllis in the 1920s and 1930s happened to be in the right place at the right time. Breeding, showing, and judging Dalmatians was becoming very fashionable, but why?

The passion for exhibitions began with the Great Exhibition in 1851 in the Crystal Palace, supported by the invention of trains,

Paparazzi around a BEST IN SHOW Dalmatian winner and its owner, 1968

which made it much easier for people in the country to travel to and from the towns. Exhibitions and dog shows became not only viable, but extremely popular, and in 1873 the Kennel Club was started in London. Charles Cruft, a British showman started holding dog shows, and when he died, the Kennel Club took them over and the Cruft name stuck. The Cruft's dog show each year is organised by the Kennel Club.

The British Dalmatian Club started life as the Southern Dalmatian Club in 1925 (after Phyllis had been taught during her school holidays by Mrs Kemp on how to breed the 'right dal type'), but by 1930 interest had grown around Britain to such an extent that it was renamed the British Dalmatian Club. It operated under the auspice of the Kennel Club. The Royal Family, with other members of the aristocracy, showed dogs regularly and also became patrons. And so, the shows held by The Kennel Club became very fashionable, drawing royalty, celebrities, and aristocrats, as well as dog breeders.

The atmosphere and status that came from a dog winning a prize at Cruft's did not really dawn on me until I saw the photograph

Phyllis Margaret MacRobert (Mother) and her prize-winning Dalmatian winning a prize at The Kennel Club, 1955

of the huge number of photographers around a BEST IN SHOW winner and its owner at the Kennel Club in 1968.[83]

Sally Ann (of Puech De Barrayre Dalmations) believes that this is a photograph of Ch. Fanhill Faune and his owner when he became the first and, to date, the only Dalmatian to be awarded the title of Supreme Champion at Cruft's.

Obviously, winning an event like that was prestigious for the dog owner and guaranteed robust demand for her puppies. Is it this that attracted Phyllis to breeding Dalmations?

1956 was a particularly auspicious year for Dalmatians, for it was then that the children's novel, 101 Dalmatians by Dodie Smith was published. This led to a film in 1961 and enormous demand for Dalmatians. Unfortunately, many people who bought Dalmatian puppies as a result of the novel or film significantly underestimated how much exercise they need and this led to a series of sad stories of neglect.

Phyllis' fluent French helped her to export some of her puppies to Europe where pedigree stock had perforce become much depleted during the war years. Sally Ann (of Puech de Barrayre Dalmatians) found records that confirmed that Phyllis' dogs were exported to Portugal and France. One of her dogs was owned by La Comtesse de Quélan. Phyllis' dogs are apparently still represented in dog lines in France and Portugal today.

Most significantly, I also obtained a couple of photographs of Phyllis from the Kennel Club, including my favourite photograph of her taken in 1955, in which she looks so pleased when her Dalmatian won a prize. Of the four photographs I have of Phyllis, this is my firm favourite. Thank you, Kennel Club.

Talking with Dalmatian breeders who remembered Phyllis

Soon after attending the Windsor Championship Dog Show, Shelagh, the Honorary Secretary of the British Dalmatian Club searched through their records and found a number of people who had known Phyllis all those years ago – fifty years ago, in fact – and were willing to speak with me. This was a tremendous opportunity and it is hard to adequately describe what these conversations meant to me.

Susan was one of the people willing to speak to me. Her mother went to dog shows with Phyllis and sometimes Susan would accompany them. I telephoned her and she invited us to visit her for a cup of tea. She lived near Durham. Rob and I were able to visit her a few months later. She and her sister welcomed us and we were most impressed with the pictures of Dalmatians on her walls and beautifully crafted porcelain dogs, each with their own name and unique markings. She continues to be a judge and breeder of Dalmatians.

'I remember your mother, Phyllis MacRobert, very well. She was a good-looking woman. She was very jolly and very keen on bridge. When she died, I had to identify her three dogs. She used to drive to the shows with two or three dogs in her car. Her champion dog was Black Prince of Bellet'.

Our visit to see Susan and her sister was invaluable because she helped to verify another strange family story. Without me raising the subject, Susan confirmed the family story that Phyllis' house burnt down in the 1950s and she had been asked to identify Phyllis's dogs after Phyllis died. I was most grateful to her for inviting us to see her.

While we were visiting, she invited us to look through the kennels. That was amazing and I learnt then that a well-regarded pedigree Dalmatian bitch could have up to fifteen puppies and selling these could help to make ends meet. This helped to explain part of Phyllis' motivation for choosing to breed Dalmatians, and also would mean she would have taken great care to ensure her own home had sufficient space for kennels.

Another very poignant, much more recent conversation was with Gwen Eady. Again, Shelagh had spoken with her and had given me her name. To my absolute delight and pleasure, Gwen had very clear memories of Phyllis and spoke very enthusiastically about her. But the very first thing she said, before I could ask any questions at all, was, 'Wasn't it sad the way she died?' I couldn't help but agree with her.

She met Phyllis at dog shows all around the country when she was young. (This must have been in the 1950s.) 'I remember her because she was so kind to me – she showed me the ropes, what to do and what not to do at the shows. That was her nature. She was also outgoing, attractive, nicely dressed, and friendly. We would meet at shows all over England. Some were more formal, but the British Dalmatian Club shows were more sociable. She also had very nice dogs.'

I could not resist mentioning that she was a spy during the War and Gwen came right back with: 'That doesn't surprise me – she had that sort of personality! She was an English lady.'

I followed up with some of the other people who Shelagh said knew her. Some of them gave very insightful descriptions of Mother. One breeder said Phyllis had a 'strong personality' and could be quite forceful! Another said that breeding Dalmatians provided her with companionship and income, and that this might have been important for Phyllis, too. The same breeder also said that Phyllis was 'well liked' and a 'very pleasant woman'.

Bellet and The Old Bakery at Barford

When Paul and I visited the Kennel Club in London, they were able to provide us with four addresses where Phyllis lived, and as Paul was not aware of all the places she lived, he readily agreed to come with me to Norfolk on two occasions to do further research. This was very rewarding for both of us. Being in country lanes familiar to Phyllis, and where she would have had her dogs running behind her, made our time there even more evocative.

One of her dogs, Black Prince of Bellet, won a prize in 1955 when she was staying in the Sculthorpe Old Rectory – a lovely two-storey home in Fakenham, Norfolk. In 1956, another dog won a prize while she was staying in Scott House, Thorpe Road, Norwich, and then another when she was staying at 'Bellet' (a name given to her home) in Barford, Norwich, also in Norfolk.

It's a little concerning that she moved around so much. I can't help wondering why? I will probably never find out.

On our second visit to Norfolk, this time also with my husband, Rob, we had a particularly interesting adventure, this time at Barford.

One evening at 5.30pm in November 2005, Rob, Paul, and I were driving towards Barford to visit Bellet when we had an incredible experience. Barford is a tiny, isolated village in East Anglia where there are no street lights, no pavements, and the houses are sometimes built right up to the road. As we approached Barford in the dark, we saw a man wearing yellow reflective clothing walking his dog coming towards us on the right hand side of the wooded lane. We stopped to ask the way to Barford, and in particular, to the house called Bellet in Barford. The man seemed friendly and so we mentioned that we were looking for the house where Alan MacRobert and Phyllis lived all those years ago.

Amazingly, he remembered Alan. He said he was eight years old at the time. 'Did Alan have a plate in his head and a Dalmatian dog, and was he a little bit mad?' he asked.

'That's him,' we said. He then told us Alan and Phyllis separated and Alan then lived in The Old Bakery.

We were intrigued by this new information and our roadside acquaintance told us how to find her house Bellet and then how to find The Old Bakery.

We found the entrance to Bellet, and then drove on looking for The Old Bakery. We pressed the bell at the gate inside an archway of an old yew hedge. Eventually, a young man came out and listened to our story. He confirmed that he was living in The Old Bakery, but that he had not been living there for long; however, there was an elderly woman living next door who would know all about Alan.

He walked with us to the house, past the front door of her white cottage, to the kitchen door at the back. He knocked on the kitchen door and introduced us to the rather surprised woman who must have been around eighty years old. It would have been unusual for her to have visitors after dark. It was a chilly autumn evening and at 6pm, she was already in her dressing gown. Despite this, she was very friendly.

She had curly grey hair and covered her mouth with her hand. She was acutely embarrassed and admitted she had not put her teeth in when she heard the knock at the door. We tried to reassure her and asked whether she knew Alan MacRobert.

'Of course I knew Alan.' She looked at me a little conspiratorially. 'He was a little mad, you know!'

This was what the man we met in the lane had said. 'Can you tell us more?'

She replied – 'Just a bit mad.'

This made me curious, so I asked a more specific question about his behaviour.

'Did he get angry?'

'Oh, no,' she reassured us. 'He was harmless!' This was strange and didn't seem to match what Phyllis had told Paul. The elderly woman explained that he was married and that his wife lived in the village.

'She left him, you know, and I can understand why she left him – I would have left him too!' She then volunteered in a reverential voice, 'She was a real lady, very attractive, and although she lived and worked here, there was a bit of mystery about her.'

I relished this rare, independent piece of information about her. We told her our story. The young man from The Bakery house excused himself, saying he would be returning.

'When you say he was a bit mad, what did he do?' I wanted to find out more about Alan.

She then started telling us strange stories. She said he would knock on her door and ask to use her bath. She clearly thought this was unacceptable behaviour. Sometimes he would entertain the children with puppets on his doorstep. Sometimes he would go into Norwich and entertain all the 'down and outs' there. The funniest story was that he set up a scaffolding plank straight up to his first floor bedroom window, which she pointed out, so that his pet rooster could visit him in his bedroom. Sometimes his rooster would visit her, too! She didn't sound quite as welcoming.

Interestingly, the lane he lived in was called 'Cock Lane'!

She continued. Alan took over two dogs from Phyllis and cared for them. She recognised Alan's 'madness' was caused by WWII and she said that sometimes he was charming, too. But, she hastily added, she could understand why Phyllis left him. She concluded our interview by saying that Alan died in hospital, but she could not remember when.

I so much appreciated meeting her and hearing about Phyllis' life there.

Just then, the young man came back. He had in his hands the

title deeds to The Old Bakery and invited us to take them away, make a copy, and post them back to him. The Deeds confirmed that Captain Alan MacRobert had indeed purchased The Old Bakery for the sum of seven hundred pounds in 1961. I was overwhelmed. This was such a kind gesture. We thanked them both profusely, drove up the remainder of Cock Lane, and turned the corner.

We were about to drive back to London, but needed some dinner. At the end of the lane was a picturesque old pub called The Cock Inn that was well-known locally for the quality of its English fare. This was perfect. We had dinner there, and as I often do, I tried the local fare. I ate the very best black pudding and fried liver I have ever tasted. We were all very jovial after such a productive, successful day.

Paul's visits to Phyllis –1957–58

In 1957 Paul received a card from Phyllis inviting him to come and stay. He visited her a few times in 1957 in Barford, the last time being over Christmas. During this visit, Paul said her relationship with Alan was 'coming down to earth'. Paul said he seldom heard Phyllis and Alan talking together. During that visit, Paul played bridge with her at the bridge club and went to an Anglican church with her, while Alan attended a Catholic church nearby. (That was the first time Paul mentioned that Phyllis went to church!) Paul said she did not drink much, and when he thought of her, it was of her chain-smoking, lighting up one cigarette with the end of the previous one, and surrounded by four dogs – three bitches and one male.

After this, Paul completely lost touch with Phyllis, his aunt, and Jeremy. He was transferred up to the North of England by Philips, the company he worked for. He said he took great care to tell her how to contact him at Philips, but he never heard from her. He then moved and changed jobs, and later, when he contacted Alan to ask about her, Alan did not know where she was either. Paul searched, but could not find her – not even to invite her to his wedding. He was distraught and never understood why she did not try and contact him at work.

However, a story about Phyllis told to me by Jan, another member of the British Dalmatian Club, about Phyllis could help to explain why she could not keep in touch with Paul. Apparently, Phyllis had a stroke in 1958 and two of her dogs were flown to Jersey to be with her sister, Barbara. Things must have been bad if she could not look after her dogs. Barbara couldn't keep them and a dedicated kennel man called Bernard looked after one, while Jan agreed to take the other, called Susie. Jan said she loved Susie 'to bits'.

Jan excused herself, saying she was in the middle of shelling five kilos of peas before supper, but she sent me a very poignant gift – a letter with a postcard inside and a stamp on her envelope featuring a descendent of Phyllis's dog, her darling 'Spot–On'.

I shed lots of tears – Phyllis felt so tantalisingly close, and yet so far away. Inexplicably, there was also a surge of pleasure and love! It was almost as if this experience was her gift to me. The pleasure her dogs gave to her lived on and continued to give others pleasure, with her dogs' genes being perpetuated through her line of dogs.

My journey exploring Phyllis's fascination with her Dalmatians and her career breeding them provided an extraordinary insight into this aspect of her life. I could not help but feel a strong sense of gratitude to Shelagh, Sally Ann, Jan, Susan, and Gwen, and to all the others who were so kind and generous in giving their advice and time and so much precious information about Phyllis, my mother.

I longed to know my mother and realised this was as close as I was ever going to be!

The Old School House at Rings End in Cambridgeshire was to be her last home. The school closed in 1949. This time, she was renting her home. The Isle of Ely Electoral register confirmed she moved into The Old School House between October 1958 and October 1959 under the name of Margaret MacRobert.

This was confirmed by two advertisements for her dogs in *The Times* in August and December 1960. Both times she gave her address as The Old School House. Interestingly, MacRobert was spelt with

The Old School House

a small 'r' and, at that time *The Times* cost just sixpence. In 1960 she placed advertisements for two house pets, giving her address as The Old School House, Rings End, Wisbech.

Paul and I visited The Old School House. It was a lovely large house with Gothic leaded windows that let in lots of light. We could hardly believe our eyes when we arrived. It still had a kennel and there were dogs; clearly dog breeders still lived there.

Relationship with her sister

Jeremy was the source of much of the information about Mother's relationship with her family. He said that Big Granny often used to confide in Barbara about her feelings towards Phyllis, and Barbara, in turn would confide in Jeremy. When Jeremy recounted these stories, he would often begin rather apologetically with, 'I love my mother deeply, but one thing I criticise her for is how she treated

Phyllis.' On another occasion he added, 'We were very close and I adored my mother, but there was one thing I did not think was good in her – there was this terrible rivalry between the sisters.' Clearly there were big issues in Phyllis's relationship with Barbara.

Jeremy said they were aware of Phyllis' role as a spy in WWII, but of course, she could not talk about it. I suspect that they did not approve of Phyllis' behaviour, even though attitudes towards marriage and women's roles changed quite dramatically during WWII. Phyllis and her mother and sister lived in two quite different worlds.

Big Granny died of liver cancer in 1943 in Barbara's home. After that, Phyllis discovered that Big Granny's will stated that Barbara would inherit most of her worldly possessions. This drove a further wedge between herself and her sister, leaving a legacy of pain with which they both struggled with for the rest of their lives.

Paul said when he met Phyllis in 1944, and for years after, she was upset about not receiving an inheritance from her mother. Jeremy said he thought that Big Granny did leave some money to Phyllis, but not as much as to her sister Barbara, because of her two little boys and her invalid husband. Big Granny did not foresee the impact it would have on Barbara. Jeremy said many times his mother grieved the loss of her relationship with Phyllis and she did try and make up for it. Later, when her godmother died and left her house and some money to Barbara, Barbara sold the house; and although there was no family obligation to do so, she sent Phyllis £1000. But she could not bring herself to contact Phyllis personally, either by phone or in writing. Our cousin said that she sent it to her bank manager in Cromer in Norfolk. The bank manager then phoned Phyllis and said to her, 'I have good news for you – someone has sent you £1000.' She apparently asked, 'Who would send me this?' and the bank manager replied, 'Your sister.'

Jeremy said Phyllis never acknowledged that she had received the money. Aunt Barbara was trying to make up for Big Granny excluding Phyllis from her will. £1000 was a lot of money in those days and the value of it became clearer after my chance meeting with the present owner of Alan MacRobert's house, The Old Bakery, at

Barham, who lent us the title deeds of his home. This recorded that the cost of The Old Bakery, which included the bakery and an apartment upstairs in 1961, was £700.

Phyllis clearly found the money useful, for when she died only half was left. What had she spent it on? Alan, her husband, was well known for episodes of madness, caused by the war, and she had left him. Had she used some of the money to help Alan buy a home, enabling her to leave him well cared for? Yet another mystery that cannot be answered.

Phyllis' death in 1963

Learning about how Phyllis died is very sad and this story stayed in the minds of many who knew her. She died of pneumonia, all alone, on 3 January 1963 at The Old School House, at Rings End, Cambridgeshire. January 1963 was one of those extraordinarily cold British winters and her body was discovered a few days after her death. She was found with her dogs all around her.

She was comparatively young, only fifty-six, and one wonders why she died so young. Did she get sick often? Had the stroke she suffered five years earlier left her with disabilities? Was she susceptible to pneumonia because she chain-smoked for most of her life? Was she depressed and had she lost the will to live? I don't know, and will probably never know.

After her death became known in the community, the bank manager telephoned her sister Barbara to tell her Phyllis had passed away. Barbara was shocked and in a terrible state, according to Jeremy, 'In fact, she was heartbroken about it for a long time'. She was shocked at the contrast to her own life and our cousin said she had 'a terrible conscience about it'. She had just spent Christmas with her eldest son and her grandchildren – it had been a wonderfully warm and happy family Christmas in comfortable surroundings. Barbara was shocked to discover that Phyllis died a solitary death in such a sparsely-furnished home.

Paul and Eileen talked of visiting her home in the Old School House at the time of her death – how the house was almost empty, but that the kennels were comfortable and pristine.

How very sad!

Phyllis' funeral

Paul attended Phyllis' funeral with our Aunt Barbara. It was held at Guyhirn Parish Church, and soon after there was an obituary in the *Wisbech Standard* on Friday, 18 January 1963.

The obituary described how the Reverend Freeman spoke about the 'good work Mrs MacRobert had done on the Isle.' Some of the people who attended included the County Medical Officer and the Clerk, a representative of the Home Help Service, the almoner from Wisbech Hospital, and fifteen Home Help Workers. The Morgan Wood Kennels and Barclays Bank were also represented, including David MacRobert (brother to Alan?). West Norfolk and King's Lynn Bridge Clubs sent wreaths. A person from London's West End, Rose Banbury, also sent a wreath. I wonder how she knew Phyllis. I recognise some of the names of her friends in the Dalmatian world. She was cremated but Paul did not know who took her ashes.

Paul's name was not mentioned as having attended the funeral and when I asked him later, he said that he was rather dazed and might not have signed the book as he entered the church. In his place, I could have easily done the same thing. Could there have been other people who attended the funeral and did not sign the book?

Sadly, I have never been able to trace what happened to Alan MacRobert or his relative, David MacRobert.

The circumstances of Phyllis' bleak and lonely death haunt me, and it is difficult to obtain closure and find peace about it. While the family says her house was almost empty, does that mean it did not have heating, either? If she had pneumonia, she may not have been able to keep her home warm, so could it be that she froze to death?

CHAPTER FORTY-THREE

My mother and me

My mother Phyllis's obituary was invaluable in helping me make sense of her life in East Anglia. It also made it possible to step back a little and view her life as a whole. How much do I know about her now, and how has she changed from just being that presence in the back of my mind when I was nineteen?

I'll be the first to acknowledge that there is much I still don't know. And despite this, I believe her character and personality shines through.

One thing is clear. Big Granny found her to be difficult and stubborn. Phyllis almost certainly grew up knowing she was not a wanted child and not the favourite in the family; perhaps, quite the opposite. She was the second daughter and not the first son! As far as her family were concerned, she was not a saint! She was an enigma, at times unbending, stern, and someone who certainly knew her own mind.

However, she also had some very positive attributes. She was fortunate to be a quick learner and grew to be an attractive, physically fit, charming young woman. Her colleagues in the Dalmatian world often referred to her as a 'real lady'.

Her mother and father taught her how to play bridge and she frequently made up as the fourth player as part of their regular evening recreation. Through studying ballet from a teacher, who would subsequently be recognised as being the best ballet teacher in all England, she was given valuable exposure to some of the earliest ballet lessons given in England. As part of her ballet introduction, she would also have attended performances and the theatre in England. She would have learnt poise, grace, balance, and confidence. It's not surprising then that she grew up loving amateur dramatics. She received an excellent education, even going to a finishing school in Belgium. Her family started going abroad for their holidays, particularly to France. When she was at home during the school holidays, she was taught how to breed Dalmatians at a local kennel by one of the first Dalmatian breeders in the UK. Her achievements and her education were recognised after school because she was offered a position in the Bank of England – no doubt a very prestigious place to work for a young woman at that time.

It would not be long before she fell in love with Jim, an eminently suitable young man who also worked at the Bank of England, and soon they married. She stopped working at the Bank just before she married – probably because it was the policy of the Bank of England not to employ married women.

Her first marriage to Jim Whicker seemed to start well, and at that time, life must have looked very rosy. Her husband was loyal, hardworking, and kind, and he reputedly never lost his temper. Four and a half years later, Paul was born. Two months after that, inexplicably, disaster struck.

Phyllis abandoned both Paul and Jim.

Paul remembered that Phyllis's brother, Boy, provided a home for her when she abandoned Paul and that when Boy died, he left his home to Phyllis. So, at least her brother, Boy, was close to her.

Three years later, Phyllis and Jim attempted to repair the marriage, but this failed when she was distracted by caring for her newborn Dalmatian puppies instead of caring for Paul. She lost her legal fight to regain custody of Paul, and then seeing and keeping contact with Paul became increasingly difficult. Her relationship with her mother and sister probably disintegrated into no relationship at all. Paul spent most of his young life in a children's home, and even after he won a place at a good school, school holidays were always a problem. He always had to ask where he would be spending the next school holidays.

Mother must have also suffered terribly. If her depression and their marital sexual issues had happened today, in our information-rich environment, these difficulties might have been a lot easier to resolve.

After she left Paul, there would be no turning back. She was now a divorcee and a woman who had abandoned her baby. From being a well-educated, very eligible young woman in the England of that time, she may well have felt her reputation was destroyed and she had little choice but to become an independent, and sometimes a solitary soul, not afraid to be different.

Her marriage to John Leonard Kleyn, a Dutchman, in 1937 must have been a very welcome relief and it would have been most exciting to leave England for the south of France. Unfortunately, this marriage lasted only six years, when John deserted her in late 1943, right in the middle of WWII. Everything in the world had changed by then.

Tragically, early in WWII, Boy, the only member of her family she was still close to, was killed.

Then, she was delighted about a new relationship she had, only to be disappointed yet again when she was deserted by the person with whom she was expecting to enter into a 'brilliant marriage', possibly my father.

After I was born, she married Captain MacRobert, victim of the appalling wartime conditions on the Burma Railway. This marriage was also short-lived. His periodic violent episodes due to his post-traumatic stress disorder destroyed her third marriage.

Initially, I found it very confronting to learn that she abandoned Paul as a newborn baby. I cannot imagine the grief and guilt she would have felt after she left Paul and wonder whether it was this experience that encouraged her to give me away for adoption.

And I wondered what this said about her. Was she just a free-spirited woman who would never have been able to cope with children and who needed to retain her independence? Or was her fate sealed when Big Granny, her own mother, mothered her so ambivalently? If she had received the right support soon after leaving Paul, might she have come back to her small baby and her husband? Did her mother and sister try to help her after she abandoned Paul? What did her family think of her after this? Did her finishing school expose her to a very different and foreign set of values that had the effect of estranging her from the principles upheld by her family? How did they view her gambling at bridge at Crockfords and mixing with the rich and famous when her own financial and social situation was so different?

Despite all of this, Phyllis was amazingly resilient, intuitive, and courageous. Her army record reported that she spoke French, German, Italian, and some Dutch, and enjoyed active sports like skiing and climbing. She was a gourmet cook, talented at amateur dramatics, and sometimes played the lead while acting in the Bank of England's amateur dramatic productions.

The careers in her life ranged from a Bank of England employee, amateur actor, and well-respected breeder of Dalmatians to formidable bridge player claiming to have partnered Iain Macleod, one of the world's great British bridge players. She was a British soldier with two war medals, reaching the rank of Junior Commander at the end of WWII, similar to the rank Princess Elizabeth achieved. She was a member of the First Aid Nursing Yeomanry, the Auxiliary Territorial Service, and a secret agent. Her acting ability may have been valuable for her spying activities in the war years. Also during the war, she was among those who led discussion groups among serving WWII soldiers about the reasons why they were fighting and who they were fighting for.

Her war medals were proof that she participated in dangerous missions in enemy territory. She risked her life for her country, travelling to Arnhem just before the Market Garden Campaign, and ominously found the German 9th and 10th panzer divisions there. After her return, and at lunch with her friend Daphne, she told General 'Boy' Browning, a high-ranking British General responsible for planning the campaign, what she had seen in Arnhem. As an undercover spy, her role would not have been acknowledged.

Could it be that her lover was also involved in WWII, perhaps also in military intelligence? Was he a factor in her being willing to risk her life for the Allied effort in the war? Was he my father?

Phyllis was not averse to the occasional name-dropping – always done meticulously and with precision. Every name she mentioned to

Paul or in her war record or even her advertisement for her Dalmatians was someone significant in their field. She was acutely aware of her place in the English class system and was discreet when this was needed.

She was an attractive, intelligent, vivacious woman, and in her younger days, she clearly enjoyed male company. I was conceived very close to her fortieth birthday in July 1946. Contraception wasn't as easy in those days as it is now.

The challenge of surviving in a war-torn London, divorced with an unwanted pregnancy, and giving birth to me must have severely traumatised her, because in 1949 she moved away – away from her beloved London, her friends and family, and settled into the small rural county of East Anglia.

I do hope that in the process of living and working in East Anglia, organising home help for those who needed care, she would have come into contact with the directness of country people, their lively humour, and the sincere expressions of appreciation that are so often offered to those in a caring role. It was suggested to me that she would have been among the early pioneers of the homecare system, organizing for homecare workers to care for the injured and traumatised war veterans, rather like her husband, Alan MacRobert.

Interestingly, while she was in East Anglia, she came into her own as a respected Dalmatian dog breeder. From all accounts, she enjoyed participating with her long-time colleagues and friends in the British Dalmatian Club dog shows all over England. She also continued to play bridge locally, and interestingly, and, according to Paul, became a regular church member of her local Church of England.

I sincerely hope that she found peace there. She was far away from her pre-war London life of gaiety, class consciousness, and keeping up appearances. Certainly, if it is fair to judge by the people who came to her simple funeral, her local community appreciated her.

In 1990, when I so hesitantly started my search for my mother, I could never have anticipated the adventures and this outcome. I know so much more and I feel fortunate and delighted to be able to respect and admire her. Despite her turbulent life, she was an extremely brave woman; resilient and willing to risk her life for her country.

Moreover, I love the fact that although while we led profoundly different lives, and I grew up quite independently of her, we have many interests, skills, and experiences in common. For example, I grew up loving travelling, walking, climbing, and skiing; and worked for nearly all my adult life in a community service role, as a social worker or a teacher in adult education. I enjoyed a brief spell breeding Bichon Frise puppies with my daughter. And I still enjoy playing bridge. But do I share her passion for gambling? I don't think I'll admit to that here.

We do have our differences. I have recently discovered that I can paint and no one has mentioned that she painted. And if there is one thing that motivates me more than anything else, it is being mum to our three children.

Still, there is much about Mother that I still long for. If only we could have met. I would have loved hearing about her life from her perspective and learning first-hand about those activities that gave her pleasure. I would have treasured listening to her about the homemaking skills she thought were important, about bridge, her work, and her dogs.

I miss not being able to laugh and joke with her, hug her, and nuzzle into her. I will never argue with her or cook with her in the kitchen, as I do with my own wonderful daughter. I miss not being able to pick up the phone for a chat, say 'happy birthday' or take her flowers on Mothers' Day. On the other hand, she has never reprimanded me or had the opportunity to point out my mistakes! If we had known each other, I think we would have had a warm, vibrant, and at times, feisty relationship – one where our closeness would probably have had to be earned.

Through searching for Mother, I have become a different, happier, and more contented self. Mother now feels real and I can accept she was my mother. I know what she looks like and something of her personality. She is no longer the ghost in the dark recesses of my mind. She now lives in my imagination.

While in life she and I led distinct, distant, and almost unrelated lives, at last I feel we are connected, linked together as mother and daughter. It is an added bonus that our stories can be told together in the pages of this book.

'Thank you, Mother, for being the person you were! I feel I know you now, but please tell me who is my father? Will I ever really know?'

Epilogue

In many ways, life is like a card game. Each of us is dealt a unique hand and the choices we make in playing the cards are all our own.

One evening early in the writing of this book, I experienced a particularly dark spell of despair. My husband, sensing this, hovered nearby wanting to comfort and hug me, but I rejected his offer and told him to leave me alone. The turmoil and pain were unbearable, but it was too late in the night to find professional help.

What on earth was wrong? I fought to keep control. Why did I feel this way? I needed answers. I also knew if I prevented the person who loved me the most from helping me, my despair might lead me down a slippery slope from which I couldn't recover.

The longing to escape the pain was overwhelming, but gradually it also dawned on me how hurtful and extraordinarily harmful this would be for him and everyone I cared about. I couldn't live with those consequences, and so I was faced with little choice but to take responsibility for my actions and heave myself out of the black hole in which I found myself.

Then I had a sudden insight – my anguish was not just a personal problem, but very much a public issue.

I remembered reading that adoptive parents often found their adopted baby 'hard to reach' emotionally. Could it be that I, even as an adult, was being 'hard to reach' as well? Was I reacting like other adoptees when I rejected the help offered by my husband? Surely this wasn't the first time an adoptee experienced this level of despair?

That night, I searched the internet and was amazed to find a newspaper article that reflected the depth and intensity of my feelings.

In *The Melbourne Age* on 30 June 1993, in an article titled, *The Painful Legacy of Adoption*, Louise Bellamy wrote that Brother Alex

McDonald, a Jesuit who worked with homeless young people in the St. Kilda area for ten years, said of the 147 suicides of young people from drugs and abuse in the area over the previous decade, 142 came from 'adoption backgrounds'.

Initially, this is hard to believe and shocking. But this was the generation that was born during the boom adoption years, from around 1950 to the late 1970s. Canada, the US, and New Zealand have similar suicide rate profiles.[84]

Adoption is a social construct created by society to provide alternate care for babies or children when their parents are not in a position to care for them. Relevant here are the ideas of the sociologist, C. Wright Mills,[85] who suggested that when the personal, social, and historical dimensions of our lives are understood, it is possible to associate 'personal troubles' with 'public issues' and that the solution is not to struggle individually, but to join forces with those who also share these experiences.

After decades of thinking there was something wrong with me, no longer were my issues ones that I had to resolve on my own. Reading about adoption being a social construct, and realising that society has a responsibility to support all those involved in adoption, made it much easier to accept what I was feeling. It felt quite reasonable, and in fact, constructive to then contact the Post Adoption Resource Centre in Sydney and ask about what assistance might be available and about the best ways to go about looking for my family and managing reunions.

The Post Adoption Resource Centre in Sydney and their library became a great resource. I discovered I am a 'late discovery adoptee' because the fact that I was adopted was not revealed until I was an adult. I found reading about all this very helpful. Finding out about the consequences of separation for both the mother and child, and the child's subsequent ability to bond, helped me understand my own experience better.

With insightful and gentle support, I have become more self-aware and the past makes much more sense. Carrying around old hurts doesn't help one's present relationships. The responsibility to sort myself out lay with me. Fortunately, I have a wonderfully supportive husband and very caring children. I cherish my family relationships above all else. This has given me added confidence in my ability to enjoy and ensure constructive relationships.

I appreciated all that my adoptive parents did for me – they loved and cared for me and provided a safe comfortable home. They were the only parents I had. But the promise I made to keep the secrets about Jonathan and my adoption became a barrier to open and honest family communication.

I believe the secrecy in relation to my adoption and the identity of my biological parents was largely imposed on them by Dr Davidson, possibly at the request of my mother or father. These restrictions distorted our relationships for a lifetime and caused a huge amount of grief and sorrow, amplified by the flawed way my adoption was structured. Fortunately, recent legal reforms to adoption law in Australia mean that the secrecy and betrayals inherent in preventing contact between adoptees and their biological parents are giving way to the right of the child to know his or her true roots and identity early in life.

Where it is possible, open honest relationships between all the parties involved encourage trust, respect, love, spontaneity, and joy. Society has the responsibility to research and understand the consequences of adoption, and most importantly, to provide the resources, expertise, and the right conditions for constructive long term relationships amongst them all. This would be an excellent investment towards encouraging happy and productive lives.

Acknowledgments

The search for Phyllis, my mother, has been an extraordinary journey, made infinitely more so by the generosity and kindness of everyone who shared it with me.

I would like to thank my wonderful husband, Rob, for standing beside me throughout the writing of this book, for his belief in me, and for his wisdom and encouragement to keep going. I became someone other than the person he thought he had married.

Intimately woven into our lives are Jonathan and our son Adam. Meeting and getting to know Jonathan and his carers was one of the most worthwhile and poignant experiences of my life. Very sadly, he died in December 2007. Adam continues to add rich meaning to the tapestry of our lives. I thank Nick and Kathryn for being who they are and for their love and steadfast support. I dedicate this book to all of you.

I'd like to acknowledge my adoptive family who, despite everything, generously gave me a home and a family, and always had the very best of intentions.

I am deeply grateful to Mary, whose support I treasured and for sensitively being my intermediary in my first contact with Paul. Thank you, Mary.

Getting to know my new family has been a truly wonderful experience: heartfelt thanks are due to my half-brother Paul and his wife Eileen, their daughter Karen, my step brothers, Howard and Peter Kleyn, and their wives, and last but certainly not least, my cousins, Jeremy and Brian, and his wife, Audrey, without whom this story could not have been told. Thank you for welcoming us so wholeheartedly into your family and for your enthusiastic support and the laughter we have shared over many a meal and glass of wine.

Very sadly, Paul, my half-brother and I, were siblings for only six years – he died far too soon in 2011. I still cherish my relationship with Eileen, his wife, and his daughter, Karen and her family. Paul

283

and I had such fun, joyfully driving around England and Europe retracing Phyllis' life.

Howard Kleyn also died much too soon. We were overwhelmed by Howard and Margaret's kindness and hospitality; and Howard even had a DNA test with me proving that, although I was Jane Kleyn at birth, John Leonard Kleyn was not my father. I miss his dry wit, his irresistible charm, and his considerable intellect.

A number of authors and other learned people exchanged emails with me, provided significant information or advice in relation to Phyllis' wartime career. Their expert contributions in analysing her army record helped considerably to establish the plausibility of her wartime spying stories. They include, in alphabetical order, Ian Bailey, who is the Curator at the Adjutant General's Corps Museum; Howard Davies, who at the time was Head of Supervision and Selection and is now the Standards Manager at The British National Archives, Kew, in London; Michael RD Foot, the much revered author of many books about the SOE; Pieter Hans Hoets, knighted at twenty-six by Queen Wilhelmina for his brazen bravery as a member of the Dutch Resistance during WWII, who confirmed the existence of the air bridge at the time of Phyllis' escape from Stockholm; and Sue Tomkins, Archivist to Lord Montagu of Beaulieu, who first raised the possibility of Phyllis being a secret agent. Researching Phyllis's wartime career has felt like a real live detective story. I could never have anticipated a stranger introduction to my mother.

I am especially indebted to the Dalmatian Club, Shelagh for inviting me to the Windsor Championship Dog Show in August 2005 and for putting me in contact with the members who knew Phyllis and Sally Ann (of Puech de Barrayre Dalmatians) in France. Their interest and expertise about Dalmatians helped me better understand the Dalmatian world in which Phyllis lived. Their information led to a number of adventures in London, Windsor, Durham, and a memorable holiday retracing Phyllis' life in the south of France. Being able to speak to Jan, Susan, and Gwen, who knew Phyllis personally in the 1950s and 1960s, provided a rich and poignant glimpse of her as a person. I am very grateful for their interest and willingness to help.

There are many dear friends whose advice and generous support I treasure. These include Dawn and Mike Jonas, Frances le Roux, Jane Drexler, Bernadette Vogel, who introduced me to John van Gorkom, Peter and Jeanne Abelson, and Cathy Gohdes for their candid feedback and encouragement. There are many others who listened, told me their stories, and gave valuable advice; thank you to you too. You know who you are.

As a new author, I especially valued receiving encouragement and suggestions from readers. Tony Voysey deserves special mention. Thank you Tony.

A week at Varuna added insight, as did my first editors, Patti Miller and Ann Cullinan. Sincere and special thanks are also due to Maria d'Marco, Josephine Pajor-Markus and Julie-Ann Harper for their kind and expert assistance through the final edit, design and complexities of the publishing process.

Adoptees' circumstances are many and varied – many do not search for their roots at all and others leave it for later in their lives, like I did. We all have different ways of making sense of our lives.

For example, although I read widely in other subject areas, only very late in the piece could I face reading about adoption. Especially helpful were books written by Betty Jean Lifton and Nancy Verrier, who are world-renowned for their work on adoption.[86, 87]

I also found the discussions on internet websites and blogs for adoptees, even adoptees like me, a 'late discovery adoptee', immensely reassuring.

Here it is appropriate to say a heartfelt thank you to Janet Henegan and other professionals at The Post Adoption Resource Centre (PARC) in Sydney, who provided encouragement, and informed empathy. The PARC library is a great resource. I am also indebted to Damon Martin, Manager, NSW Office at the International Social Service, as his understanding and skill in facilitating my search was invaluable.

A memoir not only reveals the writer's life, but also involves the lives of others. Out of respect for privacy, a few names have been changed or I have used first names only.

Considerable effort has gone into ensuring accuracy, but if any errors or oversights remain, so continues our journey of discovery. 'Errare humanum est' – to err is to be human.

Appendices

Endnotes

1   http://www.jewishvirtuallibrary.org/jsource/Judaism/reform_practices.html
2   Phyllis Margaret Kleyn's WW II Army Service Record (for an overview of her army record, see Chronology; for photographs of relevant pages from her army record, see janeeales.com).
3   Phyllis Margaret Kleyn's WWII Army Service Record
4   Lifton, B.J., *Journey of the Adopted Self*, p. 31
5   de Courcy A., *Debs at War 1939-1945*, Paperback ed. Phoenix, 2006, p. 14
6   de Courcy A., p. 14
7   Letter to the author from Jeremy, 4 April 2012
8   However, for clarity in this context, she will still be referred to as Phyllis.
9   Ross, J., (Ed) *Chronicle of the 20th Century,* Penguin Books, Australia, 1999, p. 509–20
10 John Kleyn's WWII Army Service Record
11 Hatch, A., *H.R.H. Prince Bernhard of the Netherlands*, p. 84
12 Foot, M.R.D., *SOE in the Low Countries,* St Ermin's Press, 2001, pp.18–19
13 Phyllis' army record and enclosed letter requesting compassionate posting
14 Noakes, L., *Women in the British Army: war and the gentle sex,* 1907-1948 Taylor Frances Ltd, UK, 2006, pp. 106, 115
15 Dame Whateley, L., *As Thoughts Survive*, Hutchinson, London, 1949, pp. 94-95
16 Foot, M.R.D., *SOE in the Low Countries*, p.83
17 Foot, M.R.D., p.83
18 Foot, M.R.D., p.84
19 Hatch, A., *H.R.H. Prince Bernhard of the Netherlands*, an authorised biography, George G. Harrap, London, 1962, p. 95
20 Hatch, A., p. 95
21 John Kleyn's army record
22 Cunningham, C. Beaulieu, *The Finishing School for Secret Agents, 1941 – 1945* Pen & Sword, 1998, p. vii
23 Foot, M.R.D., p. 43
24 Dame Whateley, L. *As Thoughts Survive*, Hutchinson, London 1949, p. 43
25 Foot, M.R.D., *SOE in the Low Countries,* St Ermin's Press, London 2001, p. 62
26 The National Archives, 30G 4W457 4505725
27 The National Archives, 30G 4W457 HS 8/854 4505725
28 The National Archives, 30G 4W457 HS 8/854 4505725
29 Cunningham, C., *Beaulieu The Finishing School for Secret Agents*, 1941-1945 Pen & Sword, 1998, p. 81
30 Cave Brown, A., *A Bodyguard of Lies.* Harper Collins Publishers, Inc. 2002, p. 5
31 Churchill, Winston S., *My Early Life: A Roving Commission 1874 to 1908*, Thornton Butterworth, London 1930, p. 112

32   Cave Brown, A., *A Bodyguard of Lies*. Harper Collins Publishers, Inc. 2002, p. 5
33   Cave Brown, A., p. 8
34   Cave Brown, A., p. 10
35   Cave Brown, A., p. 2
35   Cave Brown, A., p. 6
36   Cave Brown, A., p. 8
37   Foot, M.R.D., SOE: *A New Instrument of War* by Mark Seaman (ed.) (Routledge, 2005). p. 85
38   Hatch A., p. 96
39   Foot, M.R.D., *SOE in the Low Countries*, p. 193
40   Englandspiel ontmaskerd: Schijnstoot op Nederland en Belgie 1942-1944 (Dutch Ed) by Pieter Hans Hoets (Paperback 1990)
41   Foot, M.R.D., *SOE in the Low Countries*, p. 43
42   Foot, M.R.D., *SOE: A New Instrument of War* quoting Christopher Andrew 'Secret Service', p. 83
43   Hatch, A., p. 96
44   Foot, M.R.D., p. 208
45   Kelso, N., *Errors of Judgement: SOE's Disaster in the Netherlands*, 1941-44, Hale, 1988, p. 222
46   Phyllis' army record
47   Phyllis' army record
48   Email to the author from Howard Davies dated 14.03.09
49   Foot, M.R.D., *SOE in the Low Countries*, 2001, p. 208.
50   Urquhart, Sir Brian Urquhart, 'A Live in Peace and War, Conversation with Sir Brian Urquhart' on 19 March 1996 with Harry Kreisler Institute of International Studies. Source: http://globetrotter.berkeley.edu/conversations/PubEd/research/UN/Urquhart/urquhart2
51   Foot, MRD, *SOE in the Low Countries*, 2001, p. 43
52   The National Archives, Piece reference FO 371/39353, 1944
53   Hoets, P H, *Vrijgevaren!* Met voorwoord van Erik Hazelhoff Roelfzema (1976), ISBN 9061001412, p. 76
54   Hoets, P H, *Vrijgevaren!* Met voorwoord van Erik Hazelhoff Roelfzema (1976), ISBN 9061001412, p. 76
55   Personal communication by email from Pieter Hans Hoets to the author, 20 November 2009
56   Ryan, C., *A Bridge Too Far,* Wordsworth Editions, 1999, p. 59
57   Hatch, A., p. 112
58   Ryan, C., p. 61
59   Ryan C., p. 61
60   Hatch, A., p. 113
61   Ryan, C., p. 60
62   Ryan, C., p. 60
63   Ryan, C., p. 61
64   Hatch, A., p. 114
65   Hinsley, F.H., *British Intelligence in the Second World War*, Vol. 3, Part II, p. 383
66   Ryan, C., p. 61
67   Hibbert, C., *The Battle of Arnhem*, London. B.T. Batsford, p. 37
68   Hinsley, F.H., Vol. 3, Part II, p. 384

69 Ryan, C., p. 110
70 Hibbert, C., p. 38
71 Hatch, A., p. 115
72 Hatch, A., p. 114
73 Winterbotham, FW, *The Ultra Secret, The Inside Story of Operation Ultra, Bletchley Park and Enigma*, Orion, London 1974, p.166
74 Hatch, A., p.103
75 MacDonald, C.B. *US Army in World War II; The Siegfried Line Campaign*, 1963, p. 122
76 Ryan, C., based on S.L.A. Marshall's interview with Bedell Smith in 1945, p. 109
77 Horrocks, Sir Brian., *Corps Commander / Sir Brian Horrocks with Eversley Belfield and H. Essame*, Magnum Books, London, 1979, p. 93
78 Ryan, A., *A Bridge too Far: A Note on Casualties*, p. 455
79 Foot, M.R.D., p. 396
80 Foot, M.R.D., ed., *Holland at War against Hitler: Anglo-Dutch Relations 1940-1945*, Frank Cass, London, 1990, p. 162
81 Urquhart, Major-General R.E. C.B., *Arnhem*, Cassel and Company London, 1958, p. 8
82 The names of those residents on Census nights are recorded in the electoral rolls at the Camden Holborn Local History Library.
83 www.britishdalmatianclub.org.uk: British Dalmatian Club – History 6th July 2013
84 Jacobs, W., *Known Consequences of Separating Mother and Child at Birth,* Sir William Deane, Inaugural Lingiari Lecture, Darwin, 22 August 1996, p. 9
85 Mills, C. Wright *The Sociological Imagination*, New York, Oxford University Press, 1959, p. 8
86 Lifton, B. J., *Journey of the Adopted Self*
87 Verrier, N. N., *The Primal Wound, Understanding the Adopted Child*, Gateway Press, Baltimore, US, 1991

Chronology of the life of Phyllis Margaret Hogg/ Whicker/Kleyn/MacRobert

18 July 1906	Birth of Phyllis Margaret Hogg at 3 Chalfont Road, South Norwood, South London.
1918-1924	Attended *Le Couvent des Ursulines*, Verviers, Belgium
1922	Phyllis met Herbert James Whicker of Florence Villa, Hill Road, Sydenham. Sydenham was not far from South Norwood.
Up to 1924	Learnt to breed Dalmatians with Mr and Mrs Kemp in school holidays.
	She played bridge regularly at home.
1925 to 1927	Phyllis employed by the Bank of England, the same place as Jim Whicker worked.
1 October 1927	Phyllis, aged 21, of 3 Whitworth Road, South Norwood, married Herbert James Whicker (DOB 8.7.1903) in St. Mary's Church, Wellesley Road, Croydon, Surrey. Honeymoon in Menton, south of France.
1927 to 1932	Began to breed Dalmatians with three bitches and one dog. Enjoyed horse or dog racing in the evenings and weekends. Played bridge at local bridge club and met Phyllis and John Kleyn. Phyllis and Jim lived in 'Bandol', Matlock Road, Caterham, Surrey.
13 April 1932	Paul Jonathan Owen Whicker was born.
June 1932	Two months later, Phyllis abandons Paul. Paul's father moves with Paul to Worthington to stay with his mother in their hotel. Paul has a nanny.
	Phyllis told Paul she named me after her dear friend Jane, a member of the family who owned Harvey Nichols. No evidence found.
	Phyllis told Paul that as a baby, he and a Dalmatian were featured in Vogue magazine in 1932-1933. No evidence found.
	Phyllis sees Paul intermittently, about once a year.
June 1935	Phyllis and Jim Whicker with Paul move back to their home, 'Bandol' in Chalfont Street. Their attempt to stay together fails.
15 November 1937	Phyllis and Herbert James Whicker divorce. Jim Whicker marries Caroline.
20 November 1937	Phyllis marries Johannes Leonardus (John) Kleyn. Phyllis becomes known as Margaret Kleyn. They move to St. Roman de Bellet, a village just North of Nice in Alpes de Maritimes.

| February 1938 | Cruft's Dog Show, dog (Anthony Adverse) wins place in two classes as novice dog. Address given: 33 Church Street, London W.8. Then she returns to Europe. |
| 1939 | Shoots 6 dogs prior to moving back to England. John Kleyn applies for British citizenship. |

WWII Activities (from Phyllis's and John's army records)

29 April 1940	John Kleyn joins the Pioneer Corps as a Clerk
11 June 1940	Phyllis enrols in First Aid Nursing Yeomanry (FANY), and the Auxiliary Territorial Service.
21 June 1940	Called up for service at PAC Section and posted to 1st London Motor Coy.
17 July 1940	From 11.6.1940 to 17.7.1940 qualified as a cook. Additional pay 2/6d.
25 October 1940	Described in army record as 5ft 3ins and 132 lbs. Religion RC. Dark brown hair.
June 1940 to Nov 1941	Phyllis drove high ranking officials around in a Humber 27 in War Office Pool.
12 November 1941	Posted to No. 2, TS Officer Cadet Training Unit in Egham.
17 December 1941	Discharged. Para 8
18 December 1941	Form 199A completed. Posted to Chilwell Group, Northern Command, Egham. Discharged only to be appointed to a commissioned rank.
31 December 1941	Served 1 year 190 days, discharged for the purposes of becoming an Officer.
18 January 1942	Home address Northbridge, Chiddingfold, Surrey. Father died. Husband's address given as 10 Gloucester Walk, W8.
1 April 1942	Phyllis writes a letter requesting compassionate posting back to London to be with her husband. Address given: Castle Ashby.
17 April 1942	*The London Gazette.* Phyllis granted a commission as 2nd Subaltern 221999
6 June 1942	Attached to J. Company for duty with PSS platoon.
15 June 1942	Compassionate leave granted for three weeks by Chief Commander AD. ATS
10 July 1942	Posted to PSS Platoon to 12th Norfolk Platoon.
20 July 1942	Army Bureau of Current Affairs Course (for Discussion Leaders)
24 August 1942	Attached to 30th Mt Company (Feltham) 1 London District Group
10 September 1942	Attached to B Company No. 1 London District Group
8 February 1943	Posted to No. 6 London District Group.
22-24 Feb 1943	Sick in lodgings
21 May 1943	Posted to HQ London District

11 November 1943	John Kleyn announced his engagement to Diana in *The Times*. Same day, Phyllis was admitted to the ATS Reception Centre. This was probably when she volunteered to be a secret agent because from now on there are no more army service details recorded. Her mother dies 10 days later.
13 November 1943	Discharged from Reception Centre
16 December 1943	Granted Divorce – decree nisi from John Kleyn

Phyllis's army record service details blank from this time, but promotions continue.

16 June 1944	5 Little Chester Street given as Phyllis's address in John Kleyn's army record
11 July 1944	Promoted to Acting Junior Commander
11 October 1944	Promoted to Temporary Junior Commander
18 or 24 Nov 1944	Phyllis visits Paul at Barnardos Children's Home 'just before she goes on a dangerous mission'. She picks mushrooms and stays at Taunton Pub.
27 November 1944	John Kleyn, Captain Intelligence Corps marries Diana.
2 July 1945	Sick at home
10 September 1945	Class A Release
6 November 1945	Army Leave – address given as 5 Little Chester Street, Belgravia, W.1.
October 1946	Paul stays with Phyllis at 5 Little Chester Street and meets General Pieters.
7 April 1947	Jane is born
12 November 1949	Phyllis marries Alan MacRobert (aged 39)
10 February 1951	Mrs A. MacRobert won certificate at Cruft's Dog Show, with dog 4579 Cabaret Coppella of Kurnool. Address, Cheneys Lane, Tacolneston, Norwich
15 March 1954	Phyllis relinquished Commission. Granted Honorary Rank Junior Commander Auth: L.G. (S) of 11.6.1954.
11 February 1956	Mrs A. MacRobert won Kennel Club Challenge Certificate 4579 with The Begum of Bellet, Black Prince and Black Queen.
2 June 1962	Paul Whicker, Phyllis' son married Eileen – but could not find Phyllis to invite her to his wedding.
3 January 1963	Phyllis Margaret MacRobert dies in The Old School House, Rings End, Cambridgeshire alone with her dogs. She was found three days later.

References

Chamberlain D., *Communicating with the Mind of a Prenate*, JOPPPAH 18(2), 2003

Cunningham, C. Beaulieu, *The Finishing School for Secret Agents*, 1941-1945 Pen & Sword, Barnsley, South Yorkshire, UK, 1998

Chronicle of the 20th Century, Our Amazing Century – History as it Happened, edited by John Ross, et al, Viking, Penguin Books, Australia, 1999 ISBN 0670 886 068

Churchill, Winston S., *My Early Life: A Roving Commission 1874 to 1908*, Thornton Butterworth: London, 1930

De Courcy A., *Debs at War 1939-1945*, Paperback edn, Phoenix, 2006

Foot, M.R.D., *Holland at War against Hitler: Anglo-Dutch Relations 1940-1945*, Routledge, 1990

Foot, M.R.D., *SOE in the Low Countries*, St Ermin's Press, London, 2001

Foot, M.R.D., *SOE: A New Instrument of War* by Mark Seaman (ed.) (Routledge, 2005), 1985

Hatch, A. H.R.H., *Prince Bernhard of the Netherlands. An authorized biography*, George G. Harrap, London, 1962

Hibbert C., *The Battle of Arnhem*, B.T. Batsford, London, 1962

Hinsley (Sir) F.H., *British Intelligence in the Second World War*, (3v in 4), HMSO, 1990, Vol. 3, Part II

Hoets, P H., *Vrijgevaren!* Met voorwoord van Erik Hazelhoff Roelfzema (1976), ISBN 9061001412

Horrocks (Sir) B., *Corps commander / Sir Brian Horrocks with Eversley Belfield and H. Essame*, Magnum Books, London, 1979

Jacobs, W., *Known Consequences of Separating Mother and Child at Birth*, Sir William Deane, Inaugural Lingiari Lecture, Darwin, 22 August 1996

Lifton B. J., *Journey of the Adopted Self, A Quest for Wholeness*, Basic Books, US, 1994

Kelso N., Errors of Judgement: SOE's Disaster in the Netherlands, 1941-44, Hale, 1988

MacDonald, C. B., *US Army in World War II; The Siegfried Line Campaign*, Office of the Chief of Military History, Department of the Army, Washington, D.C., 1963

Noakes L., *Women in the British Army: war and the gentle sex*, 1907-1948, Taylor Frances Ltd, UK, 2006

Mills, C. Wright, *The Sociological Imagination*, New York, Oxford University Press, 1959

The National Archives, 30G 4W457 HS 8/854 450572

Pearl L., Post Adoption Resource Centre, *Why wasn't I told? Making sense of the late discovery of adoption*, Paper presented to the Tasmanian Adoption Conference, May 2000

Robinson, E. B., *Adoption and Loss, The Hidden Grief*, Clova Publications, 2000, rev. 2003

Ryan, C. A., *Bridge Too Far*, Wordsworth Editions, 1999

Urquhart, Major-General R.E. C.B., *Arnhem*, Cassel and Company London, 1958 ISBN No. SBN 85617 623 1, 16.

Verrier, N. N., *The Primal Wound, Understanding the Adopted Child*, Gateway Press, Baltimore, US, 1991

Dame Whateley, L., *As Thoughts Survive*, Hutchinson, London, 1949

Winterbotham, F.W., *The Ultra Secret, The Inside Story of Operation Ultra, Bletchley Park and Enigma*, Orion, London, 1974

CPSIA information can be obtained
at www.ICGtesting.com
Printed in the USA
BVHW082244120620
581252BV00005B/134